Walking

with

GOD

101 Lessons for Life and Ministry

Dr. Stephen A. Gammon

Are you **Walking with God?**

http://youtu.be/nhKldcSNyCQ

Walking With God

101 Lessons for Life and Ministry

Dr. Stephen A. Gammon

Walking With God – Stephen A. Gammon

Copyright © 2014

All rights reserved. No part of this book may be reproduced, stored in a retrieval system, or transmitted in any form or by any means – electronic, mechanical, photocopying, recording, or otherwise, without written permission from the publisher.

Scriptures taken from the Holy Bible, New International Version®, NIV®. Copyright © 1973, 1978, 1984, 2011 by Biblica, Inc.™ Used by permission of Zondervan. All rights reserved worldwide. www.zondervan.com. The "NIV" and "New International Version" are trademarks registered in the United States Patent and Trademark Office by Biblica, Inc.™

RELIGION / Christian Life / Inspirational

www.lifesentencepublishing.com

Printed in the United States of America

First edition published 2014

LIFE SENTENCE Publishing books are available at discounted prices for ministries and other outreach.

Find out more by contacting us at info@lifesentencepublishing.com

LIFE SENTENCE Publishing, ANEKO Press, and all logos are trademarks of LIFE SENTENCE Publishing, LLC
P.O. Box 652
Abbotsford, WI 54405

Paperback ISBN: 978-1-62245-178-4

Ebook ISBN: 978-1-62245-179-1

10 9 8 7 6 5 4 3 2 1

This book is available from www.amazon.com, Barnes & Noble, and your local Christian bookstore.

Share this book on Facebook:

Cover Design: Robert J. Hatcher

Cover Photo: Dina Marie/Moment Open/Getty Images

Editor: Ruth Zetek

Contents

Acknowledgements VII   Introduction IX

WALKING WITH GOD AS A CHILD

You Are Loved..2	We Are Stewards, Not Owners 16
Life Is a Precious Gift 4	Work Hard and Do It for God 18
Families Watch Out for Each Other...............6	With My Dad I Am Safe 20
Church Is Forever Family 8	This Is How You Plow a Straight Path............ 22
Worship Puts God First 11	Our Heavenly Father Always Watches 24
God's Word Is a Treasure to be Mined.......... 14	Following Jesus Won't Always Be Easy 27

WALKING WITH GOD AS AN ADOLESCENT

I Must Own This Faith Myself 30	Give of My Best to the Master....................... 39
When I Call He Hears and Answers 33	It Is Unwise to Plan Alone 41
Joy Is Found in Serving................................. 37	

WALKING WITH GOD AS A YOUNG ADULT

Self-Reliance Is Deceptive 45	The Lord of All Directs My Steps 64
Neglecting Fellowship Increases Vulnerability 47	God Satisfies the Thirsty With the Holy Spirit.66
When God Has Our Full Attention, He Changes Us.. 49	Christian Fellowship Is Sweet 70
He Is Lord of Where I Go, What I Say, and What I Do 52	Keeping the Main Thing the Main Thing Honors Jesus... 72
When Jesus Is Lord of All, Relationships Realign 54	Christian Marriage Partners in Love and Service 75
When Jesus Is Lord of All, Priorities Realign ... 57	God Loves Giving Good Gifts to His Children79
The Lord of All Reveals His Presence 61	Choosing Obedience Brings Reward............ 82

WALKING WITH GOD IN SEASONS OF PREPARATION

When Jesus Is at the Helm, He Steers 87	Sorrow Can Bring Us to Our Knees and to His Side 97
God Goes Before Us So We Need Not Fear . 89	
God Cares Through His Family..................... 92	Communication With God Goes Two Ways .100
Our Disappointments May Be God's Appointments 94	For God's People, Joy Comes in the Morning 103
	God Leads Us Along 106

WALKING WITH GOD AS A YOUNG SHEPHERD

I Need the Lord More Than I Know 110	God Gives Mentors 118
Do Not Even Try to Go it Alone.................. 112	God's Calling Brings His Equipping 120
Be a Praying Shepherd 115	

WALKING WITH GOD AS A PARENT

Being a Parent Is God's Blessing.................. 124	Our Children Belong to God, Not to Us 137
I Can Make a Difference for This One 127	The Best Thing That Can Happen to Our Children.. 140
You Are a Child of God's Promise................ 131	
God Desires His Children 134	Tough Love is Tough 145

Praying for Children Is a Lifelong Assignment 150

Let Children See That Death Is Part of Life 154

WALKING WITH GOD IN CHRISTIAN LEADERSHIP

Shepherd Christ's Church on His Behalf.... 157
Job #1 is to Love the Lord 159
Job #2 Is to Love the People 161
Prioritize Family 165
Make Disciples Along the Way 167
Aim for Biblical Unity 169
Aim for Increased Fruitfulness 171
See the Church as One 173
Shine as a Light in This World 175

WALKING WITH GOD IN SACRIFICIAL SERVICE

Taking Orders Is Mandatory! 178
Our Surprises Are Not Surprises to God ... 183
God Goes Wherever His Service Members Go 188
God Places Us Where We Are Needed 192
God Superintends Our Unexpected Changes 195
There Is a Cost of Discipleship 197
God Continually Watches Over Our Loved Ones 200
Marriage Is Worth the Sacrifice 203
God Keeps Reminding Us of His Love 206

WALKING WITH GOD WHILE AWAITING ORDERS

Decision Times Mandate Prayerful Listening 211
God Sees Our Future as Clearly as Our Past and Present 213
God Gives His Orders in His Good Time .. 216

WALKING WITH GOD IN SPIRITUAL BATTLE

Peace and Strength Are Available in the Battle 221
We Are Never in This Alone 223
There Are Reasons for the Chaos in the Land 226
Hidden Sin Will Be Disclosed 231
When Battles Rage, Satan Tempts Us to Run . 234
No Circumstance Is Too Difficult for God . 237
Pray with Availability for Divine Appointments 239
Live with Heaven in Mind 246

WALKING WITH GOD IN THE FOG OF UNCERTAINTY

Trust Is Foundational in Following Jesus ... 251
Make the Most of Every Opportunity to Serve Him 254
Christ, the Good Shepherd for Me and Those I Love 258
Saying Good-bye Precedes Homecoming Joy 261

WALKING WITH GOD INTO GREATER RESPONSIBILITY

Don't Ever Stop Listening 265
Never Resist God's Will 268
If You Pray, God Will Make a Way 271
Following Jesus Is the Greatest Adventure . 274
Remember, Hell Is Real 277
Leaders Must Lead With Faith 280
God Knows His Plan for Us 283

WALKING WITH GOD INTO UNEXPECTED CHANGE

Fast, Pray, and Listen 287
Proceed Boldly as the Spirit Leads 291
Say "Yes" Again 294

WALKING WITH GOD TO FINAL BREATH AND BEYOND

Keep Standing By for New Orders 297
Emulate Faithful Witnesses 299
Run the Race to the Finish Line 301
Tell His Story in You 303
Walk with God into Glory 305
About the Author 307

Acknowledgements

I compare writing a book to a baseball pitcher who pitches all nine innings of a winning baseball game. Starting the game, the pitcher has no idea how far he will get. So when the last out is made there is much joy and celebration. The story line may credit the pitcher, but the pitcher knows it was a team effort. In writing this book I had a tremendous amount of help from a great team and I want to express my gratitude.

My deepest thanks is to the Lord Jesus Christ for loving us all and making a way to walk with God, for now and eternity.

I am forever grateful to my parents, Glendon and Marjorie Gammon, for loving the Lord and living the faith and for introducing me to the joy of walking with God. Their prayer support has covered me from infancy until now, and I am forever grateful.

Thanks, too, to my children, Carl Gammon, Jonathan Gammon, and Amy Hatcher for loving and encouraging me through the years and in this process, and to my son-in-law, Joey Hatcher, for designing the cover that so beautifully conveys the privilege and theme of walking with God.

Thanks to the local congregations I have been part of thus far, including especially the two I was honored to serve as pastor – Darlington Congregational Church in Pawtucket, Rhode Island, and Trinity Evangelical Church in Peterborough, New Hampshire. You are forever family. Your love for each other and your hunger for God filled me with joy and compelled me to walk with God.

Thanks to the ministers and churches and friends of the Conservative

Congregational Christian Conference, who have been my extended family for 35 years. Your love and support when I served as your conference minister, and your unwavering biblical commitment to love God, love others, and make disciples as we go inspires me greatly, and gives pleasure to God.

I am grateful to the people of LifeSentence Publishing for your beautiful vision of glorifying the Lord and building His church, and for publishing my book toward that end.

Finally, I give special thanks to my dear wife and best friend, Helen. Your love and partnership with me through our years of life and ministry, even when it cost you much, and your particular support and encouragement in this effort has meant more to me than words can say. I will forever be thankful to God for you.

Introduction

I have been walking with God since childhood, and through every chapter of life and ministry He has taught me lessons I needed to know right then. This is the privilege I have lived and one He offers His children through Jesus.

For Christian leaders who first yielded to the lordship of Jesus in adulthood, it can be challenging to discern developmental lessons God teaches children early in life. Younger ministers might also struggle to know what particular lessons He has in store for those who are older and have journeyed longer. From the perspective of one who has walked with God for nearly six decades, I share 101 life lessons God taught me through various seasons of life and ministry.

We all have a story to tell. Whether we have walked with God a short while or for a lifetime, telling the story of what He has done for us honors Him and can bless others by pointing them to Him. My own journey with God has included two local church pastorates, military chaplaincy in various venues, serving in a leadership and support role for churches and ministers, and more. In each chapter of life and ministry God has taught precious biblical lessons I needed to know then.

It is an awesome thing to walk with God from childhood to final breath. This is what we were created to do. Should God allow, I expect to live a few more years, so I cannot yet speak firsthand as one who has walked with God until my final breath, but I have been walking with Him for as long as I can remember. As a boy I understood God is personal and invites me into relationship with Him. This insight is uncommon knowledge today, but I can say with certainty it is true because God has said so and I have lived it. The infinite God created us to know Him, live with Him, love Him, and walk with Him personally, not for a short while but from infancy to eternity.

God has woven into our spiritual DNA a longing to know Him, which is why anthropology and archaeology have yet to find a culture devoid of religious faith and practice, and why, according to the 2011 survey by the Pew Forum on Religion & Public Life, 84 percent of people worldwide identify with a religious group. In all of us there is a yearning for acceptance, depth of intimacy, purpose, peace, and hope. Such things can be found in fullest measure in relationship with God.

Renown philosopher and mathematician Blaise Pascal experienced profound insight into this when he observed: "There is a God-shaped vacuum in the heart of every man." In other words, there is a depth in our longing that can only be filled in relationship with God. This is my story of walking with God through every chapter of life and ministry. I can't yet see the finish line, but when I do I will cross over with God. In Jesus Christ this is a privilege possible for us all.

The Scriptures have much to say about walking with God. In the garden of Eden, humanity's first home, God walked with Adam and Eve. They wanted to be with Him, listening carefully and enjoying His presence. When they sinned it all came to a screeching halt. Now the thought of being with God scared them, so they hid (Genesis 3:8-9). God's intention was broken because sin cannot be in the presence of the Holy One, and the wages of sin is death (Genesis 2:16-17; Romans 6:23). When sin entered the world spiritual death became immediate and the process of physical death began. Humanity was forced out of Eden and doomed to long for a relationship with God that could no longer be. It would never be unless God in His mercy intervened to make a way.

That is precisely what God did through Jesus. By His death on the cross He made a way for sin to be atoned for and relationship with God to be restored, a way for us to walk with God through life and into eternity. The Old Testament contains God's promise to send a redeemer. Prophesies of the coming Messiah are strung like a golden thread through the Old Testament beginning with Genesis 3:15 which foretold the *offspring* (seed/sperm) of a woman (the only place in Hebrew literature where this word is used of a woman) who would one day crush the head of the serpent (the Devil). More messianic prophecies came through the centuries, giving details of His birth, death, incarnation, kingdom, meekness, priesthood, prophetic office, rejection, resurrection, sufferings, and ultimate triumph.

Why did God do this? His motivation was love (John 3:16). He did it to save us from the consequences of our sin and restore us to the everlasting life for which He created us, a relationship that begins now and lasts to our final breath and evermore. If we claim to believe this but keep God at a distance we are foolish. Many seem entirely unaware that there is a way by which they can walk with God. Jesus invites us to walk with Him through life, and along the way invite others to join us. When we walk with God through the changing circumstances of life, He illumines and applies timeless truths for our benefit and also to bless others.

I have included here 101 life lessons God has taught me while walking with Him. If you read from beginning to end you will see a chronology of life lessons God taught me in various stages of life and ministry. You may also begin reading about the particular stage of life you are in now, one you will soon begin, or one that people you care about are in. I hold no pride in sharing my story, for it is all because of God's unmerited favor. To any extent I have followed Jesus I invite you to *Follow my example, as I follow the example of Christ* (1 Corinthians 11:1).

Schools often give quizzes following periods of study to determine if students have grasped what they were taught. This practice works well with spiritual lessons too, for whenever God speaks He calls for response. For this reason I have included application questions at the end of each lesson for reflection or discussion. Please do not rush through this part but listen prayerfully to what the Holy Spirit says and how He calls you to respond.

I would like to introduce you to the man God used to plant within me a desire to write this. It was my grandfather Reverend Morley Durost. He came to faith in Jesus as a young man, then walked with God until his final breath in 1981 at age eighty-seven. In mid-life God surprised him with a call to pastoral ministry. He walked with God, living the faith he proclaimed and experiencing God's faithfulness. Along the way he shared personal stories of God's grace and lessons learned. After many requests to do so, in his later years he began writing testimonies to share with his children and grandchildren and anyone interested, but starting late he did not finish.

My grandfather died six weeks after laying hands upon me and praying over me when I was ordained for gospel ministry. Sometime later my uncle found a box containing my grandfather's loose, typed pages and he gave them to me. The pages were disorganized and incomplete but I knew they must be shared. I put into chronological order the stories contained in the box, then printed and distributed them to family. Though Reverend Morley Durost has been gone for a generation now, among his many descendants conversations are still heard about lessons he learned in his walk with God through life and ministry. I follow his example.

Walking with God through life and ministry can begin in childhood and last until our final breath, and then forevermore. I am eagerly anticipating heaven, in part because there we will have an infinite supply of time to praise God for the countless ways He demonstrated love and faithfulness to us along our life journey! As on this side of heaven we all have limited time, I thank you for taking some of yours to read my story of walking with God. Your earthly journey is different than mine, but I pray you will know the joy I have known of walking with God through every chapter of life and ministry, and learning from Him all along the way.

Part I

WALKING WITH GOD AS A CHILD

Children have much to learn and are eager to learn it, but they cannot do it alone. My grandson Levi reminds me of this. He is eager to explore new things, but he needs help. Learning to walk he held tightly to Mom or Dad's finger, while putting one foot in front of another. In the same way little children have much to learn from the big people in their lives, so do we all have much to learn from God. Learning to hold onto His hand is a good place to begin. In my childhood I learned more about walking with God than in any other chapter of my life.

1

You Are Loved

The LORD appeared to us in the past, saying: "I have loved you with an everlasting love; I have drawn you with loving-kindness" (Jeremiah 31:3)

This is an intangible lesson but we all must learn it. Developmental psychology confirms we are designed to learn in the first two years of life that we are loved, and to trust and feel secure. People who don't learn this inevitably struggle with emotional insecurities and relational dysfunction. The same is true in relationship with God. As a boy I learned that I am loved.

No one has ever chosen to be born or chosen the family into which they were born or adopted. The Bible says God created us in our mother's womb (Psalm 139:13-16). He did this because of His love: *In love he predestined us for adoption to sonship through Jesus Christ, in accordance with his pleasure and will* (Ephesians 1:5). At whatever point we begin to grasp that we are loved, it is helpful to consider how we became a recipient of such love. The only biblical answer I can find to explain this is that God loves us because He loves us. This was stated by Moses in Deuteronomy 7:7-8a: *The LORD did not set his affection on you and choose you because you were more numerous than other peoples, for you were the fewest of all peoples. But it was because the LORD loved you.*

> Developmental psychology confirms we are designed to learn in the first two years of life that we are loved, and to trust and feel secure.

When I entered this world my father was pastor of the Baptist church in Burnham, Maine. I joined my parents and eighteen-month-old brother, David. From the very beginning God showered me with gifts of life and love. The apostle John's words are ever true: *See what great love the Father has lavished on us that we should be called children of God! And that is what we are!* (1 John 3:1)

One of the first songs I learned as a boy was "Jesus Loves Me." I sang it from my heart because I believed it was true. I still know it is true.

> *Jesus loves me! This I know,*
> *For the Bible tells me so;*
> *Little ones to Him belong,*
> *They are weak but He is strong.*
> *Yes, Jesus loves me!*
> *Yes, Jesus loves me!*
> *Yes, Jesus loves me!*
> *The Bible tells me so.*

God wants us all to know that He loves us.

How can we measure if we have learned this lesson? It becomes evident in three relational ways: (1) in the way we accept His love for ourselves, finding comfort and peace and security in Him; (2) in the way we love God in return, desiring to worship Him and express to Him our loyalty and devotion; and (3) in the way we reflect His love to others, demonstrating His compassion and care, as God has shown to us. To know and accept the biblical truth that I am loved is a precious lesson taught by God to His children for the rest of life.

Life Application Questions:

1. How do you know you are loved and what is the evidence that you know it?

2. If you believe that because of God's love Jesus died for you, how does this belief affect how you see yourself and others?

3. What response is the Holy Spirit asking of you now?

2

Life Is a Precious Gift

Then the LORD God formed a man from the dust of the ground and breathed into his nostrils the breath of life, and the man became a living being (Genesis 2:7)

As we walk along with God He teaches His children that life is a gift. My parents had six children in six and a half years. First, three sons were born (David, Stephen, Gary), and then three daughters (Cheryl, Marcia, Marilee). As a child I learned that every life is a precious gift, an important lesson for life and ministry.

An early memory of this lesson happened in our 1958 Christmas celebration. I was about four years old and the season was exciting. It was joyful because it was Jesus' birthday, we had each other, and presents were expected under the tree on Christmas morning. Family preparations felt strange, though, because our mom was away for a few days. I didn't understand why she was gone but I missed her.

I went to bed Christmas Eve excited about the next day. When morning came my father lined us up for the annual tradition of having the children's picture taken standing on the stairway in descending order of age. We then ran into the living room to see the lighted tree and the presents under it, and there to my surprise was my mother, having returned from the hospital the previous night. And under the tree with other gifts piled around was a new baby sister named Marcia.

I cannot recall any other gifts received that Christmas, but I understood that day that my baby sister was a present from God. As I have walked with God in life and ministry I have grown to appreciate that every life is a gift of God, and because He loves and cares for us all, I must do the same. One of the best parts of learning this lesson has been realizing that when God makes us His children, He gives us brothers and sisters too. To Him we are family!

The Bible teaches this in Ephesians 1:3-6: *Praise be to the God and Father of our Lord Jesus Christ, who has blessed us in the heavenly realms with every spiritual blessing in Christ. For he chose us in him before the creation of the world to be holy and blameless in his sight. In love he predestined us to for adoption to sonship through Jesus Christ, in accordance with his pleasure and will – to the praise of his glorious grace, which he has freely given us in the One he loves.*

When we walk with God He teaches us that life is a gift.

I was blessed to learn this important lesson as a child and to apply it all through the years. When we walk with God He teaches us that life is a gift.

Life Application Questions:

1. Do you know that you are a precious gift of God and everyone with whom you lock eyes is also precious to Him?

2. How does this affect the way you think of yourself and others?

3. What response is the Holy Spirit asking of you now?

3

Families Watch Out for Each Other

God sets the lonely in families (Psalm 68:6)

Another lesson God teaches His little ones is how blessed we are to be in a family that watches out for one another. God designed families to support each other in good times and bad. Though some of us have lived in families with varying degrees of dysfunction, God's design has always been that families will be people we can count on, who watch out for us no matter what.

My parents had six children in six and a half years, three sons followed by three daughters, so sibling rivalry was evident in our home when we were children. My older brother David and I tussled some. He was stronger but I was bigger, so we battled evenly. My sister Cheryl told me in later years that as a little girl she feared David and I would kill each other, or at least cause major injury. But we never did, and when push came to shove we loved each other because we were brothers.

All families confront challenges, but these are God-given opportunities to learn to love and be loved.

I can recall a particular day at the schoolyard of the Lee Elementary School when a playground bully was picking on me and threatening to beat me up. On the other side of the playground my big brother saw what was going on and suddenly he was standing between me and that bully, warning him to leave me alone or he'd let him have it! I was shocked but so thankful! It was not the last time a brother looked out for me, or I for them, but it was a vivid example to me of what God designed families to do. God gives families so none of us are alone in this world. At whatever point we become God's children, He places us in families and teaches us to express His love and to be there for each other in the ups and downs of life.

How I thank God for the family I was born into, and the one He established when Helen and I married, and the family of God – the church. All families confront challenges, but these are God-given opportunities to learn to love and be loved.

Life Application Questions:

1. How have you experienced family watching out for each other?

2. Do you believe God can provide this for you? How does your answer affect the way you see yourself and how you relate to others?

3. What response is the Holy Spirit asking of you now?

4

Church Is Forever Family

Now that you have purified yourselves by obeying the truth so that you have sincere love for each other, love one another deeply, from the heart (1 Peter 1:22)

All children of God through faith in Jesus Christ are brothers and sisters together because He has made us His family forever. As such God expects us to love each other deeply. I began learning this as a boy in Lee, Maine. We moved there when I was just two years old and we stayed for nine years. The population of Lee then was about five hundred people. It was a great place to be a kid.

In Lee there was one flashing streetlight, presumably so folks going through would slow down enough so as not to totally miss the town. There were two stores on opposite corners of the intersection. One of these was Haskell's General Store, which was also the only gas station in town, and, in my expert opinion, they had the best selection of penny candy. The other was Whitten's Store right next to the post office.

Our yard abutted the back of Whitten's Store, the second floor of which was the proprietors' home. I remember playing in the yard while smelling donuts being made inside. Especially memorable were times when an upstairs window opened and a ridiculous question was yelled down. "Would you kids like some warm donuts?" Our answer was always, "Yes!" which prompted a warm gift floating down from above in a bag, every crumb of which was thoroughly enjoyed from our perches on the swing set.

Everybody knew everybody in Lee. It was home and I loved it. I loved the school, the fishing holes, the gravel pits, the baseball field, and all the places to ride a bike. Besides family and the Lee Elementary School, the most formative part of my years in Lee was spent in the Lee Baptist Church. It was the only church in town then, and my dad was the pastor. We lived in a parsonage across the street from the church and we were at the church a lot. I didn't mind this at all because friends and family were there. I learned that church is extended family.

From various people in the church I received love. There I learned by absorption what walking with God is about. Friends of all ages were there, and together we grew in faith and in the knowledge of God. People in the church felt like family to me. Mrs. Virginia Smith was one person who took a special interest in me. I stayed with her and her husband and family at their farm one week when my parents were away. We milked cows, rode horses, and ate farm-fresh food. They made me feel like part of their family. It was wonderful! Years later when I was in college they contacted my parents to ask for my address and reached out to me again to show their love. Mrs. Smith is in heaven now, preceded by her daughter and husband, but I will see them again because we are forever family.

> *I thank God for teaching me as a child that church is not merely an organization we join.*

Another memory of when I was eight years old reminds me of the intergenerational blessings of church life and the importance of older saints loving and speaking into the lives of children in the church. An older saint in the congregation, a woman who walked closely with God, came to me one day and tousled my hair. She said, "Stephen, look at me." I did as instructed. Looking intently into my face she said, "Stephen, God's hand is on you. You're going to be a preacher someday!" I have a vague recollection of blushing some and of my brother giggling, but that moment was implanted into my memory for future recall. I thank God that she cared enough to speak into my life words that later became a great blessing to me.

The early experiences I had in church have carried with me through life. I thank God for teaching me as a child that church is not merely an organization we join, or a place of worship we go to when it is convenient. Church is the body of Christ (Romans 12:4; 1 Corinthians 12:27; Ephesians 1:23; 4:12; Colossians 1:24; 2:19). And because church is the family of God (John 1:12; 2 Corinthians 6:18), we will be brothers and sisters forever. Referring to His disciples Jesus said, *"Here are my mother and my brothers. For whoever does the will of my Father in heaven is my brother and sister and mother"* (Matthew 12:49-50).

There is no perfect local church, just as there is no perfect family. Yet in the church we share with one another a perfect Father in heaven who loves us all, and who chooses us to demonstrate His care and to help us help each other grow to become more like Him. How grateful I am that God taught me this lesson as a child.

Through the years God has moved me from place to place, and saying good-bye is not easy, but He teaches His children that really we never say good-bye to each other. As forever family, even if we should not see one another again on this side of heaven, in faith we can always say, "See you later." I love that! As I think back to "forever family" members I have known through the years, some of whom are in heaven now, I rejoice in the memories of times we shared, while I look forward to eternity together. Because of Christ in the church we are forever family.

Life Application Questions:

1. Do you regard the church as the body of Christ and forever His family?

2. How does your answer affect your attitude and involvement in a local church?

3. What response is the Holy Spirit asking of you now?

5

Worship Puts God First

One thing I ask of the LORD, this only do I seek: that I may dwell in the house of the LORD all the days of my life, to gaze on the beauty of the LORD and to seek him in his temple (Psalm 27:4)

When Jesus came into Jerusalem on the day of His triumphal entry, children worshiped Him. Their childlike voices could be heard above the crowd joyfully shouting, *"Hosanna to the Son of David!"* The religious elite were indignant and said to Jesus, *"Do you hear what these children are saying?"* Jesus heard them all right! He replied, *"Yes,"* … *"have you never read, 'From the lips of children and infants you, Lord, have called forth your praise'"?* (Matthew 21:15-16).

Our heavenly Father teaches us to worship, and children often do it best, as childlike faith opens the door for worship! We do not worship because it is required or to earn His favor. Like children we worship God because we want to, because He is worthy, because in His presence we cannot help but worship Him!

David Olson of the American Church Research Project has for many years revealed the trends of declining worship service attendance in America. The Pew Forum on Religion & Public Life also confirms that an increasing percentage of Americans are religiously "unaffiliated" now, including one-third of adults under age thirty. One reason for this trend is the overemphasis in American Christianity on individual spirituality. Many conclude they can be faithful Christians on their own, but God teaches His children the importance of connection with other believers. Focusing only on our own walk with God grieves the Lord.

This trend began as early as the first century. This is why the writer of Hebrews penned strong words of exhortation to followers of Jesus about not neglecting corporate worship and fellowship, but to come together often for encouragement, worship, and exhortation: *And let us ... not [give] up meeting together, as some are in the habit of doing, but encouraging one another—and all the more as you see the Day approaching* (Hebrews 10:24-25).

God's intention is for worship to become an exuberant way of life, offered not as an occasional occurrence, but offered by joy-filled children who love their Father's presence. For God's children, worship is as essential to spiritual well-being as food and water and staying active are to our physical health.

Early in life children learn there are things we must do to stay healthy and strong. We learn to take care of personal hygiene, get sufficient sleep, eat well, drink water, take care of our teeth, and exercise regularly, to name a few. We also learn how to keep ourselves well emotionally. We learn ways of reducing stress, letting off steam constructively, and dealing with conflict by talking things out rather than allowing things to simmer. We watch and listen and learn how to take care of ourselves and others. We learn that when we do these things we feel better and relationships are healthier, but when we disregard these things there are consequences.

> *God's intention is for worship to become an exuberant way of life.*

In the same way God teaches His children that there are things we can do to stay spiritually healthy. Besides joining others for corporate worship, times of personal worship also bring reward. My parents modeled this well. Every morning except Sundays, after breakfast we had family devotions. We read God's Word, listened to the reading of a devotional, sang worship songs, shared prayer requests, and then prayed together. I recall being surprised when visiting friends reported this was not something they were used to. This was a time of family togetherness and connecting with God who loves us and promises to be with us throughout our day.

Jesus encouraged this by an illustration of a branch remaining connected to the vine and receiving life through that connection (John 15:4-6). That is what daily worship does. As a child I remember how excited I was when my dad came home or my grandparents came for a visit. I ran to them with joy, looking to be hugged and to enjoy time together. Later in life I experienced this with my own children. Our heavenly Father teaches His children to enter His presence with such longing. He comes where we are and invites us to stay with Him awhile.

Jesus took a little child to demonstrate faith, and told His disciples to come like that (Matthew 18:2-3). Sometimes we complicate things so! Little children are full of wonder, prone to trust, and love to be held and to listen when stories are read. The child that was held by Jesus on the day described in Matthew 18 undoubtedly loved it! As a boy I loved to be held, and I still do.

It hasn't always been this way for me though. I have sometimes felt distant from God or distracted by many things. But whenever I am still enough to hear His voice, and trusting enough to come near and listen, there is great reward! God longs for us all to approach Him daily with childlike enjoyment at being with Him. When we neglect to do this He still loves us but we miss out on great blessing! Ever ready to forgive, He stretches out His arms to welcome us into His presence; He meets with us when we take the time to meet with Him.

Life Application Questions:

1. Do you agree that almighty God is worthy of worship now and forevermore?

2. How is your answer seen in your corporate worship and daily devotional life?

3. What response is the Holy Spirit asking of you now?

6

God's Word Is a Treasure to be Mined

The law from your mouth is more precious to me than thousands of pieces of silver and gold (Psalm 119:72)

God's Word is a treasure! As we walk with Him through life and ministry we see that the Scriptures are more precious than thousands of pieces of silver and gold. He teaches us to approach His Word in the same way excited children approach a seashell-laden beach, excited about every discovered treasure. God calls us to come to His Word often to mine this treasure, which requires a more determined effort than taking a cursory look.

Have you ever picked up a magazine and flipped through the pages for a while? As you did so a subscription card fell out. You were just skimming to see if something might catch your eye. You were not really reading it. Do you ever approach God's Word in this way? "Mining" treasure requires more intentionality. It is approaching God's Word prayerfully, inviting Him to speak and expecting He will. We then pause to examine particular verses or themes, and with the Holy Spirit's help we dig out precious nuggets that were at first glance hidden beneath the surface. As we do this we lay up treasures that can be applied when needed, and we are prepared to pass them on to others also.

When I was a boy this revelation came gradually. I appreciated the Scriptures through church and family worship, and then I began reading on my own. God spoke to me at various times so I wanted more. In my fourth-grade year I was given an incentive to dig deeper and I took the challenge.

Our church participated in a program encouraging children to memorize Scripture. Upon reaching various milestones of memorization prizes were publicly awarded. The grand prize was offered to any child who memorized a total of 250 Scripture verses in a year – a free week at a lakeside summer youth camp! I had no idea if I could memorize that many verses, but I decided to try.

Our Bible memory program was designed for children to memorize key chapters, including Genesis 1; Psalm 1, 23, 100, and 121; John 1, 3, and 15; Romans 8 and 12; 1 Corinthians 13; Ephesians 6; and Hebrews 11, to name some I recall. It took months to accomplish this, and it was the biggest challenge I had faced in my short life, but oh, the reward! Not only did I receive a free week at summer camp, even better I received the priceless reward of God's Word planted in my soul.

God teaches His children to look for something more precious than silver and more costly than gold.

A primary motivation for diving into God's Word is to know and enjoy Jesus. From start to finish the Scriptures point toward Him, as Hebrews 1 testifies. As we walk with Him in life and ministry God teaches His children that in His Word there are so many treasures worth mining. In the days of the California Gold Rush, and later in Alaska, as people heard about it they traveled in droves to seek treasure. God teaches His children to look for something more precious than silver and more costly than gold (Psalm 119:72). We can go mining every day!

Life Application Questions:

1. Do you regard God's Word as more precious than thousands of pieces of silver and gold? How is your answer reflected in the way you approach the Scriptures?

2. What tools will you get, what fellowship will you seek, and what steps will you take to dig deeper into God's Word?

3. What response is the Holy Spirit asking of you now?

7

We Are Stewards, Not Owners

Again, it will be like a man going on a journey, who called his servants and entrusted his wealth to them (Matthew 25:14)

As we walk with the Lord He teaches us stewardship. Children who have not yet become materialistic are well positioned to learn that what they have belongs to God. The little boy who generously offered his lunch to Jesus and then saw Him use it to feed thousands is an example of this (John 6:9). God gives treasures, abilities, and opportunities through our short season of life, so we might invest them well for Him. My parents reinforced this by quoting this maxim: "Only one life, 'twill soon be past. Only what's done for Christ will last."

One way I learned stewardship was by understanding and practicing the biblical principle of tithing. In Scripture God called His children to set aside the firstfruits of their crops. The top 10 percent of earnings were to be a baseline offering to Him. It is not that God needs our money, for He lacks nothing and owns *the cattle on a thousand hills* (Psalm 50:10). God teaches His children to do this to *learn to revere the LORD your God always* (Deuteronomy 14:23).

When we tithe we worshipfully recall that all we have comes from God and we are stewards of what is His. We therefore gladly invest in the work of His kingdom. In Malachi God chastened people who failed to tithe. *"Bring the whole tithe into the storehouse, that there may be food in my house. Test me in this,"* says the LORD Almighty, *"and see if I will not throw open the floodgates of heaven and pour out so much blessing that there will not be room enough to store it"* (Malachi 3:10).

The New Testament does not teach tithing as a legal obligation but teaches us to give regularly (1 Corinthians 16:2), cheerfully (2 Corinthians 9:7), and according to our ability (Act 11:29; 2 Corinthians 8:12). My parents never had much money but they practiced tithing and taught me the joy of doing the same. In this way God looks to develop such childlike faith and surrender in all of us.

I recall applying this lesson as a little boy after earning a dime for hauling my red wagon to an elderly neighbor's house, filling it with empty water jugs, pulling it to a town spring to fill with spring water, and hauling it back to their home to off-load the water. After receiving a dime as payment I went to the store and bought a piece of penny candy, then went home to put eight cents in my bank after setting aside a shiny penny to put in the plate the next Sunday as my offering to God. I was so happy I could give a portion of what God allowed me to earn!

> *He teaches His children that we are stewards, not owners.*

Biblical stewardship applies to our material possessions. It also extends to the truth God reveals to us. The apostle Paul said God entrusts truth to us and He holds us accountable for it. *This, then, is how you ought to regard us: as servants of Christ and as those entrusted with the mysteries God has revealed. Now it is required that those who have been given a trust must prove faithful* (1 Corinthians 4:1-2).

We will all manage a finite number of dollars and days in life, as are entrusted to us by God. God gives His children opportunities to invest material treasures in His name, and to invest time and energy to do His work. As we do so we are assured of an eternal reward on our investment (Matthew 6:18-21). As we walk with God through life and ministry He teaches His children that we are stewards not owners. By word and example we must aim to pass this lesson on to our children.

Life Application Questions:

1. Do you agree that all you have belongs to God and is entrusted to you to be invested for Him? How does this affect your use of time, talent, and resources?

2. Have you told the Lord that you desire to be a good steward for Him?

3. What response is the Holy Spirit asking of you now?

8

Work Hard and Do It for God

Whatever you do, work at it with all your heart, as working for the Lord, not for human masters, since you know that you will receive an inheritance from the Lord as a reward. It is the Lord Christ you are serving (Colossians 3:23-24)

Anyone who has ever known my dad will vouch for the fact that he is a very hard worker. He could never be idle for very long. He grew up on a family farm in Peru, Maine, where there were always chores to do: cleaning the barn, feeding the animals, mowing the lawn, plowing the fields, weeding the gardens, picking the vegetables, stacking the wood, fertilizing the crops, milking the cows, fixing the equipment, repairing the fences, gathering the eggs, cleaning the chicken coop, carrying the water, raking the leaves, shoveling the snow, not to mention all the chores around the house. Hard work was bred into him as a child and he has carried it with him through life. My dad taught me to work hard, and to do it all for God.

I can't begin to list all the ways my dad has blessed people by his work ethic. Many people through the years were blessed when he arrived with toolbox in hand. He has helped more people through works of service than almost anyone I know. Because small town pastors often aren't paid well, especially as his family grew he had to do other odd jobs to make ends meet. Even then he often charged less than others would, and he could be counted on to do a superb job. My dad did carpentry, plumbing, electrical jobs, and whatever else needed to be done. I watched him in action and I have always admired his work ethic.

My parents wanted their children to develop a good work ethic. I learned that the ultimate reason we work hard in life is because there is satisfaction in doing it all for God. This is the point Paul made when writing to Christians: *Whatever you do, work at it with all your heart, as working for the Lord, not for human masters, since you know that you will receive an inheritance from the Lord as a reward. It is the Lord Christ you are serving* (Colossians 3:23-24). Whatever our work is, if we do it to please Him, there can be pleasure and reward in it. If we cannot do it for Him we should not do it at all.

When I was a child in Lee, Maine, each year at potato harvest time schools closed and every able-bodied person who wanted to went to the fields to pick potatoes. Every potato picker was assigned a number, and when they had filled a barrel with potatoes the picker put their number on the top of the barrel. When the harvest was finished pickers were paid according to the number of barrels they filled.

The year I was seven years old my brothers David and Gary and I combined forces to share a number and we worked side by side for three days filling barrels with potatoes. We didn't have to do it; we wanted to do it, assisting the family who owned the potato farm and earning some money during our school vacation week. In those days a quarter was a lot of money to me and a dollar was a fortune. So when the harvest was complete and my brothers and I were paid, between us we had earned $22.50, which was $7.50 for each of us. I cannot begin to describe how satisfying it was! I set aside a tithe for the Lord who had made it possible, and I bought my first watch – a glow-in-the-dark pocket watch that I treasured.

God teaches His children that working hard is a good thing, especially when we do it for Him. The lessons I learned about this as a child have carried with me through life. God equips His children to do whatever He calls us to do.

Life Application Questions:

1. How has God's call to work hard and for Him affected you in your life history?

2. How does this relate to the work you now do and to your future plans?

3. What response is the Holy Spirit asking of you now?

9

With My Dad I Am Safe

God is our refuge and strength, an ever-present help in trouble. Therefore we will not fear, though the earth give way and the mountains fall into the heart of the sea, though its waters roar and foam and the mountains quake with their surging (Psalm 46:1-3)

God teaches His children that we can trust Him and with Him we are safe. The story is told in Matthew's gospel about Jesus' disciples being on the lake in a storm and Jesus was with them (Matthew 8:23-27). Jesus was utterly exhausted and sound asleep in the storm. Jesus had no worries but the disciples did. They were in a storm more powerful than they were. They battled hard, but *the waves swept over the boat,* and they were afraid.

At that point they turned to Jesus who was astonished at their lack of faith. They didn't seem to know how safe they were because Jesus was with them in the boat. He showed them in a remarkable way how capable He is in every storm. He rebuked the wind and waves and calm came upon the lake that day. The disciples were amazed, and in the future when they faced other raging storms they were undoubtedly reminded of that day, and of Jesus' power over all things.

This is a lesson God wants all His disciples to carry with us on our journey with Him. One of my earliest memories of learning this lesson came when I was a boy fishing with my dad and brothers. It was a summer when the parsonage in Lee was undergoing renovations so we were staying at a cottage on Silver Lake owned by a family in the church. It happened on the boat my father had built.

The parsonage in Lee had an attached barn with a second-story loft, a favorite play area for us and neighborhood children. We had a makeshift basketball court there, which we greatly appreciated on cold or rainy days when playing outside wasn't possible. For several months the upstairs loft was off limits for play, as Dad was building a boat there. He bought plans, and piece by piece, little by little, in his spare time he built a sixteen-foot wooden boat, painted white and blue, and covered with fiberglass. It had a steering wheel, padded seats, and an outboard motor strong enough to pull water skiers.

I was amazed my dad could build such a thing and wondered how he would get it out of the second floor of that barn, but he knew what he was doing. When the project was completed the loft door was swung open, and with pulleys and ropes, and a little help from friends, the boat was pushed out the door and lowered to the ground. It was then placed on a boat trailer and hauled to the lake where it worked masterfully. For years that boat brought joy to our family.

It was in that boat on a stormy day on Silver Lake that I learned a valuable lesson about trusting that when my dad was in the boat I did not need to fear. My dad took his sons fishing that day and we were catching them too. We were so wrapped up in what we were doing we had not noticed the gathering clouds. When the storm came it was furious and strong. The skies grew dark, thunder rolled, lightening flashed, waves were white-capped, and rain fell hard and fast. It was a furious squall and I was more than a little afraid.

My instinct was fear but my dad's priority was to get us safely home. He told us to crawl under cover in the bow of the boat. We did not need to be afraid. I remember being under there with my brothers. The boat rocked and the rains fell, but our "Dad" was at the helm and He would get us safely through the storm.

There have been many times in life when like that day on the lake I have been afraid, confused, and felt small, but the lesson I learned with my father reminds me that I do not need to be afraid, because my God is with me.

Life Application Questions:

1. What does your Father in heaven want you to hold on to in the storms of life?

2. How has this lesson helped you in past storms?

3. What response is the Holy Spirit asking of you now?

10

This Is How You Plow a Straight Path

No one who puts a hand to the plow and looks back is fit for service in the kingdom of God (Luke 9:62)

God teaches His children how to follow a straight path and avoid aimless wandering. He taught me this through gardening with my dad. That man knew all about growing vegetables and every year he raised a sizable garden. As children we had assigned duties in the garden, from preparing soil to planting, fertilizing, weeding, hoeing, and harvesting. It was much work, but it was great to watch seeds and seedlings transform into food-producing plants. It was all a mystery to me. How did a seed planted into the ground become a carrot or beans or corn or lettuce or a beet? The process is miraculous and I learned a lot.

One lesson learned in the garden that I have reflected on through the years is how to plow a straight row. At planting time one year my dad placed in my grip a hand tiller and told me to lay a row for planting. I thought, *This can't be hard*, so I grabbed ahold, dug into the soil, and marched down the entire length of the garden laying a furrow for the seed. I kept my eyes a few feet ahead, pushing hard against the stubborn soil all the way to the end. When I reached the other end of the garden I turned around and was surprised to see how much I had wandered. The row I laid was as crooked as could be! My dad watched what I was doing but allowed me to get to the other end so I could see what I had done and so I would be in a right frame of mind to learn a better way.

He said, "Stephen, come back with the tiller, and I will show you how to lay a straight row." He said, "Son, if you look right in front of you, you will wander. To plow a straight row, fix your eyes on your destination and keep your focus there. Do not look down or to the right or left; keep your eyes fixed on your destination until you reach it." I did as instructed. I looked to the other end of the garden, fixing my eyes on where I was going, and I plowed ahead. When I reached my destination and looked back that row was about as straight as an arrow.

This was biblical wisdom for plowing a straight row in life. There are many things to distract us along the way, and we are prone to focus on our immediate challenges or the distractions all around. When that happens we are as prone to wander as when I laid that first row in the vegetable garden.

> *This requires ever looking forward to where we are headed.*

God tells us to fix our gaze on Jesus. *Therefore, holy brothers and sisters, who share in the heavenly calling, fix your thoughts on Jesus, whom we acknowledge as our apostle and high priest* (Hebrews 3:1). *And … fixing our eyes on Jesus, the pioneer and perfecter of faith. For the joy set before him endured the cross, scorning its shame, and sat down at the right hand of the throne of God. Consider him who endured such opposition from sinners, so that you will not grow weary and lose heart* (Hebrews 12:1b-3).

Revelation 21 offers a picture of the glories of heaven we will one day see. Jesus said he was going to prepare a place for us (John 14:1-6). God teaches us to retain a heavenly focus as we plow forward in this world. Our Father gives wisdom for plowing straight rows. This requires ever looking forward to where we are headed.

Life Application Questions:

1. What have your eyes been fixed upon along the way?

2. Where are you headed now and how will this lesson affect you looking ahead?

3. What response is the Holy Spirit asking of you now?

11

Our Heavenly Father Always Watches

For your ways are in full view of the LORD, and he examines all your paths (Proverbs 5:21)

God's children learn that He is always with us. We must know He sees us wherever we go, hears everything we say, and knows everything we think. Nothing is hidden from Him. Still, people convince themselves otherwise. Adam and Eve lived with God in the garden of Eden, but when they sinned they attempted to hide (Genesis 3:8). God saw what they did and knew where they were hiding.

Jonah thought he could run from God (Jonah 1:1-3) so he bought passage aboard a ship heading far away, but God saw. Achan took for himself things devoted to God (Joshua 7:1). He thought no one saw him, but God did. Judas thought Jesus wouldn't know when he went in secret to the chief priests to betray him (Matthew 26:14-16), but Jesus knew. Ananias and Sapphira thought no one would know if they lied about the price received from selling their property, so they purported to give it all to God while holding some back for themselves (Acts 5:1-11). God knew and He struck them dead for lying to Him.

God teaches His children that even if we choose to live as though it were not true, still nothing is hidden from God. *My eyes are on all their ways; they are not hidden from me, nor is their sin concealed from my eyes* (Jeremiah 16:17). It was impressed upon me as a child that God sees everything I do, hears everything I say, and is with me everywhere I go. There have been times when I have pretended this is not true, but still God sees. I am grateful this lesson was taught to me as a child.

I discovered I could fool my parents sometimes, but fooling God was another matter entirely. I was convicted of this after stealing candy from Haskell's store. Their penny candy display was awesome and all my favorites were there. One day I went in with a friend who was going to buy candy. He had money but I didn't. No one was watching and the temptation was great. I reasoned that Mr. Haskell would not miss it and no one would know, so I grabbed five pieces and stuffed them into my pocket. When my friend left the store I did too. No one saw me but God. *You, God, know my folly; my guilt is not hidden from you* (Psalm 69:5).

After leaving the store I found a quiet place, and one by one I peeled those candy pieces and stuffed them into my mouth. I enjoyed every piece. No one saw me. I got away with it, I thought. But God let me know that He knew. That night as I went to bed and said my prayers, God reminded me He knew what I had done that day. After all, He sees everything we do; none of our ways are hidden from Him. With this realization I confessed my sin to God and He let me know He would forgive me, but I had to make it right. I tried going to sleep but could not, so with trepidation I went downstairs to see my mom and dad. They asked what was wrong, and through my tears I told them what I did.

> He reminds us that He knows.

That event happened fifty years ago, but it affected the course of my life. It reinforced in my soul that God sees me. Nothing we say or do, and no place we ever go is hidden from Him. It also reminded me of the sweetness of forgiveness and grace when we offer true repentance, as the Bible promises: *Godly sorrow brings repentance that leads to salvation and leaves no regret* (2 Corinthians 7:10).

My parents handled that situation well. They reflected God's love and affirmed that I did the right thing in confessing my sin, and they prayed with me about it. My dad told me the next day I would have to tell Mr. Haskell what I had done and pay him for the candy I had stolen. I told my dad I had no money to pay, so he gave me a nickel. That was grace.

My walk to Haskell's store the next day wasn't easy, but I did as directed. I told Mr. Haskell I had stolen candy and that I was sorry. I asked him to forgive me, and I gave him the nickel. He thanked me for my honesty and told me he was proud of me for coming to make things right, and he said I was forgiven. There was a definite spring in my step as I walked home that day, an experience I have known many times through the years because of God's grace to forgive.

There have been too many times when I have conveniently forgotten that God watches all. Perhaps you have too. There are times when we go our own way. Whenever this happens it is our sinful nature raising its ugly head. *Woe to those who go to great depths to hide their plans from the LORD, who do their work in darkness and think, "Who sees us? Who will know?"* (Isaiah 29:15).

We can thank God for the convicting work of the Holy Spirit who does for all His children what He did for me that day. He reminds us that He knows. He shows us our sin and calls us to repentance (Micah 7:18-19). Oh, the joy of forgiveness!

Life Application Questions:

1. What difficulties have you faced in life as a result of ignoring that your heavenly Father always watches his children and corrects them as needed?

2. What blessings have you received from remembering this lesson?

3. What response is the Holy Spirit asking of you now?

1 2

Following Jesus Won't Always Be Easy

"Blessed are you when people insult you, persecute you and falsely say all kinds of evil against you because of me. Rejoice and be glad, because great is your reward in heaven, for in the same way they persecuted the prophets who were before you" (Matthew 5:11-12)

Many Christians prefer not to read things like this. Like children, we would rather focus on fun than on tests and challenges, on the rewards and benefits of following Christ rather than on the difficulties that come. Jesus, who was Himself *despised and rejected by mankind, a man of suffering, and familiar with pain* (Isaiah 53:3), announced to those who follow Him that we too will experience rejection and suffering from those who refuse the truth.

I received a taste of this lesson as a little boy. Akin to a childhood vaccination, a little exposure then would immunize me from succumbing later to a false "health and wealth gospel," which purports that following Jesus is always easy and joyful. Being raised in a home and church where people love God, I was prone to conclude that attracting people to Jesus would be easy, but one memorable day when I was just seven years old I learned otherwise.

I loved Jesus and wanted everyone else to love Him too. One day after school I was playing with a friend at his home when I asked if he believed in Jesus. When he told me no, the first thing I could think of was if he didn't believe in Jesus he would not go to heaven when he died, so I told him so. He asked me where he would go then, and I told him if he didn't believe in Jesus he would go to hell when he died. My friend said, "My mother doesn't believe in Jesus!" to which I replied, "Then your mom won't go to heaven either. She'll go to hell!" At this my friend went crying into his house to tell his mother what I had said.

While excelling in zeal that day I failed miserably at tact. Still I was unprepared for what came next. My friend's mother tore out of her house holding the broom with which she had been sweeping her floor. She waved her broom at me and let me know in no uncertain terms I must get off their property now and I was not welcome there again!

No matter how hard it gets for God's children, following Jesus is the most incredible way to live.

I went home crying, unable to comprehend this reaction. God used my parents to teach me that everyone isn't ready to accept Jesus yet, but I must keep doing what He did. I should pray and love them as Jesus does.

Jesus said, *"If the world hates you, keep in mind that it hated me first. If you belonged to the world, it would love you as its own. As it is, you do not belong to the world, but I have chosen you out of the world. That is why the world hates you"* (John 15:18-19). I have met Christians who have suffered greatly because of faith in Jesus, including some who have lost family, home, job, or freedom. No matter how hard it gets for God's children, following Jesus is the most incredible way to live because there is such sweet fellowship with Him and His family. There is very great reward, transcending any temporary struggle we may face along the way.

Life Application Questions:

1. What hardships have you experienced for being a child of God and what assignments from God have you avoided to escape such difficulties?

2. What prevents your desire to obey Him no matter the cost?

3. What response is the Holy Spirit asking of you now?

Part II

WALKING WITH GOD AS AN ADOLESCENT

Adolescence is a challenging season of life, in part because so many changes come as we transition from childhood into adulthood. Learning how to walk with God in and through our teen years lays a solid foundation for life. What follows are important lessons I learned about walking with God when I was an adolescent, each of which has blessed me all through the years.

13

I Must Own This Faith Myself

I am reminded of your sincere faith, which first lived in your grandmother Lois and in your mother Eunice and, I am persuaded, now lives in you also (2 Timothy 1:5)

Growing up in a home where God is welcomed, His presence acknowledged, and His wisdom sought is a tremendous blessing. I thank God for giving me this gift! If you were raised in such a home, give thanks to God, for this blessing is given to relatively few. If you were not raised in a Christian home but came to Christ in your teen years or later, yours too is a testimony of grace.

I have heard many remarkable stories of how people came to faith in Jesus Christ. Some come to Him later in life out of difficult circumstances. Some walk difficult paths for years before meeting the Lord. Some live long in despair or emptiness, experiencing hard consequences of their sin or of being sinned against, so when at last they meet Christ they experience what it means to be "born again." They feel like they are at last alive!

I once met a Christian leader in Eastern Europe who was raised Muslim. When asked how he came to faith in Jesus, he gave a moving testimony of Jesus appearing to him in a dream telling him that He was the Son of God and Savior. This man was brought to his knees in repentance, surrendering his life to Jesus. No matter how or when we come to Christ, it is always a miracle of grace! When we do hear Him calling us we must personally say yes to Him. Each of us must own the faith ourselves as Timothy did. Timothy's grandmother Lois was a follower of Jesus, as was his mother Eunice (2 Timothy 1:5). But of course, God has no grandchildren. So in his first letter to Pastor Timothy, Paul celebrated that this young minister was God's child through faith in the Lord Jesus Christ.

Sadly, some who are raised in Christian homes choose to go a different way. Sometimes they reject the faith altogether, adopting the irrational but so prevalent view in our culture that truth is relative and one religious persuasion is no better than another. They may decide to select only the parts of Christianity that suit them, which is ultimately a rejection of the lordship of Jesus. Others decide to table their Christian roots for now, thinking they might eventually come back to them, but there are no guarantees they ever will. Because God allows such freedom we all face choices, and with our choices come consequences.

> *No matter how or when we come to Christ, it is always a miracle of grace!*

As a teenager I confronted these choices too. Many of my friends did not know Jesus and this world offered sharply different priorities and attractions. I faced temptations and wrestled with whether I would allow my relationship with Jesus to be the foundation of my life. One support that helped tremendously was being part of a Christian youth group. We studied and worshiped and had occasional retreats together. We had fun together and encouraged each other to grow as Christians. Such support is important for teens in every generation. Learning the benefits of Christian fellowship, friendship, and accountability brings blessing in our teen years and in all the years that follow.

God wants us to arrive at the same conviction Timothy came to. Whether it happens when we are young, middle-aged, or old, He wants us to own this faith ourselves! In my adolescent years as I was being exposed to other world views, I took a hard look at the faith I had been raised in and and came to know for myself that the message of Christ is true!

In time God blessed Helen and me with three incredible children. In Part VI I have included several lessons God taught us while walking with Him through parenting. On this theme of owning the faith ourselves I will share now a conversation my oldest son, Carl, described to me. We were blessed to adopt him when he was almost two years old, and when he was eighteen years old he wanted to meet his birth mother, so I found her and arranged a personal meeting. Sometime later Carl described to me a phone conversation he had with her. He said he had been burdened for her salvation so he phoned her to discuss the matter.

Carl said, "She said, 'You believe in Jesus because that's the way you were raised.' I replied, 'Yes, that is the way I was raised, but that is not why I believe it. I've come to know for myself it is true! Jesus is the Son of God and Lord of all!'" What music to this father's ears and to his heavenly Father's ears too! Whether in childhood, adolescence, or adulthood, God calls us to own the faith for ourselves.

Life Application Questions:

1. Who has told you the gospel of Jesus and lived the faith they proclaimed?

2. When have you ever wrestled with faith to determine if you really believed?

3. What response is the Holy Spirit asking of you now?

14

When I Call He Hears and Answers

How gracious he will be when you cry for help! As soon as he hears, he will answer you (Isaiah 30:19b)

If in adolescence we learn that God hears and answers when we call, we will always know who to call when we are in trouble; we will call upon the Lord. Perhaps the prayer most common to humanity is, "Help!" You have prayed it, haven't you? How troubling it must be to God if we only call upon Him in times of crisis. Still, He loves us and He hears and answers when we call to Him in faith. He wants us to experientially know that He is *our refuge and strength, an ever-present help in trouble* (Psalm 46:1). I know firsthand this is true. God used my parents and family to teach me this when I was a teenager. To illustrate how I learned this I will share stories about my father, then my mother, and then my brother Gary.

One occasion when God taught me that He hears and answers when I call to Him happened at one of my favorite spots on earth – Madagascal Pond in Burlington, Maine. In the years we lived in Lee, Maine, much of the wooded area in that part of the state was owned by a paper company. Logging was big business as trees were harvested for lumber and paper.

One tract of land owned by the paper company included Madagascal Pond, just seven miles from our home. The company was going to lease lakefront lots so folks could build cottages there. My dad seized the opportunity and built an A-frame cottage by a sandy beach. Later he was able to buy the lot. That lake cottage remains one of my favorite spots on earth, with memories created and countless fish caught there. We call it "Camp Gammon," and I have gone there for at least a week nearly every year of my life.

It was a beautiful summer afternoon at Madagascal Pond. In those days I was the proud owner of a pair of walkie-talkies. With these, two friends could hear each other up to half a mile away. It all sounds archaic now as we use phones or Skype to talk with friends and family around the world. In those days, however, walkie-talkies were way cool!

That afternoon I decided to go fishing by myself. Into the canoe I threw a seat cushion, fishing pole and tackle box, bait, a bottle of water, a book to read, and as an afterthought a walkie-talkie. There is a little island in the middle of the lake, so I decided to canoe to the island and fish from there. The lake was calm, the sun bright, and the day beautiful, so off I went.

After a few hours of catching fish, reading, and enjoying solitude it was time to return. I hadn't noticed the change of weather. The wind was whipping now and the lake was covered with whitecaps. I don't know if you have ever navigated a canoe through rough waters, but it's a hard thing to do even if you have two strong people operating the paddles. With only one person sitting in the back of a canoe it is impossible. I tried, though, and it soon became apparent I was in trouble. The canoe bounced around like a cork. Water splashed into the canoe and I was in danger of capsizing. Foolishly I had not brought a life jacket. No one was in sight on the lake and I was a long way from shore. I was scared.

The only thing I could think to do was to cry out to God, "Help me Lord!" That's when I remembered the walkie-talkie on the floor of the canoe. Somehow I managed to reach it without capsizing the canoe. I had no reason to expect anyone was listening on the other end, but I turned it on, pressed the speak button, and said, "Can anyone hear me? This is Stephen. I'm in trouble and I need help NOW!"

Immediately I heard my dad's voice. "I hear you son. I'm on my way." What music to my ears! My father jumped into the motorboat and in a few minutes he reached me. He helped me tie the canoe alongside the boat, I crawled into the boat with him, and in a short time I was standing with him on terra firma. I then thanked him for rescuing me. When I asked how he heard my cry for help, he said he was working on the car and his citizens band radio was on. Though his radio had a couple dozen channels on it, that day it was tuned to channel 9 – the same channel my walkie-talkie operated on! My dad was tuned in to my frequency so he heard my cry and responded. My heavenly Father has often done this for me. He hears my cry and answers my call, and comes to me when I call to Him in faith.

Later the Lord used my mother to reinforce this lesson. One occasion happened when we were living in Fair Haven, Vermont, where we had moved a few days before I started my freshman year in high school. My dad was pastor of the Fair Haven Baptist Church in Fair Haven and the Hydeville Baptist Church in nearby Hydeville. In the late fall of 1970 I required surgery to correct a deviated septum in my nose. The surgery was scheduled in Burlington, Vermont, a ninety-minute drive from our home. I expected to remain one night in the hospital post-surgery, but I spiked a fever for unknown reasons, perhaps as a reaction to the anesthesia, which meant I was required to remain in the hospital for a few days.

> *Her coming when I needed her, her love expressed in countless ways, her praying for me day after day through the years, taught me much about God's love.*

Because it was not a short drive and my parents had five other children and my dad had Sunday responsibilities, I didn't expect to see any of my family at the hospital on Sunday morning. I was feeling sick and sore and miserable and alone. I was awake late Saturday night when the nurse came in to check my temperature. She told me it was snowing hard outside and more than a foot of snow was expected. That clinched it for me. I was now sure no one from my family would come to see me the next day, so I leaned on the One I knew was always with me.

From my bed I prayed, thanking God for being with me. I said, "Lord, I'd love to see someone from my family tomorrow, but it doesn't look like it's going to happen. Be with them all even as you are with me." Soon after, I drifted off to sleep. A few hours later I opened my eyes and I couldn't be sure, but I thought someone was sitting in the chair next to my bed. "Is someone there?" I asked.

I heard, "It's me Stephen; it's your mother."

"Mom! You came?" It was snowing so hard outside, but she was determined to come, and there she was! I have never forgotten that. Her coming when I needed her, her love expressed in countless ways, her praying for me day after day through the years, taught me much about God's love. His love is faithful, tender, and constant. He comes when we need Him, every time!

I recall a time when I was scared for my brother Gary and I called upon the Lord for him. Gary was seventeen months younger than me and one school year behind me, so we were together a lot growing up. One year our high school Explorer's Club went on a camping and canoeing expedition for several days in New York. We were enjoying the great outdoors, paddling through a chain of lakes and camping along the way. This expedition was in May when the water was cold and the whitewater rapids were rough. Each aluminum canoe had two people paddling. At one point I stood on the shore watching while other canoes navigated a patch of rough whitewater. I watched in horror as the canoe my brother Gary was in capsized. His canoe was flipped upside down and pressed sideways against rocks in the middle of a strong current. I saw one head pop up – the other rider in Gary's canoe. Gary's head did not come up right away. Several seconds went by.

No one was in the water to help Gary. As this scene unfolded, God reminded me that I knew who to call on and He was in the river with Gary. I cried, "Jesus, help him!" I expect under the water Gary was praying too. Suddenly, up he popped – soaked and cold to the bone but all in one piece. How I praised God that day.

As I have walked with God through life and ministry I have often seen the promise of Isaiah 30:19 fulfilled. *How gracious he will be when you cry for help! As soon as he hears, he will answer you.*

Life Application Questions:

1. Can you recall a time when you needed His help but neglected to ask?

2. Have you experienced God answering when you called to Him in faith?

3. What response is the Holy Spirit asking of you now?

15

Joy Is Found in Serving

And do not forget to do good and to share with others, for with such sacrifices God is pleased (Hebrews 13:16)

Jesus' followers are called to serve, and in doing so there is joy. If we learn this when we are young we will want to serve Him all our days. I learned this in my teen years. It started with "customers" for whom I provided regular summer lawn services or winter snow shoveling. Most of my regulars were elderly people, many of them widows. I was initially motivated because I wanted money. Grass needed to be mowed weekly in the summer, so that income was regular. Shoveling snow was needed when it snowed, so I became excited whenever a winter storm was predicted, or snow began to fall, as this meant my pockets would soon be full.

Over time I regarded many of my customers with love. Some of the elderly women were homebound in winter. I knew they didn't get out often and some were lonely. Going from house to house with shovel in hand, I knocked first to let them know I would be working on their driveway, sidewalk, and steps. When I did this I often received an invitation to come inside when finished.

After accepting such invitations I often found a cup of hot cocoa waiting with a plate of cookies. They wanted me to stay a bit to talk. Sometimes I was annoyed as I wanted to get going, but to be polite I generally stayed a little while before going to the next house. As I drank cocoa and ate cookies, I enjoyed the conversation and listening to life stories. By the time I reached the third or fourth house, my appetite for cocoa or cookies was waning, but I always welcomed a glass of water or a few minutes of conversation. In time I looked forward to seeing them. I discovered that joy is found in having a servant's heart.

I thank God for teaching me as a teenager that there is joy in serving others. I have noticed that those who experience such joy when they are young are more likely to continue serving through their lifetime. Our sin natures are inherently self-focused, which conflicts with Christian discipleship. Jesus demonstrated the heart of a servant, and He calls His followers to do the same. When we learn this we can know a lifetime of joy in His service!

> *Jesus demonstrated the heart of a servant, and He calls His followers to do the same.*

Life Application Questions:

1. Was there a formative time in your life when you learned the joy of serving?

2. How is Jesus' example of serving reflected in your life now?

3. What response is the Holy Spirit asking of you now?

16

Give of My Best to the Master

Then Mary took about a pint of pure nard, an expensive perfume; she poured it on Jesus' feet and wiped his feet with her hair. And the house was filled with the fragrance of the perfume (John 12:3)

God asks for our best. Nothing less will do. When I was young I learned many hymns. At Sunday evening or Wednesday evening services in our church's tradition, folks were invited to select favorite hymns and we sang them. One hymn that spoke to me then was "Give of Your Best to the Master." The refrain says:

> *Give of your best to the Master;*
> *Give of the strength of your youth;*
> *Clad in salvation's full armor,*
> *Join in the battle for truth.*

I remember reflecting on what it means to give Jesus the best I have. There are two people in the Gospels Jesus commended for giving their best. One was a poor widow who gave two small copper coins. *"Truly I tell you,"* he said, *"this poor widow has put in more than all the others. All these people gave their gifts out of their wealth; but she out of her poverty put in all she had to live on"* (Luke 21:3-4).

Another person Jesus commended for giving her best is Lazarus's sister Mary who took a pint of expensive perfume and poured it on Jesus' feet, wiping his feet with her hair and filling the house with the fragrance of the perfume. Such a thing was exorbitant, and seemed foolish to some, but Mary wanted to give Jesus the best she had and He commended her for it.

Teenagers make many decisions that affect the course of their lives. Decisions to explore new interests or begin new habits can have a lifelong effect. As a Christian teenager I wrestled with many things, including trying to grasp what it means to give God my best. I came to understand that ultimately giving God my best means giving Him my all (Matthew 22:37).

For teenagers and Christians of any age for whom there are many paths to choose, the primary issue isn't what career path we will take. Rather, it's about whom we are living for. As we walk with God He teaches us to give Him our best, which is to do it all for Him. *And whatever you do, whether in word or deed, do it all in the name of the Lord Jesus, giving thanks to God the Father through Him* (Colossians 3:17). *And He died for all, that those who live should no longer live for themselves but for Him who died for them and was raised again* (2 Corinthians 5:15).

Giving God our best includes recognizing His ownership of our life. This is how we establish our life upon a firm foundation, on what really matters and will leave an enduring legacy (1 Corinthians 3:10-15). I was in high school when this awareness came, which caused a significant internal struggle for me. I wasn't sure I was ready to give God my best, so a tug of war began in me. Part of me wanted to give God my all and part of me wanted to hold back. That tug of war still raises its ugly head at times, as it does in every Christian's life. I thank God for teaching me then and teaching me still that giving to Him my best and giving lavishly, this is what He wants and in doing so is great joy. Only those who do this can realize what Mary realized – that Jesus is worth our all!

Giving God our best includes recognizing His ownership of our life.

Life Application Questions:

1. What motivates someone to want to give Jesus their very best?

2. What would it look like for you to give Jesus your best?

3. What response is the Holy Spirit asking of you now?

17

It Is Unwise to Plan Alone

Now listen, you who say, "Today or tomorrow we will go to this or that city, spend a year there, carry on business and make money." Why, you do not even know what will happen tomorrow. What is your life? You are a mist that appears for a little while and then vanishes. Instead, you ought to say, "If it is the Lord's will, we will live and do this or that" (James 4:13-15)

As we walk with God through our transition from adolescence to young adulthood, He teaches us to seek Him and lean on Him in decision making. He wants us to know how unwise it is to make life plans alone. When our oldest son was a little boy I learned this lesson the hard way when I bought his first tricycle. It came in a box with a gazillion pieces and I procrastinated until Christmas Eve to put it together. There was a picture on the box showing what it should look like. I reasoned, *It's only a tricycle! I can do this!*

I poured the pieces on the floor, took a cursory look at the instructions, and occasionally peaked at the picture on the box. It seemed obvious where the pieces went. As the tricycle took shape I was proud of myself until I tried rolling it toward the Christmas tree. When I did that, it bobbed up and down, which I was quite sure it was not supposed to do. That is when I knew I had to back up, this time paying careful attention to the manufacturer's instructions. As I worked to fix my mistakes, I was left to reflect that if I had done this first, that night would have gone so much easier! This time it came together the way it was supposed to.

I learned this next life lesson the hard way. As my high school graduation approached, I began making plans for my future. You know how it is with high school seniors. People ask, "What are you going to do with your life?" We need an answer so we make some plans. I thought I knew what I was doing. My brother was in pre-med, so I thought I would become a dentist or medical doctor, which required similar college preparation.

I applied first to the University of Maine and was accepted. I thought I knew what I was doing, but the thought of praying about it and seeking counsel from people who knew me well and listening carefully to God to discern what direction He had for me – this I did not do. I wasn't praying much then, but thankfully I had people who were praying for me. Parents and grandparents and others who knew me well were praying, and God heard their prayers.

He wants you to know you can depend on Him. He will show you the way.

One day that summer while doing custodial duties in the Fair Haven Baptist Church I picked up an issue of *Campus Life* magazine. Pausing for a break from my work I began turning pages. It featured Christian colleges across the country, listing schools, costs, and majors offered. For the first time in my decision-making process I wondered if I had made the right decision about where I would attend college. I wondered if maybe God had another plan. So I asked Him.

It was a feeble but heartfelt prayer. "Lord, if there's something here you want me to see, show it to me." I turned the pages wondering if there were any Christian colleges in New England offering pre-medicine and pre-dentistry programs. There were, one of which was Barrington College in Rhode Island. I had heard of that school and recalled that my dad attended Providence Bible Institute which, during the years he attended, relocated and became Barrington College. (If you look for Barrington College now you won't find it; in the mid-1980s it merged with Gordon College in Massachusetts.)

Reading about Barrington College I wondered if God wanted me to go there. It was mid-summer and I had announced my plans to go to the University of Maine, but as I sat that day in the basement of the church I asked God if He wanted me to change course. There probably was not enough time to make this change anyway, I reasoned, but the only way I would know was to ask. I called the school and asked if it was too late to apply. A few days later I received an application in the mail. I completed the form and put it in the mail along with an application for financial aid. In mid-August I learned I was accepted and financial aid was offered. Sensing God was in it, I attended Barrington College.

I had no idea then how that decision would affect my life, but God knew. I was a young adult and I lacked wisdom. I needed to learn that it is unwise to make decisions alone. When God's children ask Him to lead them, He will. When I tried to put that tricycle together myself, assuming I knew what I was doing, God was teaching me to lean on Him. He leads us in ways we may not understand at the time, but His grace greatly exceeds our foolishness.

We all can look back in life and recall some decisions we made based on our own limited understanding. We did not bother with the "manufacturer's instructions" or ask God to show us the way to go. We wrongly presumed we knew what we were doing, but we did not. So the tricycle wobbled. Still by God's grace He teaches us, even through the hard lessons of life. If you are a young adult now or at whatever age you may be, as you walk by faith in Jesus Christ He wants you to know you can depend on Him. He will show you the way. If you stubbornly choose to go your own way He will still teach you, but it will be a harder way to learn!

Life Application Questions:

1. Has there been a time when you learned it was unwise to make plans alone?

2. Can you describe a time when applying biblical principles allowed things to go better for you?

3. What response is the Holy Spirit asking of you now?

Part III

WALKING WITH GOD AS A YOUNG ADULT

Young adulthood is when we step out to begin assuming our place in this world. To thrive we need some degree of maturity, and hopefully we are ready. We are full of dreams and aspirations and are aiming at new things, perhaps big challenges. Our parents realized this season would come and so did we, but it doesn't mean it is easy for any of us. Leaving home is generally part of young adulthood, which requires leaving the comfort zone of what we have known.

God knows we need to lean on Him. God knows we need to walk with Him through our young adulthood, lest we veer off the path marked out for us and find ourselves in distress, dealing with the painful consequences of unwise decisions. Learning how to walk with God in and through young-adult years is important, for we are laying a foundation for our future. What follows are invaluable lessons God taught me while walking with Him in young adulthood.

18

Self-Reliance Is Deceptive

I will instruct you and teach you in the way you should go; I will counsel you with my loving eye on you. Do not be like the horse or the mule, which have no understanding but must be controlled by bit and bridle or they will not come to you (Psalm 32:8-9)

As we walk with God in young adulthood He teaches us to exchange self-reliance for God-reliance. He wants us to enjoy the benefits of relationship with Him, but self-reliance precludes closeness with God because we have wrongly reasoned we can do this ourselves. On the road of pride we convince ourselves we are on the right course, even when we are heading the wrong way entirely.

I can recall a summer night when I drove onto the interstate in Pennsylvania to head east toward New England. After driving a couple of hours I began looking for a rest stop. I saw one that said, "Welcome to Ohio!" Presuming I was driving the right way, I had actually been heading the wrong way entirely! Pulling off the highway to turn around, I kicked myself for being so foolish. If only I had paid closer attention, if only I had watched the road signs, or asked the friend asleep in the seat next to me to keep watch with me, I would have avoided this trouble. I didn't do those things because I was convinced I knew what I was doing. I was self-reliant.

I did something similar in my first year of college. Entering the on-ramp of my college years, I was sure I knew where I was going and how to get there. I majored in chemistry and studied hard. In my second semester I took twenty credits, including calculus and chemistry and vertebrate zoology. I worked so hard I did little else. I got one B+ and all the rest were A's, and I won the freshman award for highest achievement in chemistry. I was on my way.

Proud and self-reliant, I convinced myself I should graduate from a larger school. Meanwhile I was communicating with a girlfriend who would be attending the University of Vermont (UVM). These factors influenced me to apply for transfer to UVM. I was accepted and informed Barrington College I would not return. In all of this I did not ask for counsel or pray about it. I was self-reliant and forgot who I was walking with. Thinking I knew where to go, I headed the wrong way.

Psalms 32:8-9 offers a beautiful promise and a strong warning. The promise is in verse 8: *I will instruct you and teach you in the way you should go; I will counsel you with my loving eye on you.* This is a sweet gift to all who follow His direction, but verse 9 contains the warning: *Do not be like the horse or the mule, which have no understanding but must be controlled by bit and bridle or they will not come to you.* This warns us that life will be much harder when we resist God's will, fighting to go our own way. When we do that it will hurt. But even still there is a grace-filled promise. God loves us enough to break us until, like a horse or a mule, we at last trust Him and gladly go where He leads.

At the end of my first year of college I was like the horse or mule. I had no understanding and was determined to go my own way. I had not yet learned how deceptive self-reliance can be. God is the one who strengthens us and teaches us to trust Him. *He will also keep you firm to the end, so that you will be blameless on the day of our Lord Jesus Christ. God is faithful, who has called you into fellowship with his Son, Jesus Christ our Lord* (1 Corinthians 1:8-9).

Joshua 9 describes a time when the leaders of Israel made a foolish decision based on their own wisdom, and they *did not inquire of the LORD* (Joshua 9:14). The Scriptures provide many such examples of what happens when God's children neglect to seek Him and His wisdom in decision making. God offers us a better way. He wants us to exchange self-reliance for God-reliance.

Life Application Questions:

1. Can you describe a time when you gave in to the sin of self-reliance?

2. When have you depended on God for guidance and found Him making the way clear for you?

3. What response is the Holy Spirit asking of you now?

19

Neglecting Fellowship Increases Vulnerability

And let us consider how we may spur one another on toward love and good deeds, not giving up meeting together, as some are in the habit of doing, but encouraging one another—and all the more as you see the Day approaching (Hebrews 10:24-25)

Christians get into spiritual trouble when they neglect Christian fellowship. I learned this firsthand as a young adult. I attended church services occasionally, but only when I felt caught up in my studies. I never attended small group fellowships or Bible studies because I had other things to do and presumed I didn't need those things. Since I had been a Christian for many years and read my Bible, I wrongly reasoned I did not need to worship or fellowship regularly with other Christians.

The above-quoted passage from Hebrews 10 offers an important lesson God teaches us as we walk with Him. He teaches us the importance of regular worship and being in fellowship with other Christians. If we neglect such fellowship, how can we *spur one another on toward love and good deeds*? If we stay to ourselves, how can we encourage one another in Christian living?

Over the years I have seen this attitude evidenced among professing Christians, including young adults. While claiming to be in Christ we neglect relationships of accountability and fellowship with brothers and sisters, preferring to walk alone. I do not pass judgment on those who go down this path for I once did it too. But God taught me this important life lesson in His Word by allowing me to see detrimental consequences in friends who walked alone. He taught me in my college experience that whenever Christians neglect fellowship with other

Christians our vulnerability increases, and we become at increased risk of yielding to temptation.

For a season I went off course from God's best for me because I was not allowing anyone to pray with me or challenge what I was doing or why I was doing it. The Scriptures remind us to *encourage one another daily, as long as it is called "Today," so that none of you may be hardened by sin's deceitfulness* (Hebrews 3:13).

> *If we neglect such fellowship, how can we spur one another on toward love and good deeds?*

I learned this life lesson while walking with God as a young man. In the years since I have so enjoyed sharing life with brothers and sisters who have spoken into my life. God has used them to give me guidance if ever I was going off course, or to offer affirmation and confirmation when I was on the right course. I became resolved to never neglect Christian fellowship again.

Life Application Questions:

1. What consequences have you known from neglecting Christian fellowship?

2. Can you recall a time when God used Christian fellowship to strengthen you?

3. What response is the Holy Spirit asking of you now?

2 0

When God Has Our Full Attention, He Changes Us

He fell to the ground and heard a voice say to him, "Saul, Saul, why do you persecute me?" "Who are you, Lord?" Saul asked. "I am Jesus, whom you are persecuting," he replied. "Now get up and go into the city, and you will be told what you must do" (Acts 9:4-6)

When we give God our full attention He changes us. This happened to me as a young adult. For some it happens later in life, as it did for Moses and Paul, but at whatever point God has our full attention, He changes us.

Moses was tending sheep on the far side of the desert when God appeared to him and changed the course of his life. He saw a bush on fire that was not being consumed so he went closer to investigate. *When the LORD saw he had gone over to look, God called to him from within the bush, "Moses! Moses!" And Moses said, "Here I am." "Do not come any closer," God said. "Take off your sandals, for the place where you are standing is holy ground." Then he said, "I am the God of your father, the God of Abraham, the God of Isaac and the God of Jacob"* (Exodus 3:4-6a).

When Moses heard God speak that day and he gave God his full attention, the course of his life changed. Henceforth God led him in ways he never dreamed possible! God used Moses to lead Israel from bondage in Egypt to the edge of the Promised Land. God brought Moses into friendship with Himself. In time he climbed the mountain again, entering God's glory and receiving God's Word. All of this was God's grace. Moses was changed when God received his full attention.

The same happened to Saul of Tarsus (Acts 9). Zealous in his faith and a persecutor of the church, Saul was sure he was on the right course. With arrest warrants in hand he was traveling to Damascus to arrest

Jesus' followers when the risen Lord met him and Saul was changed. Imagine his shock when, knocked off his horse and blinded by a brilliant light, he heard a voice speaking his name. Utterly terrified he cried into the darkness, *"Who are you Lord?"* The reply changed his world: *"I am Jesus, whom you are persecuting."* God now had Saul's full attention, and he would never be the same! From that day forward he took direction from the Lord who immediately gave His first instruction: *"Now get up and go into the city, and you will be told what you must do."*

I have seen it many times. When by God's grace He has our full attention we are forever changed. We cannot go back to life as it was before. This happened for me on August 17, 1974. It had been a busy summer as I worked at the Grand Union Supermarket in Fair Haven, painted my neighbor's house, and mowed a number of lawns every week. I also filled in as custodian of Fair Haven Baptist Church. Saturday evening came and I realized I had not yet cleaned the church building in preparation for Sunday so I bolted down to the church to do so.

> *How about you? Have you given Him your full attention?*

In two weeks I was to begin my sophomore year at the University of Vermont, as I had transferred there from Barrington College. My girlfriend would also be attending UVM. I had arranged for an apartment and a roommate and I was enrolled in pre-med classes including organic chemistry and physics. I had my plans, but that August night God got my full attention and I was changed.

While dust-mopping the floors of the sanctuary I suddenly became aware of God's presence as His glory seemed to fill the room. I could not stand in His presence and fell prostrate before Him, like the prophet Ezekiel responded when he became vividly aware of God's presence (Ezekiel 1:28; 3:23; 44:4). I did not know what to do. I only knew I was in His presence and must be still and give Him my full attention. I cannot say if it was an audible voice or the Holy Spirit speaking to my spirit, but I heard God speak that night. He said, "Steve Gammon, who is going to be Lord of your life, you or me?" He had my full attention!

The lordship of Jesus is the essence of Christianity! Agreeing that Jesus was a great religious leader, or insightful and inspiring teacher, or even a miracle worker, is a beginning. But He was and is much more than that. As Peter proclaimed on the day of Pentecost: *"Therefore let all Israel be assured of this: God has made this Jesus, whom you crucified, both Lord and Messiah"* (Acts 2:36). Jesus Christ is Lord, and this truth brings life-changing implications to all who believe it.

Although cognitively I already knew Jesus is Lord and He cares about us, in that moment on August 17, 1974, I was aware and astounded that Jesus knew my name and was speaking to me! I was simultaneously filled with terror and joy! As to the Lord's question, I could only give one answer. With repentance and deep sorrow for having ignored this reality so long, yet with great joy at what it was going to mean I said, "You Jesus! You are Lord of all! Be Lord of all in my life!" With this resolved I could now stand. I was changed and I knew it. I had no idea how the course of my life would go but I knew He would direct me now.

God works in His children in various ways. He relates to each of us in ways unique to how He made us, but this is true for all who walk with the Lord through life and ministry: God desires our full attention. He wants us to be still and know He is God (Psalm 46:10). He wants us to listen carefully to His still small voice (Psalm 81:13). He wants us to acknowledge His lordship (Philippians 2:11) and yield our will to His (James 4:15). God is speaking! The question is, are we listening? How about you? Have you given Him your full attention?

Life Application Questions:

1. If you have ever given God your full attention, how were you changed?

2. If you believe Jesus is lord of all, how is this evidenced in the way you live?

3. What response is the Holy Spirit asking of you now?

21

He Is Lord of Where I Go, What I Say, and What I Do

But when they arrest you, do not worry about what to say or how to say it. At that time you will be given what to say, for it will not be you speaking, but the Spirit of your Father speaking through you (Matthew 10:19-20)

As we walk with Jesus in young adulthood He teaches us to let Him be lord of where we go, what we say, and what we do. This is an important lesson, and I began learning it the night I gave Him my full attention. I had to respond in some way, so I went to the piano where I played and sang from my heart to the Lord a hymn that expressed my commitment. I sang, "I'll Go Where You Want Me to Go." The words I sang are as follows:

It may not be on the mountain's height,
Or over the stormy sea;
It may not be at the battle's front,
My Lord will have need of me;

But if by a still, small voice He calls,
To paths that I do not know,
I'll answer, dear Lord, with my hand in Thine,
I'll go where You want me to go.

Refrain:
I'll go where You want me to go, dear Lord,
O'er mountain, or plain, or sea;
I'll say what You want me to say, dear Lord,
I'll be what You want me to be.

The light went on. I understood my first priority was to stay close to Him, so I would go where He wants me to go, say what He wants me to say, and do what He wants me to do. This was the only response I could give to His lordship. In the years since then I have often reflected on the words I sang to the Lord that night, as they were prophetic. I have gone wherever He has sent me, having ministered in nearly every state and on every continent but Antarctica. I have preached the gospel on the mountain heights including Mount Fuji in Japan and the Himalayas of Nepal, and in the navy on stormy seas. I have served and preached in wartime to troops on their way to war, and to churches in spiritual battle. I have gone to places and peoples He has sent me, to love them and proclaim His truth.

The light went on. I understood my first priority was to stay close to Him, so I would go where He wants me to go.

Two weeks after Jesus confronted me with His lordship I arrived at the University of Vermont. I attended my classes and did my work, but my perspective was changing because this critical issue was settled and I was beginning to grasp the implications. At whatever point in life we commit to the lordship of Jesus Christ, we will be changed because we have come to realize He is lord and we are not. This means He will now be lord of where I go, what I say, and what I do.

Life Application Questions:

1. But in your hearts revere Christ as Lord (1 Peter 3:15). What does this mean?

2. How is the lordship of Jesus affecting where you go and what you say and do?

3. What response is the Holy Spirit asking of you now?

2 2

When Jesus Is Lord of All, Relationships Realign

Anyone who loves their father or mother more than me is not worthy of me; anyone who loves their son or daughter more than me is not worthy of me. Whoever does not take up their cross and follow me is not worthy of me (Matthew 10:37-38)

In young adulthood we begin thinking about marriage and long-lasting friendships. Walking with God through this season of life we are amazed to learn that He is very personal and relational, and even cares about our personal relationships. God has eternally been in perfect relationship within the fellowship of the Trinity. We first see this affirmed in the plural pronoun of the creation account in Genesis 1:26: *Then God said, "Let us make mankind in our image, in our likeness."* God, who is personal and relational, created us in His image for relationship with Him.

The biblical story of humanity's creation describes Adam (Hebrew for "humankind") being created from the earth (Adama). Humanity's first personal relationship was with God Himself. Adam lived with God in the garden of Eden, enjoying fellowship with God. God created Adam before creating Eve, showing that the primary relationship for which humanity was created is with God. The greatest commandment emphasizes this too: *Love the LORD your God with all your heart and with all your soul and with all your strength* (Deuteronomy 6:5; Matthew 22:37).

Being in personal relationship with God we now come to Genesis 2:18: *The LORD God said, "It is not good for the man to be alone. I will make a helper suitable for him."* Having created humanity as a relational being in His image, the Designer then says it is *not good* for us to be alone. God's created purpose is that human relationships be founded upon reciprocal love with Him. God wants to be our first love, and on

PART III ~ WALKING WITH GOD AS A YOUNG ADULT

this foundation He wants us to enjoy relationships with others. His design for the covenant of marriage is for a relationship between one man and one woman, with each in personal fellowship with God, so they can thus enjoy and reflect His character through relationship with each other.

Jesus made it very clear to His disciples that love for Him takes precedence over all other relationships. *"Anyone who loves their father or mother more than me is not worthy of me; anyone who loves their son or daughter more than me is not worthy of me. Whoever does not take up their cross and follow me is not worthy of me"* (Matthew 10:37-38). These are hard words. Only those who have discovered how precious Jesus is can understand them.

Arriving at UVM to begin my sophomore year, I was nineteen years of age. A primary factor in my deciding to transfer there was a girl I had known for a few years who was dear to me. We enjoyed each other's company and loved each other, but it soon became clear to us both that there were important differences between us. We viewed our relationships with God differently. She believed in God and took her faith seriously, but she did not understand my faith perspective. This was not something we could share, and I knew I could only pursue a lifelong relationship with a woman who shared my first love.

That October I received a phone call from my friend Paul Morse, whom I had known the previous year at Barrington College in Rhode Island. He invited me to come to Barrington for homecoming weekend. He was very persistent. When I told Paul I had schoolwork to do, he encouraged me to bring it with me. When I told him I had no way to get there he said he would come and get me.

I agreed, and I am forever grateful I did. That Friday Paul drove to Burlington, Vermont, to pick me up, then we immediately drove together back to Barrington, Rhode Island. Saturday morning I entered the college library for a couple hours of study. Leaving the library I locked eyes with a student named Helen whom I remembered from the previous year when we attended a class together.

She asked, "Didn't you used to go here?"

I replied, "Yes I did," and so we began a conversation. Helen was quite direct in her questioning. She asked if I would be attending the homecoming soccer game later and we agreed to look for each other in the crowd. We spent considerable time together that afternoon at the game, and following an evening banquet we shared a long walk, talking about what God was doing in our lives and what He was teaching us, and talking about our families and how we looked forward to a life of serving Him, however He would lead. We agreed to meet the next morning to attend church services together, and before I left Sunday afternoon to return to Vermont we exchanged addresses. A few days later we both received from each other the first of many letters.

A few weeks later my friend Paul called saying that he and a few friends would be coming to Vermont for a skiing weekend and asked if they could sleep on the floor of my apartment. I agreed. When he arrived, to my joy one of the friends with him was Helen. We listened to contemporary Christian music albums and talked incessantly during her visit. Before they left to return to Rhode Island I called my parents in Fair Haven, Vermont, to ask if I could bring my friends by for breakfast on their way back to college. In a little over an hour five of us pulled into my parents' driveway.

After breakfast, as their car pulled out of the driveway, my mother said to me, "Stephen, there's something about that girl I really like!" This was the first time my mother had met Helen, but immediately she saw something special in her. She saw we were good for each other and we shared the same first love. Helen has a similar story of how her personal relationships realigned after yielding to Jesus' lordship. When we walk with the Lord through life and ministry He teaches us that when our relationship with Him is primary, other relationships will realign with His will.

Life Application Questions:

1. In what ways has the lordship of Jesus affected your personal relationships?

2. Read again Matthew 10:37-38 and also read 2 Corinthians 6:14. Why does Jesus want your love for Him to take precedence over all other relationships in life?

3. What response is the Holy Spirit asking of you right now?

23

When Jesus Is Lord of All, Priorities Realign

So I went down to the potter's house, and I saw him working at the wheel. But the pot he was shaping from the clay was marred in his hands; so the potter formed it into another pot, shaping it as seemed best to him (Jeremiah 18:3-4)

Jeremiah's picture of a potter molding the clay is a beautiful image of God's work of transforming us in every way. God is the potter and we are as clay in His hands. The clay does not determine how the potter shapes it; that is the potter's call. Our part is to be moldable in His hands so He might form us as He desires for whatever purpose He intends. Jeremiah saw and described this picture of God's grace. When the pot is *marred in his hands*, the potter does not leave it that way or discard it. He keeps working the clay, *shaping it as seem[s] best to him* (Jeremiah 18:4).

The apostle Paul made a similar point in 2 Corinthians 5:17: *Therefore, if anyone is in Christ, the new creation has come: The old has gone, the new is here!* When we allow Jesus to reign on the throne of our hearts a transformation begins. Indeed, *The old has gone, the new is here!* Now we do as Jeremiah encouraged: *Let us examine our ways and test them, and let us return to the LORD* (Lamentations 3:40).

Acts 2 describes the birth of the church. When the Holy Spirit descended in power at Pentecost, new life came upon believers in Jesus and they were never again the same. Verse 42 describes changes they shared: *They devoted themselves to the apostles' teaching and to fellowship, to the breaking of bread and to prayer.* Four priorities were evident among early Christians as they *devoted themselves* to these things. In the months I attended UVM God established these priorities in me.

(1) When Jesus is Lord of all to us we become hungry for God's Word. *They devoted themselves to the apostles' teaching.* Early Christians could not get enough of the apostles' teaching. They wanted to learn all they could about Jesus. This priority grows in us as we yield to Him. As the psalmist said, *How sweet are your words to my taste, sweeter than honey to my mouth!* (Psalm 119:103)

In my days at UVM I attended classes and did my homework, but it did not satisfy me like studying God's Word did. I read the Bible daily, savoring passages that spoke to me, and I kept a journal. What I was learning was so incredible I could not keep it to myself. Like early Christians described in Acts 2, I wanted to learn more and to discuss these things with others who loved Him too. Just as it is more enjoyable to eat a good meal with friends than to do so alone, I began seeking opportunities to enjoy His Word with others. Are you devoted to God's Word?

(2) When Jesus is Lord of all to us we become hungry for Christian fellowship. *They devoted themselves to ... fellowship.* Early Christians loved coming together. They had no concept of individualized Christianity. They were God's family and wanted to enjoy family, so they devoted themselves to fellowship. The book of Acts goes on to describe how they demonstrated love for each other by sharing their resources. Who wouldn't be attracted to a fellowship like that?

While at UVM I began attending InterVarsity Christian Fellowship meetings where I met people who loved Jesus and wanted to grow in faith. I gathered around me Christian brothers. We held each other accountable, prayed for each other, and studied God's Word together weekly, applying passages like 1 Corinthians 8:9 that teach us to look out for weaker brothers. I led the study. I loved it and could not get enough of it. When Jesus Christ is Lord of all to us we will become hungry for Christian fellowship. Are you seeking and enjoying such fellowship?

(3) When Jesus Christ is Lord of all to us we become hungry for communion with Him. *They devoted themselves ... to the breaking of bread.* The early church was led by the apostles who had known and enjoyed Jesus' presence during His years among them. Surely they missed that, but when they gathered and broke bread with other disciples they

remembered His promise to be with them whenever they gathered in His name, even as they shared in the Lord's Supper that He instituted.

Early Christians devoted themselves to the breaking of bread because they loved communion with Jesus. When He is Lord of all in us He satisfies our spiritual hunger as nothing else can. Jesus said, *"I am the bread of life. Whoever comes to me will never go hungry, and whoever believes in me will never be thirsty." "But here is the bread that comes down from heaven, which anyone may eat and not die. I am the living bread that came down from heaven. Whoever eats this bread will live forever. This bread is my flesh, which I will give for the life of the world"* (John 6:35, 50-51).

> *A lifestyle of worship became part of my life, with quiet times sitting at His feet and resting in His presence.*

While attending UVM I increasingly longed for communion with Jesus. A lifestyle of worship became part of my life, with quiet times sitting at His feet and resting in His presence. I listened to Christian music that expressed my desire to adore Him. I spent time with Jesus every morning and throughout every day. I wanted to walk with Jesus as the disciples did on the road to Emmaus (Luke 24:13-35), to invite Him into my home as Mary and Martha and Lazarus did (John 12:1-11), to sit at His feet and hang onto every word as Mary did (Luke 10:38-42), and to go wherever He would send me as His disciples did (Mark 6:7). When Jesus Christ is Lord of all in us we will become hungry for communion with Him; we won't be able to get enough of Him. Are you longing for such communion with Jesus?

(4) When Jesus Christ is Lord of all to us we will become hungry for prayer. *They devoted themselves ... to prayer.* The apostles lived a lifestyle of prayer because Jesus taught them to live this way. They often saw Jesus pray (Luke 5:16) so they asked Him to teach them how (Luke 11:1-13). After Jesus ascended into heaven what did they do? *They all joined together constantly in prayer* (Acts 1:14). Why did they do that? Because prayer connected them with Him. The story of the early church in Acts shows the apostles and the church often in prayer. This is essential in all for whom Jesus Christ is Lord.

Prayer is far more than something we do when in trouble. Prayer is like our spiritual oxygen supply; we need it to breathe. The privilege we are offered through Christ to approach God's throne is too priceless to ignore. *For we do not have a high priest who is unable to empathize with our weaknesses, but we have one who has been tempted in every way, just as we are—yet he did not sin. Let us then approach God's throne of grace with confidence, so that we may receive mercy and find grace to help us in our time of need* (Hebrews 4:15-16).

I began developing my prayer life at UVM. I started my days in prayer, prayed throughout the day, and at times joined with others to pray. All for whom Jesus Christ is Lord will increasingly learn to devote themselves to prayer, to hear whatever He has to say. We will want to share what is on our heart, laying it all out and seeking His direction. We will pray because we need His power and grace in every situation. We will long to enter the tent of meeting as Moses did to share communion with God. When Jesus Christ is Lord of all to us we become hungry to pray!

These priorities give evidence that Jesus Christ is Lord of all to us. As was true for the first Christians, we will be hungry for His Word, hungry for Christian fellowship, hungry for communion with Jesus, and hungry for prayer.

Life Application Questions:

1. If being a devoted follower of Jesus was a crime and you were charged and brought to trial for this, what evidence would there be to bring a conviction?

2. How does your life reflect each of the four priorities listed in Acts 2:42?

3. What response is the Holy Spirit asking of you now?

2 4

The Lord of All Reveals His Presence

If you remain in me and my words remain in you, ask whatever you wish, and it will be done for you (John 15:7)

God wants us to believe His Word. Knowing what it says is not enough. He wants us to stand on it in faith! When we do so He reveals His presence in ways we would not see otherwise. There are many examples in Scripture of people who stood in faith on God's promises and thus saw God's deliverance. He wants the same for us. God taught me this lesson when I was a young man.

Shadrach, Meshach, and Abednego were young men who trusted God in the midst of a fiery furnace. As they did so God revealed Himself, standing with them in the flames and delivering them from harm (Daniel 3). Consider also Daniel in the lions' den, when God closed the mouths of hungry lions (Daniel 6). Or consider the apostles in the public jail praying and trusting God to meet them in their time of need. During the night an angel of the Lord opened the doors and brought them out, which brought forth praise in the early church, increasing the opportunities to tell the good news of Jesus (Acts 5:17-42). God has not changed since the days of the Bible! *Jesus Christ is the same yesterday and today and forever* (Hebrews 13:8).

I will not forget the day my Lord taught me this lesson in remarkable fashion. That morning as I read God's Word the Holy Spirit challenged me to believe it. The Scriptures that day were familiar as I had read them before. They included God's promise to hear whenever I called upon Him, that He would give me what I asked of Him in faith (John 15:7).

When the Holy Spirit asks a question I am often prone to give a quick response, without prayerfully considering the implications of my answer. But that day the Spirit pressed in. "Do you really believe this, Steve?" God was promising to hear me when I prayed in faith, to demonstrate His glory when I call upon Him. He was asking if I believed this. I wrestled with this question for a while, then by grace I resolved, "Yes Lord, I do believe it. I believe you will hear and answer me anytime I call to you in faith."

That evening God gave me an opportunity to stand on this promise. It was a stormy winter night in Vermont. Snow was falling fast and getting deep. It was cold and the wind was blowing. Not realizing how bad driving conditions were I ventured onto the roads. I saw very few cars. It appeared everyone heeded the warnings to stay off the roads except me.

Driving up a small hill I lost traction and slid off the road into a ditch. The car was tilted sideways in the ditch at about a thirty-degree angle, stuck in deep snow. It would be a long walk to get help, and this was before cellphones. It was cold outside and I saw no signs of life to wave down help. My inclination was to panic.

God reminded me of His presence and I felt the warmth of His peace. He reminded me of the Scripture I had read earlier and again asked if I believed what I had read, that He would hear and answer when I called to Him in faith. I said, "Yes Lord, I believe." Then He said, "Then ask me." With the car tipped sideways in the ditch and my hands on the steering wheel I bowed in a prayer of faith. "Dear Lord, standing on your promise I look to you now. I do not know how you will do it, but I ask you to get me out of this ditch, and when you do all the praise and glory will be yours!"

He has reminded me that I am not alone, for He hears whenever I call.

When I lifted my head I saw two men in my rear-view mirror, standing behind the car. One of them motioned for me to put the car in gear. Though startled, I obliged. The two men literally picked up the back of the car, so with front-wheel drive I got traction and drove out of the ditch to the top of the little hill. I then got out of my car to thank the men who had lifted me from that ditch, but no one was there. There were no cars; there were no people; no one was there!

I sat on the side of the road dumbfounded, overflowing with praise to God for His remarkable answer to my prayer of faith. I thought of Hebrews 1:14 which speaks of angels as *ministering spirits sent to serve those who will inherit salvation,* and Hebrews 13:2 which speaks of entertaining *angels without knowing it.* In the years since then there have been many more occasions when I have confronted fear or faced a situation that on the surface seemed to be impossible. In those times, as I have walked with God He has reminded me that I am not alone, for He hears whenever I call. That promise is for all His children.

Life Application Questions:

1. Has there been a time when God revealed His presence to you in answer to your prayer of faith?

2. Read John 15:7. What does Jesus desire from you whenever you confront what appears to be an impossible situation?

3. What response is the Holy Spirit asking of you now?

25

The Lord of All Directs My Steps

LORD, I know that people's lives are not their own; it is not for them to direct their steps (Jeremiah 10:23)

As we walk with the Lord He directs our steps and we must let Him do so. Several years ago I saw a bumper sticker that said, "God is my copilot." At first I liked it, but then God reminded me He has no desire to be the copilot, going wherever I wish to go. His desire is to be the pilot of my life, taking me wherever He wants me to go.

At the beginning of my adult journey I regarded God as my copilot. I was happy to have Him come along, but I decided where to go. When I decided to prepare for medicine or dentistry, I never asked God if this was the direction He intended for me. Now something was changed inside of me. Now I began to pray, "Show me your will, Lord. Lead me in the way you want me to go, for I belong to you."

Praying a prayer like this is wise for every disciple of Jesus Christ. This is the sort of prayer God loves to answer. For me, direction came through the group of friends with whom I studied the Bible. At the conclusion of one of our studies my friends said, "Steve, we have something we are agreed about and want to discuss with you."

"What is it?" I asked.

"What you have been doing with us, we believe this is what God has created you to do. You are called to this, Steve! You need to be someplace where you can prepare to do this with your life." I immediately knew this was a message from the Lord. They were right! Nothing gave me more joy than shepherding God's people, making disciples of Jesus, and studying and teaching God's Word. I thanked them profusely for sharing this with me and I began to pray for God to steer me the way He wanted me to go.

As I prayed about this, my excitement began to grow about devoting my life to the service of Jesus Christ, shepherding His church, and introducing people to Him. As time went by Paul's words in 1 Corinthians 9:16 expressed what was burning in my soul: *For when I preach the gospel, I cannot boast, since I am compelled to preach. Woe to me if I do not preach the gospel!*

So I began to ask, "Where do you want me now, Lord? Where can I study and learn and grow for the life of service you intend for me?" As I prayed I knew the answer. Barrington College, the school I had attended the year before, had a great biblical studies department. I contacted the school to inquire about transferring back as a biblical studies major. I was accepted and again offered financial aid, so after just one semester at UVM I was headed back to Barrington College, but in a very different place spiritually than I was the year before. God was steering my course now. I knew it and determined this was how I wanted to live the rest of my days.

> *His desire is to be the pilot of my life, taking me wherever He wants me to go.*

The Bible promises this to all who will trust Him. *Trust in the LORD with all your heart and lean not on your own understanding; in all your ways submit to him, and he will make your paths straight* (Proverbs 3:5-6). *Whether you turn to the right or to the left, your ears will hear a voice behind you, saying, "This is the way; walk in it"* (Isaiah 30:21). What wonderful promises of God for all who trust in Him, allowing Christ to be Lord of all in our lives.

Life Application Questions:

1. In what ways has your life gone off course because of failure to yield to the lordship of Jesus?

2. In what ways has the Lord Jesus provided clear leading in your life?

3. What response is the Holy Spirit asking of you now?

26

God Satisfies the Thirsty With the Holy Spirit

On the last and greatest day of the festival, Jesus stood and said in a loud voice, "Let anyone who is thirsty come to me and drink. Whoever believes in me, as Scripture has said, rivers of living water will flow from within them." By this he meant the Spirit, whom those who believed in him were later to receive. Up to that time the Spirit had not been given, since Jesus had not yet been glorified (John 7:37-39)

As we walk through life with God our spiritual thirst is satisfied. Jesus promises to quench our thirst by the Holy Spirit and He teaches us to come often and drink.

When I returned to Barrington College, I was thirsty spiritually. I wanted more of God and I was beginning to become acquainted with the third person of the Trinity, whom Jesus promised to all who love Him (John 14:15-17). I read the Scriptures describing the Holy Spirit's work in the life of believers and in the church. I understood that the Spirit is God Himself empowering and satisfying all who trust in Jesus and are spiritually hungry and thirsty for Him. I pondered Jesus' instructions to His disciples to *wait for the gift my Father promised, which you have heard me speak about* (Acts 1:4). I wanted the power He promised for being His witness: *"But you will receive power when the Holy Spirit comes on you; and you will be my witnesses in Jerusalem, and in all Judea and Samaria, and to the ends of the earth"* (Acts 1:8).

Being spiritually thirsty I asked for more of Him, and when I asked He satisfied completely. Jesus said, *"Which of you fathers, if your son asks for a fish, will give him a snake instead? Or if he asks for an egg, will give him a scorpion? If you then, though you are evil, know how to give good gifts to your children, how much more will your Father in heaven give the Holy Spirit to those who ask him!"* (Luke 11:11-13)

Within Christ's church there are various theological understandings concerning the work of the Holy Spirit in the lives of Christians. We are called to love and respect one another regarding these differences. With Christ as our first love, and the Scriptures as our infallible guide, we must always approach our search for truth humbly, committed to love and fellowship with brothers and sisters who are equally committed to the authority of Scripture but whose experience or understanding differs from our own.

> We should examine our experiences through the filter of Scripture, for God's Word is infallible but our experience is not!

Recognizing our human frailty we are wise to avoid examining Scripture only through the filter of our own experiences. Rather, we should examine our experiences through the filter of Scripture, for God's Word is infallible but our experience is not! With this in mind, as a young man I resolved to seek the Holy Spirit to more fully understand Christ's revelation about Him. I asked my heavenly Father for the fullness of the gift He promised. I asked Him to empower me, reveal Himself to me, and work in me any way He would choose, even if I did not fully understand. I prayed and trusted Him to answer.

The last part of my prayer was a breakthrough for me, because though I loved the Lord, I was limiting my faith to my ability to comprehend. I struggled with accepting truths I could not grasp. God began reminding me that He is God and I am not, so my faith must transcend understanding. He brought me to Isaiah 55:8-9 which I meditated on for many days: *"For my thoughts are not your thoughts, neither are your ways my ways,"* declares the LORD. *"As the heavens are higher than the earth, so are my ways higher than your ways and my thoughts than your thoughts."*

Because He is God and I am not, of course He will work in ways beyond my understanding. I resolved to invite Him to work in me, through me, and around me, even if I could not fully understand His ways. Toward this end I prayed, and He answered my prayer. One way He did so was by giving to me a prayer language I did not understand.

I had read of this in chapter 14 of Paul's first letter to the church at Corinth, but because I did not comprehend it, previously I passed it by.

My assigned roommate upon my return to Barrington College was a young man with an intimate knowledge of the Holy Spirit. I still chuckle at the memory of entering our room my first week there and hearing him in the shower singing away in his prayer language. When I asked about it, he pointed me to 1 Corinthians 14:2, 14-15, which describes speaking in a language that speaks not to men but only to God, uttering mysteries with the spirit. I observed that Paul encouraged praying and singing with our mind and with our spirit.

I could not wrap my mind around these Scriptures and I wrestled in prayer about it. God challenged me yet again, asking if I was willing to trust Him to work in my life even in ways I would not understand. Being thirsty for more of Him I said, "Yes, Lord. Work in me in any way you desire! I want the fullness of your Spirit in my life." (See Acts 1:4-5; Ephesians 5:18.) I invited another student to pray with me.

After praying in this way at first I felt no different. Though I had no emotional reaction I was fully resolved to allow the Holy Spirit to have all of me. The next day while kneeling alone in prayer I opened my mouth to praise the Lord and heard myself speaking a prayer language I had never before heard and did not understand. The joy in my soul and praise in my heart was full! Through the years since then I have prayed with my mind and also with my spirit (1 Corinthians 14:15). I have worshiped God with understanding and in ways that transcend understanding. The Holy Spirit is the one who increases our thirst for God and then satisfies us with streams of living water flowing from within.

The apostle Paul made it clear the Holy Spirit does not work in all of us the same way. This implies that every Christian will not speak in tongues (1 Corinthians 12:18-20; 27-31). Do I believe the gift of tongues is the sign of the baptism of the Holy Spirit or every Christian should speak in tongues or have a prayer language? Though I respect those who interpret Scripture this way, my answer to each of these is no.

Still, Paul was not hesitant to let people know he personally spoke in tongues (1 Corinthians 14:18) and he instructed, *do not forbid speaking in tongues* (1 Corinthians 14:39). He prohibited people from overemphasizing this gift, however, teaching that it was much more important to seek gifts that edify others, and that none of it matters unless we demonstrate Christ's love.

While walking with God I have learned that He loves to satisfy people who are thirsty for more of Him. I was so thirsty for God then that I longed for a river of life to flow from within, so I asked Him to have all of me. In the years since then there have been times when I have allowed sin or the distractions of this world to block the flow of His Spirit. Perhaps you have done the same. But God is ever merciful and He forgives. He keeps inviting us into deeper waters with Him.

Life Application Questions:

1. What is it like to be hungry and thirsty for God?

2. Are you willing for God to work in you in ways you may not fully understand?

3. What response is the Holy Spirit asking of you now?

27

Christian Fellowship Is Sweet

*Now you are the body of Christ, and each one
of you is a part of it* (1 Corinthians 12:27)

God teaches us to treasure the sweet gift of fellowship with other Christians. The book of Acts describes a church composed of disciples who loved being together! *Every day they continued to meet together in the temple courts. They broke bread in their homes and ate together with glad and sincere hearts, praising God and enjoying the favor of all the people. And the Lord added to their number daily those who were being saved* (Acts 2:46-47).

Followers of Jesus are to care for each other, share life together, and be real with each other. Led of the Spirit, they open their homes to one another, speak into each other's lives, pray and worship together, grow and love together, and reach out to people who don't yet know Him. In my travels among churches I have witnessed and experienced this often, and it is wonderful!

Such fellowship reflects Jesus' character. That is why the apostle Paul referred to the church as *the body of Christ*. When we experience loving fellowship with one another Jesus' life is expressed in us. He inhabits His church in wisdom, power, and love, and people are drawn to Him because they experience Him in the church! This is why Acts 2 says He added to their number daily those who were being saved. These Christians did not go to church; they were the church.

For many churches this kind of Christian fellowship is a foreign idea. For such congregations the church is a place to go to or an organization to be a part of, to participate in whatever worship format they are comfortable with, and to hear a message that reinforces what they believe or that helps them feel better. But they will not risk being vulnerable or share their true selves with each other. They do not fervently pray together, or cry and grieve together, or laugh and rejoice together. Because of this they cannot possibly show unbelievers how wonderful Jesus is, so they rarely if ever see anyone come to newfound faith.

I have also seen and been part of churches that do offer genuine expressions of Christian fellowship, as people sacrificially give and love each other tangibly, and because of it people are drawn to the Lord. My own eyes were opened to the sweetness of such fellowship after returning to Barrington. I met faculty and students who had a deep relationship with Jesus. We were from many denominational backgrounds and attended various local churches, but we loved each other, we loved Jesus Christ together, and we regularly met to worship Him and support each other. We were a family in Christ, a privilege He offers us all.

> *God teaches us to treasure the sweet gift of fellowship with other Christians.*

Life Application Questions:

1. Where and how have you experienced Christian fellowship?

2. How are you experiencing such fellowship now, or how will you seek it?

3. What response is the Holy Spirit asking of you now?

28

Keeping the Main Thing the Main Thing Honors Jesus

Finally, all of you, be like-minded, be sympathetic, love one another, be compassionate and humble (1 Peter 3:8)

As we walk with God through life and ministry He teaches us to keep the main thing the main thing. If we learn this well when we are young we can be His instruments for bringing unity among those who follow Him. If we do not learn this well, we may presume we are pleasing Him when we are dishonoring Him. In Jesus' prayer in John 17 He prayed for His disciples and all who would become His disciples. He prayed for us. He prayed this on the night before His crucifixion, knowing what was coming. In the context of this prayer, we know with certainty that the things for which Jesus prayed were enormously important to Him!

A primary focus of His prayer was that those who walk with Him will not be divided, but will be one. The words of His prayer included these: *that all of them may be one, Father, just as you are in me and I am in you. May they also be in us so that the world may believe that you have sent me. I have given them the glory that you gave me, that they may be one as we are one—I in them and you in me—so that they may be brought to complete unity. Then the world will know that you sent me and have loved them even as you have loved me* (John 17:21-23).

Why did Jesus focus on this theme before His arrest, suffering, and death? He was intentional in all He did so this emphasis, too, was purposeful. Considering what I know of church history and in view of what I have witnessed in churches, I believe Jesus passionately prayed these things because He knew that Satan would lead an all-out assault against the unity of the church to divide us by our differences. He knew if the church becomes divided, its witness is made ineffective.

Because Christian unity would not come easily, Jesus prayed fervently. Those who walk with Him must follow suit. We too must pray for biblical unity, lest differences divide us. Paul reminded the church that attaining spiritual unity requires effort. He said, *Make every effort to keep the unity of the Spirit through the bond of peace* (Ephesians 4:3). Other New Testament letters include this message too. The early church had to be reminded not to allow their differences to divide them (1 Corinthians 1:10; 1 Peter 3:8).

God gave me this vision for biblical Christian unity when I was a young man attending Barrington College. There I became friends with people from a wide range of denominational and theological perspectives. I had friends who were Baptist, Presbyterian, Congregational, Episcopalian, Catholic, Methodist, Assembly of God, Pentecostal, Evangelical Covenant, non-denominational, Christian and Missionary Alliance, Evangelical Free, Evangelical Friends, Plymouth Brethren, Orthodox and more. In biblical survey or theology courses it led to very interesting discussions at times, even more so when we studied the Bible together.

When people of different backgrounds, perspectives, and interpretations who love and follow Jesus also love and respect each other, we reflect His heartbeat.

I learned to love and respect brothers and sisters in Christ who walked with the Lord and were equally committed to the authority of Holy Scripture, yet who appreciated other traditions and interpreted Scripture differently on various matters. In most cases I found in the core essentials of our faith – including matters of salvation by grace alone through faith alone in Jesus Christ alone – we were fully agreed. God is honored when those who follow Him achieve unity on the core essentials of faith and who love and respect one another regarding our differences.

In every local church I have been part of there have been Christians with varying understandings on many matters. This is not a bad thing; it simply reflects the breadth of the church. When people of different backgrounds, perspectives, and interpretations who love and follow Jesus also love and respect each other, we reflect His heartbeat. Such love draws people to Him.

Life Application Questions:

1. What does biblical Christian unity look like, and how have you witnessed it?

2. How is Jesus' prayer for unity in the church having an impact on you?

3. What response is the Holy Spirit asking of you now?

29

Christian Marriage Partners in Love and Service

But for Adam no suitable helper was found. So the LORD God caused the man to fall into a deep sleep; and while he was sleeping, he took one of the man's ribs and then closed up the place with flesh. Then the LORD God made a woman from the rib he had taken out of the man, and he brought her to the man (Genesis 2:20-22)

For young adults who follow Jesus and hope to experience marriage as God intends, learning about the ultimate purpose of Christian marriage is of vital importance. Genesis 2 makes it clear that only God could provide what Adam needed, and He did. There is considerable theology in these few verses. The designer of the universe and of humanity was establishing the first human relationship, the foundation of all civilization.

Again, the first relationship humanity enjoyed was with God Himself. We see this in Adam who lived in relationship with God in Eden. Though this was God's created intention for humanity, this relationship was broken by sin, as God cannot allow sin in His holy presence. Then at the right time Christ came as the second "Adam" to re-establish what was irreparably broken by Adam's sin, so humanity could be restored to relationship with God (1 Corinthians 15:22, 44-50).

On the foundation of relationship with God by grace through faith in Jesus, God now offers the potential of a right relationship with others, including marriage. Biblically defined marriage is a man and a woman in a lifetime commitment, loving and serving Him together. This was His design for Adam and Eve and it remains His design today. The apostle Paul quoted from Genesis 2 and added that marriage is a picture of the love and commitment between Christ and His church.

"For this reason a man will leave his father and mother and be united to his wife, and the two will become one flesh" (Ephesians 5:31).

I imagine Adam's joy when he awoke from his sleep, shook off his drowsiness, and saw Eve for the first time. Genesis 2:23 provides a glimpse of his excitement. His dream was more than fulfilled. Eve was a suitable helper, a life partner to love, with whom He could serve the Lord.

I sometimes thought about such things as a child. I knew I would marry when I grew up, so now and then as a child, I remember asking Jesus to watch over the little girl whom I would one day marry. I asked God to give her a good day. Helen and I have laughed about it, wondering how this may have affected her as a child, as we know God hears the prayers of His children.

As a young man, when I realized God was leading me into ministry I knew I would need a life partner. I wasn't looking for a spouse then; I just grew to love Helen. I loved being with her, watching her, listening to her, and dreaming with her. After one semester back at Barrington College I was smitten. I was just twenty years old, so I didn't want to think about marriage yet, but I knew I wanted to spend my life with Helen.

That summer Helen was in Europe ministering with the Slavic Gospel Association. Living in France she went on excursions into Eastern Europe smuggling Bibles in the back of a Volkswagen van to deliver to Christians. While she was in Europe I was in Pennsylvania working with a painting contractor. I worked hard that summer saving money for college, and Helen and I exchanged letters, but the time apart was hard. She had one year of college remaining and then would be gone, a prospect that disturbed me greatly. When we returned to school that fall I was glad to be with her again. I envisioned spending the rest of my life with Helen as partners in love and service.

This was a decision I would not make without wise counsel. I decided to seek it from three men I respected: my father, Helen's father, and Harold Fickett, the president of the college. I first scheduled an appointment with Dr. Fickett, as I had become acquainted with him through ministries including student government.

When I entered his office, Dr. Fickett asked what I wished to discuss with him. I told him I was considering asking Helen to marry me, but as I was only twenty years old, I wanted to be sure I wasn't rushing things. At this he leaned back in his chair, smiled warmly, and said, "Stephen, my wife and I have been married for thirty-five years, and I have just one regret."

I asked, "What's that, sir?"

Laughing, he replied, "I didn't marry her sooner!" He then said, "Readiness for marriage has little to do with age and everything to do with love and commitment to God and the one with whom you are making a lifelong covenant." He was giving me the green light.

The next person I asked was my father, which required a trip home. I got a few minutes alone with him and said, "Dad, I love Helen and want to spend my life with her. Do you think I'm old enough to get married?"

He looked at me with a grin and said, "A-yuh!" For those of you who aren't from Maine, that means "Yes!" He had a few more things to say, but the bottom line was I had his blessing too! Others could see our relationship was right, and in my heart I knew it was. Helen and I shared a similar goal, to love and serve the Lord wherever He would lead us. We could do this better together than alone. I was excited about being her husband.

> *His intention is that marriage be founded upon a shared love for Him and a prayerful commitment to love and serve Him together.*

The last person I asked was Helen's dad, Bob Richter, as I wanted to formally ask for his daughter's hand in marriage. My opportunity came when he and Nancy, Helen's mom, visited Barrington College during homecoming weekend. Requesting a moment of his time, I told Bob I loved his daughter and wished to spend the rest of my life with her. I then asked for his blessing. At first I thought he was upset, as he wept, but soon he smiled and said these were tears of joy as he loved me and he knew Helen and I would be good for each other, and yes, he would give his blessing. At that I knew this was the right course.

Many years have gone by since then. Recently I visited Christian friends who have been married longer than Helen and I have and remain much in love and active as partners in His service. The wife said, "I love my husband more now than ever!" I can relate, as Helen and I feel the same way.

We all live in a broken world in which many people have not known what Helen and I have experienced in marriage. Perhaps heartache and broken promises have been part of your life experience. If so, I am sorry for your pain. God wants you to know He loves you and His love never fails. If you are currently in a marriage, even if it is far from what you want it to be, I hope you will pray for God to have His way, to help you love your spouse as Jesus loves you. If you need godly counsel please ask God to lead you to someone who can provide it. If you are not currently in marriage but desire to be one day, please don't settle for anything less than God's best for you. His intention is that marriage be founded upon a shared love for Him and a prayerful commitment to love and serve Him together.

Life Application Questions:

1. What does God's created intention for marriage look like, and how have you experienced or witnessed it?

2. What impact could it make if you regularly prayed for yourself and the people you love, for God's created intention for marriage?

3. What response is the Holy Spirit asking of you now?

30

God Loves Giving Good Gifts to His Children

If you, then, though you are evil, know how to give good gifts to your children, how much more will your Father in Heaven give good gifts to those who ask him! (Matthew 7:11)

God wants us to discover that He loves giving gifts to His children. I learned this in a memorable way. Though I knew Helen would become my wife, I had not yet formally asked her. I wanted to do it in a way that would put a smile on her face for the rest of her life. I knew she would want an engagement ring. I learned her ring size and went to a jewelry store to price one. For three hundred dollars I could get a diamond ring she would love, but I had no money to buy a ring. All the money I saved was for tuition and room and board, and the money I was earning during the school year was for day-to-day expenses. Three hundred dollars was a fortune to me.

I wrestled with asking God to meet this need. Could I expect Him to care about something like my desire to buy Helen an engagement ring? I wondered if it was presumptuous to ask, but God invites us to *Cast all your anxieties on Him because He cares for you* (1 Peter 5:7), so I prayed, offering Him this concern. When I prayed He reminded me that He is my heavenly Father and He loves to give good gifts to His children who ask Him (Matthew 7:11).

I prayed like this: "Heavenly Father, you know I love Helen and want to marry her. I want to formally ask her to marry me so we can begin making plans for our life together. When I do this I want to give her an engagement ring. To buy a ring will cost three hundred dollars which I do not have. I have no idea where to get such a sum of money, so I turn to you. I know you can provide in a way that is totally unexpected to me. So I am asking you to please make a way for me to buy a ring for Helen. I trust you for the answer and I ask this in Jesus' name. Amen."

I told no one about my need or about the prayer I had prayed, but God heard me. He definitely heard me! Two or three days later when I opened my mailbox at the college post office I found a letter from Lee, Maine, where I had lived as a little boy. The return address on the envelope said it was from Mrs. Virginia Smith. I was surprised to receive a letter from her, as I had not seen her since I was a child. Holding her letter in my hands my mind reviewed memories of her as my Sunday school teacher, of her husband Hershey and their children, and of the special week when I stayed with their family while my parents were away.

> *I marvel at how God loves to give good gifts to His children.*

I opened the envelope and read her letter, which said, *Dear Stephen, I have been praying for you. When Hershey and I asked the Lord what He wanted us to do with extra tithe money from income he earned this summer, He told us to send it to you. We think you might have a special need of some kind for which this gift can be used. We know God has great plans for you in His service, and with our prayers and this gift we want to encourage you. With much love, Mrs. Virginia Smith.*

After reading the letter I looked in the envelope and found a check, and you guessed it! The amount of the check was three hundred dollars, the exact amount I had asked God to provide. I don't mind telling you I stood in that post office with tears of joy trickling down my face. My joy came from the fact that I now had the funds needed to buy my sweetheart an engagement ring, but even more my heart overflowed for this vivid reminder of my heavenly Father's care. Our Father loves to give good gifts to His children! Praise His name!

A few days later I bought the ring and told Helen I wanted to take her to dinner in Boston, after which we would continue north to Maine to see my parents and sisters, whom we had not seen for a couple of months. She agreed, so I made reservations at the Top of the Hub restaurant on the highest floor of the Prudential building in Boston. It was an elegant restaurant with a fantastic view of the city, and the food was great! Helen was chatty and enjoying every bite of her dinner, while I nervously picked at my food until before dessert I popped the question and gave her the ring. She let out a yelp and answered with an enthusiastic, "Yes!"

With joy we traveled on to Maine and shared our good news with my family, then called Helen's family to let them know too. What a memorable day that was! I still marvel at how God loves to give good gifts to His children. Has He not taught this lesson to you? He teaches it as we walk with Him in faith through life and ministry.

Life Application Questions:

1. Do you recall a time when your Father in heaven showed how He loves to give good gifts to you?

2. Why is it so important to remember and thank Him for His gifts to us?

3. What response is the Holy Spirit asking of you now?

3 1

Choosing Obedience Brings Reward

*May your fountain be blessed, and may you rejoice in the wife
of your youth. For your ways are in full view of the LORD,
and He examines all your paths* (Proverbs 5:18, 21)

The further we walk with the Lord through life and ministry, the more we learn that choosing obedience brings great reward. We do well to pay attention to this when we are young. Since the dawn of history God has reminded His people that He is God and we are not. He has taught that when we obey His Word we know His blessing, but when we disregard His Word we will face consequences.

In Eden God said to Adam, *"You are free to eat from any tree in the garden; but you must not eat from the tree of the knowledge of good and evil, for when you eat of it you will surely die"* (Genesis 2:16-17). Adam and Eve presumed to know better. They thought they were wise enough to decide for themselves whether to obey God's commands, and they willfully sinned. Then they faced the consequences. The fellowship previously enjoyed with God was broken and they were forced from Eden. The intimacy they had known with each other was broken too, and the long-term consequences upon family and humanity were catastrophic. Their firstborn son Cain murdered his brother! Consequences of disobedience are very real.

But God teaches those who walk with Him that the consequence of obedience is blessing. *Be careful to obey all these regulations I am giving you, so that it may always go well with you and your children after you, because you will be doing what is good and right in the eyes of the LORD your God* (Deuteronomy 12:28). The apostle Paul emphasized that as we grow in Christ and yield to the Holy Spirit we become empowered to choose obedience over disobedience. *So I say, walk by the Spirit, and you will not gratify the desires of the flesh* (Galatians 5:16).

The Bible provides many illustrations of God enabling His people to choose obedience, thus experiencing blessing. Consider Daniel. The people and leaders of Judah willfully disregarded God's commands. Despite numerous warnings and calls for repentance, the people lived their own way, and as a consequence their land was conquered by Babylon, multitudes died, and many were led far away into captivity. While in exile Daniel and his friends resolved to obey God. Living in a culture with standards vastly different from God's Word, they faced constant temptations to adopt the standards of the culture around them. Still, with faith in God they chose obedience, and because of it God used them in ways that spread far the fame and glory of God. What a very great reward!

> *The Bible provides many illustrations of God enabling His people to choose obedience, thus experiencing blessing.*

Another biblical example of this principle is Joseph who also lived in a foreign land, having been sold into slavery by his brothers. Invited by the wife of his master Potiphar to *"Come to bed with me!"* (Genesis 39:7), Joseph could have yielded, thinking, "No one will know" or "It's not a big deal." But he refused. He faced this temptation saying, *"How then could I do such a wicked thing and sin against God?"* (Genesis 39:9) Joseph's obedience ultimately led to great reward for himself and for the people of Israel and generations that followed.

Throughout history Christians have confronted dilemmas like those faced by Daniel and Joseph. The church was born in the days of the Roman Empire when sin and sexual permissiveness was rampant but Christians were taught, *But among you there must not be even a hint of sexual immorality, or of any kind of impurity, or of greed, because these are improper for God's holy people* (Ephesians 5:3; see also Ephesians 4:17-19; Colossians 3:5-8; 1 Thessalonians 4:3-8). Sexual temptation was prevalent in the first century, as it is today. Regarding marriage Hebrews 13:4 says, *Marriage should be honored by all, and the marriage bed kept pure, for God will judge the adulterer and all the sexually immoral.* These lessons still apply.

In the early church, congregations were planted in places where the culture around them was pervasively wicked. Christians had to choose between obeying God and adopting the world's standards. Christians of every generation and culture have faced such choices. When God's Word is disregarded painful consequences follow, but when His Word is obeyed there is reward. This includes in our sexual life.

Helen and I knew God's Word teaches that sexual intimacy is a beautiful gift created of God for a man and a woman committed to each other in the holy covenant of marriage. We were tempted to disregard God's Word on this matter, but we resolved to obey. Our wedding was scheduled for August 1976, but earlier that summer we signed a lease on an apartment and Helen moved in. I continued paying rent at another apartment I shared with friends. I was not going to live with Helen until after we had married. We rightly determined that if God's Word was going to be our guide throughout our life together it must be so now, so we agreed to wait. Obedience is always the right call!

> *Whatever our past sins have been, if we will now walk with the Lord, He reveals to us our sin and in grace offers forgiveness as we come to Him in humble repentance.*

God is merciful whenever we step off the path of obedience. He forgives through the sacrifice of Jesus, but His forgiveness does not absolve us of all the consequences of our sin. I have counseled many struggling couples through the years, and many promiscuous men and women, and I can emphatically bear witness that the painful consequences of sexual intimacy outside of marriage are considerable. Still, whatever our past sins have been, if we will now walk with the Lord, He reveals to us our sin and in grace offers forgiveness as we come to Him in humble repentance. *If we confess our sins, he is faithful and just and will forgive us our sins and purify us from all unrighteousness* (1 John 1:9).

At whatever point along your life journey you turn to God in faith, determined henceforth to live according to His Word, from that point forward the choice of obedience will bring great reward! I thank God that when Helen and I married we could give each other a gift that can only be given once, our virginity. That day we made a covenant before God that until death separates us we will be faithful to each other

(Malachi 2:14-15). To do this I have needed to need to walk closely with the Lord, leaning on Him along the way. Beginning marriage on a biblical foundation of faithfulness to God and each other has allowed us to weather every storm, remaining strong and secure.

Life Application Questions:

1. When God's Word is disregarded painful consequences follow, but when His Word is obeyed there is reward. How have these truths become evident to you?

2. Why is sexual faithfulness in marriage God's command, and what are the consequences of disobedience and the rewards of obedience?

3. What response is the Holy Spirit asking of you now?

Part IV

WALKING WITH GOD IN SEASONS OF PREPARATION

We all have seasons of preparation in life. In such seasons God invites us to walk with Him. Transitions by their nature are stressful, because we are leaving our comfort zone to go where we have not been before. As we walk with the Lord He teaches us to lean on Him, and we realize He is with us. He is ready to teach us and prepare us well for the future He created us for. He also knows that the extent to which we lean on Him in our seasons of preparation is a good reflection of our intent to lean on Him in the chapters of life yet to come. What follows here are priceless lessons God taught me as I walked with Him in seasons of preparation.

32

When Jesus Is at the Helm, He Steers

As Jesus went on from there, he saw a man named Matthew sitting at the tax collector's booth. "Follow me," he told him, and Matthew got up and followed him (Matthew 9:9)

It is important for disciples of Jesus to learn that as we walk with Him our sole responsibility is to go wherever He leads us, to do whatever He calls us to do, say whatever He calls us to say, and be whoever He calls us to be. After all, He is Lord and we are not! This is true through every season of life, especially in our seasons of preparation. When Jesus called His first disciples He did not ask them where they wished to go. He simply said, "Follow me," and they did. Along the way He was preparing them for their destiny. This aspect of discipleship is the same today.

In seasons of transition it's important to know who is in command, and for Christians it is not us; it is the Lord. Using navy imagery, there is only one captain and everyone aboard ship is under the captain's authority. In the same way, disciples of Jesus know He is Head of His church and Lord of our lives. So as we move out, we want Him to steer us on whatever course He determines. With Jesus at the helm He steers, and that is how we want it!

Helen and I were married on August 21, 1976. She graduated three months before, and I would begin my senior year of college two weeks after our wedding. We were agreed that the following year we would move to wherever God would lead us, as I would attend seminary to prepare for pastoral ministry. I did research prayerfully, requesting information from a number of seminaries, and speaking with pastors and professors about the various seminaries I was considering.

Helen and I trusted God to direct our steps. In November I took a road trip with a friend to visit seminaries. One school we visited was Covenant Seminary in St. Louis, where we toured the school and sat in on classes. We spent a night there as guests in an apartment occupied by seminary students. God used a conversation there to assure me He would direct me in the way He wanted me to go.

I expressed to one of the students my fear of making a wrong choice and missing God's best. That student wisely said, "God is far more concerned about who you are than where you go. If your heart belongs to Him, and you love Him and desire to please Him, you can look at the options before you and make whatever choice you wish, confident He is leading you and will surely bless you." In other words, I could trust His leading. I recall the release I felt that evening, as my fear was lifted and peace settled on me. I knew God was leading and the choice I made would be His choice for me.

> *I thank God for teaching me that when we allow Jesus to be at the helm of life, He steers.*

The next stop on our trip was Bethel Theological Seminary in St. Paul, Minnesota. I sat in on some classes and conversed with students and faculty. I learned about their balanced emphasis on spiritual life, academics, and practical pastoral experience. As I prayed throughout my visit I knew God wanted me there.

I thank God for teaching me that when we allow Jesus to be at the helm of life, He steers. We do not need to go through life fearful of making wrong decisions. We have the privilege of following Jesus, knowing He knows where He is leading us and He will show us the way.

Life Application Questions:

1. When did you first hear Jesus say, "Follow me," and what have been the implications of your reply?

2. Looking ahead, what will be the effect of having Jesus at the helm of your life?

3. What response is the Holy Spirit asking of you right now?

33

God Goes Before Us So We Need Not Fear

So do not fear, for I am with you; do not be dismayed, for I am your God. I will strengthen you and help you; I will uphold you with my righteous right hand (Isaiah 41:10)

Because none of us sees the future or knows what is around the next corner we can at times be afraid. When we walk with Christ, facing the unknown presents a clear choice: We can face the approaching change using our own strength to confront our fears, or with dependence and trust in His faithfulness we can turn to God. As young adults in a time of uncertainty Helen and I turned to God in faith, and He answered us in remarkable fashion.

In the summer of 1977 we prepared to move fifteen hundred miles west. We had saved enough money for my first semester of seminary but we had no more. We had no jobs awaiting us and no place to live, and we did not know anyone in Minnesota. We asked God to lead us. A worship song we sang in those days quoted Isaiah 41:10, which declares this beautiful promise of God: *So do not fear, for I am with you; do not be dismayed, for I am your God. I will strengthen you and help you; I will uphold you with my righteous right hand.* Standing on this promise Helen and I asked God to go before us, and we believed He would. We asked Him to lead us to a church home that would be our family in Minnesota, from which we believed He would guide us to jobs and a home.

Before we left Rhode Island a friend ran to my car. I rolled down my window and he said, "As you're going to St. Paul I have a friend I want you to look up." With that he wrote down a name and gave it to me on a slip of paper. I thanked him and placed it in my wallet, grateful for the name of someone to contact upon our arrival.

Helen and I then took two weeks to visit family and friends and say good-bye. We went first to Maine for a few days with my family, then to upstate New York where Helen's family lived. The last day of our stay was a Sunday. We went to church services with Helen's parents, after which they hosted a farewell meal, inviting Ed and Sandy Whitman, their pastor and his wife, to join us, presuming they might have words of wisdom for us.

After dinner we prayed with Helen's parents and with Pastor and Mrs. Whitman, and then we loaded our car to start the journey. We gave hugs and said good-byes and then got in the car. As I backed out of the driveway Pastor Whitman ran to my car. When I rolled down the window he said, "As you're going to St. Paul I have a friend I want you to look up." He then wrote a name and gave it to me on a slip of paper. I took a quick look, thanked him, and placed it in my wallet, grateful for another name of someone to contact upon arrival.

We pulled out of the driveway and made our way to the interstate, heading west. Driving along we thanked our God for His faithfulness and claimed His promise to go before us, directing our steps along the way. About an hour into our journey an astonishing thought crossed my mind and I pulled over to the side of the road. As Helen asked why we were stopping I opened my wallet to look again at the name I had been given by the friend in Rhode Island, and now at the name given by Pastor Whitman in New York. On both slips of paper was the same name! I said to Helen, "Well, honey, we are definitely going to call this man!"

Two days later when we arrived in Minnesota tired from our journey, we went first to the seminary housing office to inquire about places to live. We were informed that all seminary housing units were full. Asking for other options I was given a list of apartment complexes with phone numbers. Helen and I returned to our car and drove out of the campus, heading south on Snelling Avenue. She asked, "What will we do now?"

I replied, "We'll find an inexpensive motel tonight and worry about it tomorrow, but first let's find a phone." Spotting a phone booth I pulled over. Opening the thick book hanging on the chain, I located the name I wanted, inserted a dime, and made the call.

When the phone was answered I asked for Reverend Clifford Christensen, the person whose name had been given to me by friends in two states. When Cliff came to the phone I told him I had just arrived with my wife to begin studies at Bethel Seminary, and that two East Coast friends had encouraged me to call him upon arrival. I mentioned their names and expressed their greetings. He then asked, "Where are you calling from?" I looked at the street signs and gave our location.

He said, "Write down these directions; you're coming to our house for dinner."

At this I covered the mouthpiece and whispered to Helen, "Free food!"

We made our way to the Christensens' home, and over dinner got acquainted with Cliff and Carol and their four children, Peter, Eric, Matthew, and Rebecca. During dinner Cliff reached across the table holding something in his hands. I put my hand under his into which he dropped a chain full of keys. "What is this?" I asked.

He said, "Tomorrow we're going on vacation for two weeks. Our house is yours!" How grateful we were! Surely God had gone before us!

Over the next two weeks Helen got a job, we found a place to live and moved in, and the youth director who had served for the past three years at the church where Cliff served as pastor abruptly resigned. You guessed it; the position was offered to me and I accepted! We had found our home! God went before us, confirming His promise that if we desire Him we have no cause to fear, for He is with us always! God teaches this priceless lesson to all who will walk with Him in faith.

Life Application Questions:

1. How has God's promise to care for you and direct your steps impacted you along your journey?

2. As you look to the future, what choices are you facing regarding trust?

3. What response is the Holy Spirit asking of you now?

34

God Cares Through His Family

God sets the lonely in families (Psalm 68:6)

As we leave childhood behind and launch into adulthood, God wants us to know we are never disconnected from family. Wherever we go in life and ministry He wants us to remain connected, living in the fellowship of His family, the church. He is our Father and all who love Jesus are our family in Christ. The apostle Paul taught this concept to the churches, mentioning various people by name as brothers and sisters (Romans 16:1-2; Ephesians 6:23; 2 Timothy 4:19-22). He envisioned the church as God's family, and his letters indicate this was happening. God cares for His children through the church. Helen and I learned this lesson in St. Paul.

If you are part of a local church family, I pray you remain closely connected with brothers and sisters, allowing the church to be God's family to you.

The family God led us to was called University Avenue Congregational Church. In our three years there they prayed for and with us, opened their homes to us, encouraged and laughed with us, worked with us, and embraced us. They demonstrated love in countless ways as we lived and grew together. We loved and served them as I coordinated ministries to youth. In addition I was given opportunities to teach and occasionally preach, and they encouraged me. Helen partnered with me in ministry and the congregation allowed her to flourish. We made dear friends in the church, some of whom we remain in contact with still. Some are in heaven now, but we remain forever family.

As Helen and I have walked with God through life and ministry He has blessed us through His family the church. He desires this for all

His children. If you are part of a local church family, I pray you remain closely connected with brothers and sisters, allowing the church to be God's family to you. If you are not currently part of a local church family, I hope you will ask God to lead you to a congregation who will help you grow in Christ. Pray for a church you can love and serve as family, joining with them to honor and serve the Lord. This is a request He will answer!

Life Application Questions:

1. Why does God call His children to be part of a local church family?

2. How is God caring for you through church family life?

3. What response is the Holy Spirit asking of you now?

35

Our Disappointments May Be God's Appointments

You intended to harm me, but God intended it for good to accomplish what is now being done, the saving of many lives (Genesis 50:20)

Nearly every young adult confronts several disappointments. Perhaps a relationship fails, or an application to a school or for a job is denied, or a promotion falls through, or financial loss occurs. In such times of disappointment God reminds His children that He is still on His throne and we can trust Him. Our disappointments may be God's appointments.

In Romans 8:28 Paul emphasized this truth in a sweeping way. He did not use the word "some" concerning the events in our lives God can use. He used the word "all." *And we know that in all things God works for the good of those who love him, who have been called according to His purpose.* What a comforting promise in times of upheaval! It is important to learn this truth so our faith is strengthened and we do not despair in the face of disappointment. As we walk with God through life and ministry He wants us to learn to trust Him in every circumstance.

Helen and I wanted to make our way through seminary without borrowing money. We intended to start a family and we were not expecting to make much money in pastoral ministry, so we wanted minimal debt. Every month we set aside funds toward the next semester's tuition. We got by with one car, and we ate a lot of pasta and bread with peanut butter. We lived frugally, paycheck to paycheck. With my part-time job as youth director at our church and with Helen's fulltime income as secretary for a CPA firm, we had just enough money to pay our monthly bills including our tithe to the Lord, but we had no more.

PART IV ~ WALKING WITH GOD IN SEASONS OF PREPARATION

Helen was grateful to have a job. Her college degree was in social work, but with a bachelor's degree and limited social work experience there were few positions available to her so she took what she could find. She did not like her job. She never complained about it, but it wasn't easy for her. Many evenings over dinner when I asked how her day went at work she struggled to find anything good to say. We talked about her looking for a new job, but she had neither time nor energy to do so. She determined to keep doing what she was doing, asking God to change her attitude. We prayed about this together.

Our disappointments may be God's appointments.

One Friday afternoon when I picked her up from work she was distraught. When I asked what was wrong she said she had just been fired. Her employers said they liked her and appreciated her effort but it was not a good fit. Helen was not upset about leaving that job, nor did she disagree with their conclusions, but she was very disappointed because of this sudden loss of income. Her concern and mine was that we needed her income to pay our bills and put food on our table.

We held each other that day and laid the matter at Jesus' feet. We prayed, "Lord, none of this is a surprise to you. You know Helen was unhappy in her job, and we asked you to intervene, so thank you for doing so. You know our precarious financial situation, so we ask you now to open a door and put her in a job where she can serve you and be fulfilled in doing so. Thank you for providing our daily bread."

After praying, we walked from the seminary to the college placement office to see if there might be any listings for social work positions. We found one that had just been posted for a Director of Social Services at a place called Maranatha Nursing Home. The word *Maranatha* is an Aramaic word used as a greeting among early Christians, which means "Our Lord, come" (1 Corinthians 16:22; Revelation 22:20). We presumed this might be a Christian nursing home.

Late Friday afternoon Helen made a phone call to the Maranatha Nursing Home to inquire about their social work position. An interview was scheduled for Monday morning. On Sunday our church family gathered around us in prayer about this matter. Monday morning Helen had her interview and they hired her on the spot. She did not miss one day of work – not one! On Friday she was in a job she did not like and where she did not fit, and on Monday she was in a job she loved, doing work for which she was trained to do. God did that!

This was not the first nor last time we faced disappointments in life, just as I know you too have faced many disappointments. He teaches us to rest in this assurance: *And we know that in all things God works for the good of those who love him, who have been called according to His purpose* (Romans 8:28).

As we walk with God He lets us see that our disappointments may be His appointments. God is the only one who can do this, and He does it for those who will trust Him always, no matter our circumstances.

Life Application Questions:

1. How have you experienced the truth of Romans 8:28?

2. What will be the effect of trusting Jesus when you face disappointments in life?

3. What response is the Holy Spirit asking of you right now?

36

Sorrow Can Bring Us to Our Knees and to His Side

Naked I came from my mother's womb, and naked I will depart. The LORD gave and the LORD has taken away; may the name of the LORD be praised (Job 1:21)

Sorrow is part of life for all who follow Him. Sometimes when sorrow strikes it doesn't make sense. Consider Job. He loved and served God and he was exceptionally blessed. Job had ten children – seven sons and three daughters. He owned 7,000 sheep, 3,000 camels, 500 yoke of oxen, and 500 donkeys, and he had a large number of people who worked for him. He was a wealthy man. The Bible says Job was *blameless and upright; he feared God and shunned evil* (Job 1:1). Then in one horrific day he lost his entire fortune and all his children. I have known people who lost everything. It is hard to describe the waves of grief that wash over someone who loses everything.

What is the qualitative difference between those who grieve without faith and those who grieve but with faith in God? Job's response was remarkable. Job got up and tore his robe and shaved his head. Then he fell to the ground in worship and said: *"Naked I came from my mother's womb, and naked I will depart. The LORD gave and the LORD has taken away; may the name of the LORD be praised." In all this Job did not sin by charging God with wrongdoing* (Job 1:20-22). Job's sorrow brought him to his knees and to God's side.

Through my years of walking with God in life and ministry I have witnessed this many times. I have walked with people through tragedies and loss and seen firsthand the qualitative difference between those who grieve without hope, and those who grieve with hope in Jesus Christ. For Christians, our grief is real because our loss is painful, but as Paul wrote to the church, though we grieve we do not *grieve like the rest of mankind, who have no hope* (1 Thessalonians 4:13). In our grief we turn to Jesus in faith and He brings comfort and hope.

Helen and I learned this lesson in the spring of 1979. We were overjoyed to be expecting our first child. Though we had not planned to start a family this soon, we were excited about it and adjusted our plans accordingly. We intended for Helen to cut back to part-time work after the baby was born and I would slow down my seminary studies to finish a year later, thus allowing me to earn a higher portion of our income and allowing Helen more time with our baby. This would be the first grandchild on both sides of our family. Our parents were ecstatic as were we. Friends began giving us baby clothes and I painted furniture and set up a nursery. From an ultrasound we learned we would have a son and we chose his name. His name was Matthew.

> Sorrows come to all God's people. When they come God is with us calling us to our knees and to His side.

Then something went wrong. At twenty-six weeks along in her pregnancy Helen went into labor. I rushed her to the Ramsey County Hospital where unsuccessful attempts were made to stop her labor. We were terrified as they rolled her into labor and delivery. They asked if we wanted to try to save the baby's life, as he was coming so early. We said, "Of course we do!" The preemie neonatal team from the adjacent children's hospital joined us. I held Helen's hand and prayed as she went through the delivery, and little Matthew was born.

We heard him cry! We cried too, praying and hoping for a miracle. He was hooked up to all kinds of tubes and monitors and placed in an incubator to be rolled over to the neonatal intensive care unit (NICU). On their way out with our baby boy, they rolled him to Helen's bed so we could see him. He looked tiny and helpless, but he was alive. He was beautiful to us. Helen said he looked like me. We blessed him and told him we loved him; then they rolled him away.

We called Pastor Cliff who met us at the hospital and prayed with us; then I ran to the NICU to check on our son. They said they were doing all they could, and promised to call if anything changed. The next day

I received the call. Matthew had died. I was grief-stricken and knew Helen was too, so I prayed all the way to the hospital, asking God for His presence and help. When I arrived at her hospital room I could tell Helen had been crying, but she was at peace.

She smiled. She said during the night, before Matthew was ushered into heaven, as she prayed God led her to Romans 14:8 which she claimed in faith. *If we live, we live for the Lord; and if we die, we die for the Lord. So, whether we live or die, we belong to the Lord.* The Lord comforted us with the sweet assurance that our firstborn, Matthew, belongs to God and was forever in His embrace.

Losing someone we love is always painful. Even after all these years there are still times when my heart aches for our firstborn, but Matthew belongs to the Lord, so our grief is tempered by hope and confident assurance of what is yet to come. Sorrows come to all God's people. When they come God is with us calling us to our knees and to His side.

Life Application Questions:

1. When and how has sorrow brought you to your knees and to His side?

2. What is the qualitative difference between grieving without eternal hope and grieving with hope in the Lord Jesus Christ?

3. What response is the Holy Spirit asking of you now?

37

Communication With God Goes Two Ways

"Then you will call on me and come and pray to me, and I will listen to you. You will seek me and find me when you seek me with all your heart. I will be found by you," declares the LORD (Jeremiah 29:12-14a)

It is so amazing that we can converse with God! You and I can approach His throne and lay our burdens at His feet (Hebrews 10:19-22). We can cast all our anxieties upon Him for He cares for us (1 Peter 5:7). This privilege is much too precious to ignore! But if ever our prayer life becomes only talking to God it is out of balance. As with all relationships, healthy communication requires speaking and listening.

God taught me this lesson in the summer of 1979. After losing baby Matthew I was doing much more talking to God than listening. I was now determined to speed up my seminary studies to graduate in June of 1980. As I would be applying for pastoral positions in just one year, Helen and I agreed I should apply for a summer internship position at a church to gain pastoral experience. She would take a leave of absence from her job while we served together in a church.

I considered various internship openings and applied to two. One was in South Dakota and one in Michigan. Both applications required submitting written essays and personal references followed by telephone interviews. I trusted God to open the door of His choosing and I was determined that if either church invited me I would go. When both churches called on the same day within a few minutes of each other to invite me to come, I had to pray and listen very carefully.

Helen and I prayed for wisdom and then agreed to go to Midland, Michigan, to serve on the staff of Midland Baptist Church from

Memorial Day weekend to Labor Day weekend. God blessed us! I led youth groups and a youth retreat, and co-led a family retreat weekend. I made hospital visitations, spoke at men's breakfasts, and preached six Sundays, receiving comments from a team who offered positive reviews of my preaching.

Helen and I worked together as partners in ministry that summer. Helen counseled young women and I counseled young men. Together we established and led a young couples Bible study, and we loved it. It was wonderful, increasing our excitement about a life of ministry together. A primary lesson we learned was the importance of balancing speaking and listening to God. One sermon I preached at Midland was based on 1 Samuel 3:1-10. I titled the message "Communication with God." Young Samuel was growing up in the Lord's temple. He believed in God, and was raised in His service, but he had no idea how to listen to God. *Now Samuel did not yet know the LORD: The word of the LORD had not yet been revealed to him.*

> *As with all relationships, healthy communication requires speaking and listening.*

God took the initiative with Samuel, just as He does with us today. God called Samuel by name until at last Samuel answered (v. 10): *"Speak, for your servant is listening."* When Samuel came to the place of listening to God, a lifetime of fruitful service began. He prayed and listened to God for the rest of his life, and God blessed and used him in incredible ways. But those who never learn to listen to God cannot and will not know the fullness of His blessings (Zechariah 7:13).

In my preaching I sometimes use object lessons to illustrate a point. That Sunday I held a telephone and simulated a short conversation with God. I then said that just as a mouthpiece and an earpiece are both necessary for a telephone conversation, so are speaking and listening both important in communication with God. Following the service, as I stood at the back of the sanctuary greeting departing worshipers, a little boy approached with his parents. I overheard him say to his mother in childlike wonder, "Mommy, THAT man talked with GOD!" I got down on one knee and agreed with him that it is amazing. I explained that we don't need a telephone; we only need to pray believing God hears us and asking Him to speak to us too! I told him I was about his age when I began to pray, and that Jesus likes it very much when children pray.

Whether you're a child or an adult, good communication with God must go two ways. Samuel's prayer is a good place to start: *"Speak, for your servant is listening."*

Life Application Questions:

1. How does your prayer life reflect a balance of speaking and listening?

2. What might happen if every day you said to God, "Speak Lord, your servant is listening"?

3. What response is the Holy Spirit asking of you now?

38

For God's People, Joy Comes in the Morning

Weeping may stay for the night, but rejoicing
comes in the morning (Psalm 30:5)

Sorrow is part of life. Good friends at Bethel Seminary were expecting their first child and went into early labor. Their son was born prematurely and waged a battle for life. As we prayed over many weeks for our friends and their baby we asked God to comfort them by His Word. One day when I saw my friend and inquired how they were holding up he quoted David's words in Psalm 30:5. Though this was a difficult season for them they believed in faith that rejoicing would yet come. As time went on their son became strong. The promise quoted by my friend in the early days of his struggle became very dear to me: *Weeping may stay for the night, but rejoicing comes in the morning.*

My final year of seminary was busy. I was taking an increased course load to finish by June, which increased tuition costs. Helen had returned to her job at the nursing home and I continued working at the church, but I needed additional income so I took another job at a loading dock. Meanwhile I prepared a profile to search for a place of pastoral service.

Then we learned that Helen was again with child. We were ecstatic and thought the timing couldn't be better. I would finish seminary in June, then we would move to wherever God would lead me to pastor, after which we would have a few weeks to get settled. Then in early November our baby would come! An ultrasound confirmed we would have a girl. My heart was so filled with joy I wanted to name her Joy. We had not yet agreed definitively on what her name would be, but I referred to her as "Baby Joy."

In May I graduated from seminary. My parents and Helen's parents were with us and Helen was looking very pregnant. We were excited about our next adventure in ministry, as we waited on God to confirm the place of His calling. We were also excited about welcoming our daughter, the first grandchild of our parents.

In June I accepted a call to a church and Helen and I prepared to move. We were so happy. Then two weeks before we were scheduled to move tragedy struck. We were shopping at a grocery store when suddenly Helen's water broke. She was just twenty-two weeks along. I raced her to the hospital where attempts were made to stop the labor, but it was unsuccessful. They told us the baby was coming and could not be stopped. It was too early for any chance of survival.

We were both weeping as they rolled Helen into the delivery room. I gowned up quickly to be with her. In a few minutes our tiny baby arrived. They showed her to us, then whisked her off until Helen's labor was finished and she was cleaned up. They then brought us our little girl. Her lungs were not developed enough to breathe, though she tried. Helen and I held "Baby Joy," kissing her and praying over her until her little heart beat its last. We held each other and cried. We then made the difficult calls to inform our parents, and I called Pastor Cliff who came to grieve with us. Our pain was intense. It hurt so much I could hardly breathe.

> *God reminded me that although I did not feel it yet, it was still true and I would see His promise fulfilled.*

Grief is like that sometimes, isn't it? Pat answers won't do. In this broken world, sometimes pain and sorrow are horrendous. Platitudes do not help, but leaning on the everlasting arms of God does. In our time of sorrow I had no answers.

I still called her Joy. I cried to God for answers. "Lord, you took my Joy from me! Why?" I received no answer except that God knew my pain. I repeated in my mind the words of the psalmist quoted by my friend in his time of trial: *weeping may stay for the night, but rejoicing [Joy] comes in the morning.* God reminded me that although I did not feel it yet, it was still true and I would see His promise fulfilled.

When Jesus faced the suffering of the cross He pointed His disciples toward resurrection morning. In biblical history God often spoke to

His people in their time of hardship, pointing them to a future when He would yet bless them. Ezekiel addressed the people of Judah who were suffering then and would yet suffer more. God promised, *I will make them and the places surrounding my hill a blessing. I will send down showers in season; there will be showers of blessing* (Ezekiel 34:26).

Walking with God through life and ministry we discover it can take a while before rejoicing comes, just as it takes a while for planted seeds to produce fruit. God grows grace from our pain, and He allows us to share with others the comfort we received in our time of sorrow (2 Corinthians 1:3-4). God's promises are not dependent on our circumstances or on how we feel, but are based on His faithfulness.

Life Application Questions:

1. How have you ever experienced God's promise of Psalm 30:5?

2. What is required to go beyond painful circumstances to trust God's promises?

3. What response is the Holy Spirit asking of you now?

39

God Leads Us Along

*I am with you and will watch over you
wherever you go* (Genesis 28:15)

God promises His children that He will lead us along, for He has a plan for us. One such promise is Ephesians 2:10: *For we are God's handiwork, created in Christ Jesus to do good works, which God prepared in advance for us to do.* God taught me this lesson as Helen and I waited on Him for our first pastoral call. Though I attended seminary in Minnesota, and Helen and I were willing to serve God wherever He would lead us, I was particularly drawn to New England. We prayed, asking God to lead us to the place He prepared for us to live and serve. I prepared a pastoral profile and submitted it to several churches in various states.

As my graduation approached I conversed with churches and interviews began. Meanwhile, Pastor Cliff Christensen asked if he could give my name to the pastoral search committee of Darlington Congregational Church, a CCCC Church in Pawtucket, Rhode Island. As Helen and I had come from Rhode Island to Minnesota, and as we had good friends in Rhode Island, I was interested.

When I asked Cliff what he knew about the church he said he had served on staff there while attending seminary, then served for seven years as their pastor. He said he thought we would be an excellent fit. I invited him to give my name to their search team. As I was just twenty-five years old then. I expect a primary reason the search team considered me was that their former pastor had given a strong recommendation and their esteem for him was high. After much correspondence through mail and telephone, Helen and I flew to Rhode Island to meet with the search team. We were impressed with how prayerful and thorough they were. We talked at length about many things, including the needs of the church and community. I learned that the church had experienced a painful departure of the previous pastor.

Dr. Lloyd Dean, a man who later became a trusted friend and mentor to me, was serving as interim pastor then and the church had achieved some degree of stability, but it was clear that considerable work still needed to be done to effect biblical unity. When the search committee invited me to be their candidate, Helen and I agreed. Returning to Pawtucket for the candidate weekend, we had a precious time with church leaders and the congregation. My heart was drawn to the people. Through conversations and meetings in those days I also discerned that some disunity remained in the church. I knew I should only accept this call if God very clearly directed so. I asked God to show me what to do.

> *God promises His children that He will lead us along, for He has a plan for us.*

A congregational meeting was scheduled for two weeks later to vote on calling me as pastor. During those two weeks Helen and I visited my family in Maine and then her family in New York. On the day of the scheduled congregational meeting we were with Helen's parents. While praying that morning I asked God to confirm beyond all doubt if this was His will for us. I asked for a miracle: a unanimous vote. I determined that only if it was a unanimous call would I immediately say yes. I told this to no one but Helen and she agreed.

That Sunday afternoon the phone rang at the home of Helen's parents. It was the chairperson of the board of deacons at Darlington Congregational Church informing me that the congregation had just voted to extend me a call to be their pastor. Before I could ask he said, "Steve, you should know the vote was 100 percent." Tears came as God reminded me in that moment that He will always provide what we need. I knew He would go with me and be with me as I assumed my new responsibilities. I agreed to come. Looking back over so many years of life and ministry since then, I thank God for the timeless truth of this lesson! In every step God has reinforced this promise, allowing me to know His call with certainty.

When Moses contemplated his assigned responsibilities he was very afraid. God knew what Moses needed and spoke to him these reassuring words: *"My Presence will go with you, and I will give you rest"* (Exodus 33:14). When Jesus was about to ascend into heaven and His disciples contemplated the task before them without His physical presence, Jesus spoke these words of reassurance: *"And surely I am with you always, to the very end of the age"* (Matthew 28:20). These are promises we can hold on to.

Life Application Questions:

1. In what ways has God given you confirmation of His will?

2. How have you experienced God's promise that He goes with you and that whatever He calls you to do He also equips you to do it?

3. What response is the Holy Spirit asking of you now?

Part V

WALKING WITH GOD AS A YOUNG SHEPHERD

It's a sacred trust when a parent entrusts the responsibility and care of their child to someone else. Wise parents assign such responsibility very carefully, to ensure their children are loved, safe, and well cared for. That is what God does with His children. He chooses pastors, shepherds, and leaders and entrusts them with caring for His children on His behalf. The good news is that when He calls us to do this He is also with us. What follows are invaluable lessons the Lord taught me when I walked with Him as a young shepherd of His flock.

4 0

I Need the Lord More Than I Know

I can do all this through him who gives me strength (Philippians 4:13)

In my early years of pastoral ministry God kept teaching me that I needed Him more than I knew. I will never forget our move from Minnesota to Rhode Island. We were still grieving and deeply wounded from the loss of our baby girl, but it was time to move on and we did. I rented a U-Haul truck with a tow bar to pull our car behind. We piled all our things into the truck and headed east. On the way we did much praying, asking God for safety on our journey and for a smooth transition as we began serving our new church family.

On the way we entered an enormous storm. It had rained for days and roads were flooded. We came to a place on the highway where cars were stalled out and some were bobbing in the water. We could not go back. The only way was forward. Our choice was to stay where we were or drive through the waters. I judged the depth of the water and determined we were riding higher than the cars that had stalled out. So we asked God to help us and driving very slowly we went ahead, through the waters.

The water reached the bottom of the truck doors but we made it safely to the other side and our journey continued. As I drove on conversing with God, I heard Him remind me that anytime I confronted deep waters in my life and ministry I could lean upon Him and He would get me through. He reminded me this was also true for the people I would serve. This promise encouraged me deeply!

The congregation welcomed us with open arms. They had filled the parsonage cupboards with food and extended so many expressions of love. Our first few Sundays went well, and Helen and I felt loved and at home. We began counting our blessings, but it wasn't long until I felt like I was driving through deep waters. Though people seemed glad we were there, it became apparent that restoring unity in the church would be a challenge.

As I visited families and conversed with members I learned there was still mistrust between various brothers and sisters in Christ. People with opposing views tried convincing me of the correctness of their perspective, which required my agreeing that others in the congregation were in the wrong. This was not going to be easy. It appeared some were so accustomed to animosity in the church that they had lost vision for what God could do. Though I was troubled by all of this, God reminded me of the lesson He taught on our move to Pawtucket. He reminded me that He was with us and He would get us through these waters.

As I struggled with what to say and how to preach, God revealed that He is the one who gives words and anointing, and if I leaned upon Him I would be given the right words. *Do not worry about what to say or how to say it. At that time you will be given what to say, for it will not be you speaking, but the Spirit of your Father speaking through you* (Matthew 10:19-20). I determined then that Philippians 4:13 would be a theme verse for me in life and ministry, for Jesus gives all I need. *I can do all this through him who gives me strength.*

Has God given you responsibility? If you feel like you are in deep waters and you don't know how to get to the other side, join the club! That feeling is a gift from God; it is His invitation to lean upon Him. Tell Him you are depending on Him to see you through! You cannot do this in your own strength, nor can the people you lead do this for you, but Christ is the power and love of God. As the prophet Joel proclaimed: *Let the weakling say, "I am strong!"* (Joel 3:10). Believe it and drive on, for He will see you through!

> As the prophet Joel proclaimed: Let the weakling say, "I am strong!"

Life Application Questions:

1. Has there been a time when you had to drive through deep waters, trusting God to bring you to the other side?

2. As you look to the future, how does the promise of Philippians 4:13 affect you?

3. What response is the Holy Spirit asking of you now?

4 1

Do Not Even Try to Go it Alone

The work is too heavy for you; you cannot handle it alone (Exodus 18:18)

Moses was giving maximum effort to his responsibilities, but it wasn't working. He was burning out. When his father-in-law came for a visit he identified the problem and stated the obvious to Moses: *The work is too heavy for you; you cannot handle it alone.* Jethro counseled Moses to share the load. Moses listened to this wisdom and his effectiveness improved.

God intends that we do not walk alone. Solomon said, *If either of them falls down, one can help the other up. But pity anyone who falls and has no one to help them up* (Ecclesiastes 4:10). New Testament churches were exhorted to *Carry each other's burdens* (Galatians 6:2), and Paul pointed out that doing so *fulfill[s] the law of Christ.* When we fail to do this we fall short of His will.

These principles offer two applications as we walk along with Him in life and ministry: (1) God wants us to help brothers and sisters who struggle under a heavy load, to do what we can to help each other; and (2) God wants us to allow brothers and sisters to help us carry our heavy load; He does not want us to carry it alone either.

I learned this lesson the hard way. As a young pastor I dove into my work. There was so much to learn and do. There were people to meet, weddings and funerals to arrange and conduct, Bible studies to lead, sermons to prepare and deliver, newsletters to write, counseling sessions, home and hospital visits, leadership and committee meetings to plan, and more, plus involvement in the local community and with area clergy. After about six months of this it wasn't working well! I was putting in the time, but my energy and motivation were waning. I was depressed.

The root of my depression was unresolved grief from losing two children. I was trying to drown my pain in a sea of busyness, but it wasn't working. I told no one I was hurting or angry with God, or that Helen and I were distant from each other, each of us grieving our own way. I told no one I was depressed or fearful I might never be a father, or that someone might find out I was angry with God, or that God might withdraw His anointing from me because of my weakness. I was trying to carry it alone. I wasn't allowing anyone to speak into my life then, so the Holy Spirit spoke to me directly as I prayed.

> *God intends that we do not walk alone.*

At a weak point I cried out to God, "Lord, I'm a mess! You know I'm hurting. You know my confusion and pain, and that I have been angry with you and don't know what to do about it! You know my fears that I might never be a father, and that Helen and I are stressed and seem incapable of helping each other with this. Lord, I cannot do this alone! Help me!" That is when I heard the Holy Spirit speak to my spirit as clearly as if He had spoken audibly. He said, "Tell them. Stop carrying this heavy load alone." I resolved to obey at the earliest opportunity.

Small groups from our church family met in various homes, led by lay leaders from the congregation. Home group meetings included times of worship and Bible study along with corporate prayer and carrying each other's burdens. That evening I attended a home group in the living room of one of our church families.

When prayer time came that evening, as requests were shared from group members someone asked, "What about you, Pastor Steve? How can we pray for you?" I knew I had to tell them, so I did. For the first time I shared the depths of my grief. I described my fear of never having children and even admitted I had been angry with God. Though embarrassed by my vulnerability, I knew the Lord was directing me to do this so I risked it. I said I was telling them this because God directed me to do so, so they might pray with me and help me carry my burden.

Though I feared judgment, I received Christ's love through brothers and sisters. God touched me as we called on Him together. God assured me I would yet be a father, a story I will tell more fully when I share lessons God taught me as a parent. One enduring lesson He taught that has blessed me through the years is that God's children must never attempt to go it alone.

God wants us to strengthen one another. Whenever we attempt to live as solo Christians, bearing our burdens alone, we become spiritually weak and we stumble and fall. Allow God's family to help you carry your burdens, as you also help them carry theirs, for *in this way you will fulfill the law of Christ* (Galatians 6:1).

Life Application Questions:

1. The work is too heavy for you; you cannot handle it alone. How have you learned this lesson?

2. How have you seen church family as God's support system for His children?

3. What response is the Holy Spirit asking of you now?

42

Be a Praying Shepherd

And pray in the Spirit on all occasions with all kinds of prayers and requests. With this in mind, be alert and always keep on praying for all the Lord's people (Ephesians 6:18)

Jesus was a praying shepherd. Though faced with many demands and filled with compassion for the flock of God (Matthew 14:14), Jesus often took time to pray (Matthew 14:23; Luke 5:16). If we are called to lead believers we must remember that the flock we are called to serve ultimately belongs to the Chief Shepherd, who is Christ (I Peter 5:4). He wants His under-shepherds to regard every lamb in the flock the same way He does, with love.

The prophet Jeremiah described what happens when shepherds fail to pray. *The shepherds are senseless and do not inquire of the LORD; so they do not prosper and all their flock is scattered* (Jeremiah 10:21). I did not want to go down that path, so I disciplined myself to pray for the church collectively and for members of the church family individually. I prayed through the church directory and through the church leadership roster. I knew that God alone knows the hearts of the people and He alone knows what is necessary to effect healing. I also realized my perspective was limited, so I turned in prayer to the One whose perspective is faultless.

As I prayed a breakthrough came. I asked for healing for every relationship. I did not want anyone to be left behind, but after several months it was apparent that while some in the church were hungry for God, collectively we remained far from what God intended. I grieved for the lack of unified vision among leaders, because leaders must always model among themselves what God intends for the church, and to the extent we fail to do this the health of the congregation suffers. I prayed that God would make our leaders one in the Spirit (John 17:20-23) so we could rightly discern His will and reflect His character together.

After months of praying this way, on one particular Saturday night as I prayed through the sanctuary in preparation for the next day, the Holy Spirit led me to pray another way. He asked, "Do you trust me?"

I replied, "Yes Lord."

"Then pray accordingly," He said.

I said, "Lord, I have been praying for some time that you would bring unity to our leaders and to our entire body. I do trust you to answer this prayer however you choose." To my prayer I added for the first time: "Lord, if you need to move anyone out so we can go forward together, then do it." God was preparing me for what was about to happen.

Though faced with many demands and filled with compassion for the flock of God, Jesus often took time to pray.

The next morning two church leaders approached me separately to say they were resigning from leadership and leaving the church. If this had occurred the previous week, or if I had not prayed as I prayed the night before, this turn of events would have devastated me. But that day I was at peace. I did not regard it as failure, but saw it as God answering prayer for the health of His church.

Some amazing things began happening then. I witnessed some who previously exited through opposite doors on Sundays in order to avoid seeing someone they did not like now purposefully crossing the sanctuary to greet one another. I witnessed hugs and tears and healing. I saw God answer prayer for His church! Our leaders came to unity, reflected in shared and fervent intercession. It was wonderful!

Our church leadership covenanted with one another that because the Holy Spirit is a Spirit of unity, our decisions would always be bathed in prayer and made in unity. We agreed that if ever we were not united about a matter – because God is neither confused nor divided – rather than accepting the disunity we would press into prayer, listening carefully until God united us. This is what we did and God honored it. I also gathered with other local ministers for prayer. We prayed for each other, asking God to move in our community, bringing people to Him.

Being a praying shepherd is a critical lesson for leaders as we walk with God. We must be faithful to pray for those in spiritual authority over us. As church leaders we must realize that God calls us to pray for the people entrusted to our care. The church is always to be a house of prayer (Isaiah 56:7; Matthew 21:13). We are called to devote ourselves to prayer (Colossians 4:2). In this way we will remember our utter dependence on God. We must have and be praying shepherds!

Life Application Questions:

1. Why are we to pray for those in spiritual authority over us?

2. How does it benefit the church when leaders pray for the people over whom they have been given spiritual authority?

3. What response is the Holy Spirit asking of you now?

43

God Gives Mentors

While they were worshipping the Lord and fasting, the Holy Spirit said, "Set apart for me Barnabas and Saul for the work to which I have called them." So after they had fasted and prayed, they placed their hands on them and sent them off (Acts 13:2)

When Jesus sent out the twelve, He sent them out two by two (Mark 6:7). Jesus knew they would be stronger, safer, and more effective if they served alongside a brother. The Bible has much to say about this. We all need others to lean on.

As a third-generation pastor, and because I had been affirmed for pastoral ministry, I presumed I was prepared for any ministry challenge. In my first week as pastor I learned otherwise, when I had to do a wedding and a funeral and I had no clue how to do either one! God had given me biblical insight and the anointing of His Spirit, but the complexities of dealing with church conflict, pastoral counseling, leadership development, sermon and worship preparations, and home life combined to show me that I needed wise counsel. I needed a mature brother to share godly wisdom with me, encouraging me when I was on the right course, and suggesting a course correction if I was not. I needed a mentor.

When the Holy Spirit directed the church in Antioch to send out church planters, Barnabas and Saul were sent together. Barnabas's name is listed first (Acts 13:2), suggesting he initially took the lead. He was an encourager, friend, and partner with Saul. Saul needed Barnabas, a ministry peer and partner. I needed someone like Barnabas too, as does everyone who is called into His service. God has provided friends and encouragers for me in every chapter of life. He does this for His children who are willing.

In time, Saul became known as Paul, a leader in a great church-planting movement. Paul discipled many elders, pastors, and church leaders. Among them was Pastor Timothy who was like a son to Paul (2 Timothy 1:1-2). I too needed people I could disciple, and God gave me people who were hungry to grow.

Timothy was mentored by Paul, but in my early years as pastor I had no one to mentor me. I lacked someone with whom I could meet often for counsel and prayer. There were a number of people who shared wisdom and prayed with me occasionally, but I needed someone to meet with me regularly for this purpose. I asked God to provide for this need and He did by connecting me with Reverend Bill Silbert, a retired Presbyterian pastor living in nearby Lincoln, Rhode Island. Bill and his wife, Betty, took Helen and me under their wings and loved us, offering extra measures of encouragement. They had a love for the Lord and His Word and the church, and they loved us. I looked forward to my appointments with Bill. I treasured the wisdom he shared, appreciated the stories he told, and relished our times of prayer. Bill is in heaven now, but the impact of our time together remains.

Do you have a mentor who is helping you grow in your walk with God through life and ministry? If not, will you ask God to guide you to someone? As you pray He may fix your heart upon someone to approach about meeting with you for this purpose. If you are not sure who to ask, let your pastor or another Christian leader know of this need. We all need partners in ministry to hold us accountable and stand with us as we serve. May God bless you and make you a blessing in every Barnabas, Paul, and Timothy relationship!

Life Application Questions:

1. Who have been your mentors and how did God use them for your growth?

2. Who are you now mentoring like Paul mentored Timothy?

3. What response is the Holy Spirit asking of you now?

44

God's Calling Brings His Equipping

*"Do not be afraid, you who are highly esteemed," he
said. "Peace! Be strong now; be strong." When he spoke
to me, I was strengthened and said, "Speak, my Lord,
since you have given me strength"* (Daniel 10:19)

Moses did everything he could think of to run from God's call. He offered excuse after excuse for why he wasn't up to the task. For every objection God offered a remedy. Moses said, *"Who am I that I should go to Pharaoh and bring the Israelites out of Egypt?"* (Exodus 3:11). God said, *"I will be with you"* (3:12). Then Moses said, *"Suppose I go to the Israelites and say to them, 'The God of your fathers has sent me to you,' and they ask me, 'What is his name?' Then what shall I tell them?"* (3:13). Then, *God said to Moses, "I AM WHO I AM." This is what you are to say to the Israelites: 'I AM has sent me to you'"* (3:14). Moses tried again. *"What if they do not believe me or listen to me and say, 'The LORD did not appear to you'?"* (4:1). God promised to confirm his message through signs and wonders.

Moses then objected that he was not a good speaker (4:10). God's reply to Moses speaks to all who have offered such an objection: *"Who gave human beings their mouths? Who makes them deaf or mute? Who gives them sight or makes them blind? Is it not I, the LORD? Now go; I will help you speak and will teach you what to say"* (4:11-12). Still Moses tried running from God's calling. *"Pardon your servant, Lord. Please send someone else"* (4:13). This reply brought God's anger but He extended mercy, agreeing to speak to Moses and allowing him to use Aaron as spokesman.

I can relate to Moses' initial reluctance for I too approached ministry with fear and trepidation. I knew my weakness and feared I might not be up to the challenges, but I also knew I had heard God's call and I did not want to do as Jonah did and run from His call. So I prayed and claimed His promise through Zechariah (4:6) that it would be not by my own might or power, but by His Spirit.

I asked God to do for me what He did for Moses, giving me everything I needed to honor Him and to accomplish what He called me to do. I asked for confirmation of His calling by helping me produce fruit that pleased Him. I savored the promise of God to Daniel (Daniel 10:19), and Isaiah (Isaiah 6:1-9; 51:16), and Paul (Philippians 4:13), that whenever God calls anyone to do something for Him, He always gives what is needed to do it.

> *Whenever God calls anyone to do something for Him, He always gives what is needed to do it.*

Within Congregationalism, local churches ordain pastors by setting apart for gospel ministry those whom they have discerned to be called by God for this purpose (see Acts 13:1-3). Recognizing their connection to the wider body of Christ, a local church ordains a minister only after receiving a favorable recommendation from a Vicinage Council of pastors and lay leaders who have gathered from nearby churches to prayerfully examine the candidate.

In preparation for the Vicinage Council, candidates prepare an extensive paper presenting their theological convictions with biblical references about major doctrines of the Christian faith. In addition such papers include a section in which candidates describe their conversion to faith in Jesus Christ and how a call to ministry was heard and confirmed. The completed paper is provided in advance to pastors and lay leaders who have registered to attend the Council, so they can read it and be prepared to interview the candidate. I have attended many Vicinage Councils through the years, and each has been a holy obligation.

My own Vicinage Council took place February 7, 1981. It started at 9:00 a.m. and did not conclude until 4:00 p.m., with lunch served in the middle. I fielded many questions that day, presenting my understanding of various biblical truths. I also fielded questions about my relationship with Christ and my personal and married life, and about how I came to hear God's call. Helen was invited in for part of the Council and asked about her reflections on my call to pastoral ministry, and whether she was supportive of this, which she answered affirmatively.

Near the end of the Council, leaders from Darlington Congregational Church asked for an opportunity to speak, as by now I had been their pastor for six months. I was moved to hear them volunteer their assessment of how God's anointing was upon me and how He was using me to bless them. After I left the room the Council prayed and deliberated and then called me back in, confirming their unanimous assessment that Jesus had both called and equipped me for pastoral ministry. They recommended that the church proceed with my ordination. I was humbled.

The ordination service was held Sunday afternoon, February 22, 1981. The congregation worshiped; the choir exalted the Lord; my father, Reverend Glendon Gammon, preached the Word; and several Christian ministers took part and laid hands upon me, with my grandfather, Reverend Morley Durost, offering a prayer of ordination. Since then, as I have walked with God, there have been many times when I have felt like I was in over my head, but the message God spoke to me when I was young continues ringing true. With God's calling comes His anointing. He always gives what we need to do what He calls us to do. This realization removes any pride or sense of "look what I did," and it gives confidence for the tasks before us.

Life Application Questions:

1. When you felt inadequate for what you were called to do, what did you learn?

2. Are you facing challenges now or in the future for which you do not feel up to the task? If so, what is God's message to you?

3. What response is the Holy Spirit asking of you right now?

Part VI

WALKING WITH GOD AS A PARENT

Being a parent is a major responsibility, one that requires love and wisdom along the way. Walking with God as a parent means we are not in this alone; we always have someone to lean on. It also means knowing God watches over our children even when we cannot, and that He helps us love our children. Parenting is not easy, but when God gives us this privilege He promises to equip us for the task. What follows are lessons God taught me while walking with Him as a parent.

45

Being a Parent Is God's Blessing

> *Children are a heritage from the LORD, offspring a reward from him. Like arrows in the hands of a warrior are children born in one's youth. Blessed is the man whose quiver is full of them. They will not be put to shame when they contend with their opponents in court* (Psalm127: 3-5)

Being a parent is a blessing of God! When Jacob introduced his family to his brother, Esau, he said, *"They are the children God has graciously given your servant"* (Genesis 33:5). Years later when Jacob came to Egypt to see his long-lost son, Joseph introduced his children to his father saying, *"They are the sons God has given me here"* (Genesis 48:9). The psalmist said, *Children are a heritage from the LORD, offspring a reward from him* (Psalm 127:3). This is true.

Growing up in a big family I presumed I would be a dad someday. After Helen and I were married a few years I began longing for children. Because on two occasions we had expected a child and then suffered loss, my anticipation of becoming a father was intensified. I longed to be a dad but understood this was God's call not mine. Helen and I prayed, trusting God to work it out in His time. He introduced us to parenting in a way we did not expect.

In the year after we arrived in Pawtucket a nonprofit abused children's home was established in the city. The founders determined it would be good to have a member of the clergy on their board of directors so they asked me, the newest member of the local clergy. I agreed to serve. This was an eye-opening experience for me, one God used to bless me.

As Christmas approached I obtained a list of first names, genders, and ages of the children living at the home so we might buy and wrap gifts for them. Families of the congregation were given the age and gender of a child and shopped for gifts. The location of the home was not public knowledge, but being on the board of directors I knew where it was, so I called to arrange a time to deliver the gifts. That experience changed my life.

On my way to the home I asked God to let me show His love to these little ones. Entering the home I removed my winter coat, gloves, and hat, and carrying a large box of gifts I entered the living room to meet the little boys and girls. Being a tall man I towered over them, so to be at their eye level I sat on the floor. Calling each child by name I gave them their presents and watched as they opened them. I enjoyed their laughter and treasured the joy the gifts brought these children. As I played with them I had a conversation with God.

> *God will give us what we need, and the love we can give a child will be worth more than any pain it might cost us.*

My prayer was something like this: "Lord, this isn't right! These little ones are here through no fault of theirs. They need the love of a family. Why aren't there more Christian families willing to take in little ones like this?"

God's response was an elbow in the ribs. "What do you mean, 'Why doesn't someone open their home to a child?' What about you?"

Sitting on the floor playing with these little children, I sensed God was telling me that He wanted us to become foster parents, offering a home for a child who needed to be loved. Driving home I asked God to confirm if this was His leading by bringing Helen to the same conviction. Becoming foster parents would require lots of training, background checks, and interviews. It would be considerable work and there would be risks.

The purpose of foster parenting is typically to provide care in a temporary home while a birth parent makes progress toward resuming responsibility for the child. The emotional risk for foster parents prevents many from doing this. As foster parents and foster children become attached, it can be very painful when the time comes for the child to leave, perhaps returning to the birth parent. Reviewing this risk in my mind as I drove home, I hated any thought of Helen going again through the pain of loving and losing a child. So wanting to obey

God I prayed, "Dear Lord, remove all fears and bring Helen and me to unity on this matter."

When I arrived home that day Helen wanted to know about my time at the children's home. I told her all about it, including the conversation I had with God while sitting on the floor. I then asked if she would consider foster parenting. To my joyful surprise she immediately said, "Yes." I reminded her of the pain that could be in store if we loved a child who was then taken from us, but Helen's reply showed it was okay to go forward. She said, "God will give us what we need, and the love we can give a child will be worth more than any pain it might cost us."

We then called the Rhode Island Department of Children and Families to initiate the process toward becoming foster parents. The interviews and home visits, combined with training and insights shared by other foster parents all served to confirm our decision. Now we would trust God to bring us the child of His choosing.

Life Application Questions:

1. How have you experienced or observed parenting as a blessing from God?

2. How could God use you to bless children?

3. What response is the Holy Spirit asking of you now?

46

I Can Make a Difference for This One

*And whoever welcomes one such child in my
name welcomes me* (Matthew 18:5)

Helen and I knew we could not help every child, but with God's help we could make a difference for one. That is what we wanted to do. Believing in the sovereignty of God we prayed and trusted that He would match us with the one He had chosen. Then we received a call from a Rhode Island Department of Children and Families (DCF) caseworker telling us about an eight-month-old boy they wished to place with us. For about six months he had been in a group home in Providence. They asked if we would like to see him and we agreed to meet the caseworker and child at the St. Vincent dePaul home. I will never forget the first time I saw him.

Helen and I and the caseworker were in a waiting room when a nun entered carrying little Carlo. When I saw him my first words were, "Isn't he beautiful!" At this he stretched his arms toward me, struggling to get out of the sister's arms and into mine. When I took him we held onto each other and he laid his head on my shoulder as my heart melted. Helen and I sat together to get acquainted with him. He put his hands all over my face and hers and we laughed. I tried passing him over to Helen or putting him down but that day he would have none of it! He was where he wanted to be and so was I.

We sat together a while and I introduced him to a stuffed Winnie the Pooh bear we had brought for him, which he clutched. It was a happy visit. When it came time to leave and hand him to one of his caregivers he wasn't happy about it. Clutching his Winnie the Pooh tightly he cried as he was carried from the room. There was no doubt in my mind; this was the child who was to be in our home. After a few more meetings we were cleared to bring him home to live with us.

We quickly gathered what we would need – a crib, changing table, high chair, baby bottles, diapers, car seat, clothes, and other things. Then little Carlo came to our home. His birth mother had weekly visitation rights, so we were offered a choice of having her visit him at our home or having him picked up and delivered to her at a neutral location. We opted for her visiting at our home, thinking we might be able to encourage and support her too.

Carlo was nine months old when he arrived. He was already sleeping through the night, so our sleep was not detrimentally affected as typically happens when a new baby arrives. As every parent can attest, though, when children enter a home, life changes. Previously Helen and I had a weekly practice of going out to breakfast on Mondays, so the first week we took Carlo with us. He made a racket, making sure everyone knew he was there.

Our church family loved Carlo from day one. He had uncles and aunties who gave him love and attention, all of which he enjoyed. His birth mother visited our home weekly and we came to love her too. She could see he was loved and well cared for, which pleased her immensely. We treasured every day as Carlo grew. When he began talking he called Helen "mama" and me "dada." His birth mother continued visiting, but as he saw her only once a week he recognized her but was not bonded with her as he was with us, which disturbed her greatly.

One day after her visit in our home she came to my church office and told me she would soon get her son back, and not allow us to see him anymore. She meant it. Dread came upon me because I knew what she threatened could well happen. Rhode Island's DCF bent over backwards to reunite children with birth parents, and there was nothing I could do to alter this plan.

All I could do was pray, so I did. I prayed the entire night like this: "Father God, this little boy belongs to you. You gave him the gift of life and He is precious to you and to Helen and me. You placed him with us and you know we love him. Lord, his destiny is in your hands. If you let us raise Him we will do all we can to show him your love and

PART VI ~ WALKING WITH GOD AS A PARENT

point him toward you! We will teach him your truth so he can see how wonderful you are! Lord, take this child into your hands. Protect him so he will have the opportunity to know you, and by your grace may he one day be with us and you in heaven."

I prayed this throughout the night. Soon after the sun rose my burden was lifted and I knew it would be okay. I knew God had answered my prayer. I was tired but at peace. A couple of hours later as we were finishing breakfast the phone rang. I recognized the voice of our DCF caseworker. She asked if I was sitting down. I said I was. "You won't believe what just happened!" she said. Mentioning Carlo's birth mother she said, "She was just here and announced she made a decision last night to terminate her parental rights releasing her son for adoption!"

> No matter what struggles or challenges you have faced or will yet face in parenting, be assured that God chose your children for you, for their blessing and yours.

Tears flowed and my heart filled with praise for answering my prayer so quickly. I then heard the caseworker ask, "Can I presume you and Helen wish to adopt Carlo?"

"You bet we would!" was my reply. Our God is a prayer-answering, miracle-working God. There was no doubt in my mind or Helen's, nor has there been any day since then, that God blessed us to be the parents of that child.

A highlight of my life so far was the day we entered Providence County Family Court to adopt our son. Helen and I stood with our attorney, holding our little boy. The judge spoke our full names and asked if we were ready and willing to take full parental responsibility for this child, to love and provide for him as our own son. With solemnity and joy before the court and God we said, "Yes, your honor!"

"What will be his name?" we were asked.

"Carl Richter Gammon," was our reply. The judge hit his gavel and proclaimed the adoption complete.

I wish I could describe what my son Carl means to me and how dearly I love him. He is the son of answered prayer. He is God's blessing. The name *Carl* means "Free man, strong," reminding me of what God has given my son. Carl's story is one of grace, just as all who are God's children have become so through adoption because of His love for us. *In love he predestined us for adoption for sonship through Jesus Christ, in accordance with his pleasure and will* (Ephesians 1:4b-5).

If you are a parent, I am sure you too have learned that parenting is not easy and we do not always get it right. Along the way as parents we are invited to walk with God, for we need His grace and strength and wisdom for this great responsibility. No matter what struggles or challenges you have faced or will yet face in parenting, be assured that God chose your children for you, for their blessing and yours.

Life Application Questions:

1. What is your reaction to the notion of making a difference to one child?

2. Have you ever been moved to fervently pray for someone for many hours? Is there someone for whom God is calling you to do so now?

3. What response is the Holy Spirit asking of you now?

47

You Are a Child of God's Promise

"I prayed for this child, and the LORD has granted me what I asked of him. So now I give him to the LORD. For his whole life he will be given over to the LORD" (1 Samuel 1:27-28)

First Samuel tells the story of a woman named Hannah who for many years longed to be a mother, but her dreams were unfulfilled. She was barren, a condition that in her culture prompted pity or contempt, as it was interpreted to mean that for good reason God had chosen not to bless her. Hannah's heartache increased as month after month and year after year went by without her knowing the joy of bearing a child. This sorrow eventually brought Hannah to her knees in the house of the Lord in Shiloh where she cried out to God.

In her deep anguish Hannah prayed to the LORD, weeping bitterly (1 Samuel 1:10). Hannah asked God for a miracle, vowing that if He gave her a child she would *give him to the LORD for all the days of his life.* Eli the priest blessed her saying, *"Go in peace, and may the God of Israel grant you what you have asked of him"* (v. 17). When Hannah left the house of God her faith and hope were restored for she knew God had heard and answered her prayer. In time she became pregnant and carried to term. She gave birth to Samuel and consecrated him to God.

Earlier I described a time in late 1980, more than a year before Carl entered our lives, when my heart was like Hannah's, for I too feared I would have no children. As I prayed one day God told me to share my pain so others could pray with me. I did as directed and my burden was lifted. He removed all doubt that I would yet become a dad. Here I will finish the story of what happened that evening.

In the living room of a church family with a group of believers gathered around for Bible study, fellowship, and prayer I was asked,

"How can we pray for you, Pastor Steve?" At this invitation I obeyed the Lord and shared my heartache from losing two children and my fear of never becoming a dad. Christian brothers and sisters gathered around and prayed, and God met us.

As we prayed for God to lift Helen's and my burden of grief and fear, and to grant peace and faith that He would yet bless us with children, the Holy Spirit did something none of us expected. He gave a vision to John Bandilli, a man who had not before had such an experience. With trembling and joy John described his vision. He saw Helen with a baby, in particular a blond-haired little girl. Others in the group bore witness that this was indeed God's promise. The moment I heard John describe this vision, my burden was lifted and in faith I knew in God's good time Helen and I would have a blond-haired little girl.

> *Christian brothers and sisters gathered around and prayed, and God met us.*

We all rejoiced that evening, as we read Peter's words on the day of Pentecost (Acts 2:17) quoting Joel: *"'In the last days, God says, I will pour out my Spirit on all people. Your sons and daughters will prophesy, your young men will see visions, your old men will dream dreams.'* Arriving home I shared with Helen what God did, and together we claimed His promise. Though we had lost two children, we believed it would not happen again, and we anticipated with joy that God would yet give us a daughter, a child of promise.

The following year when we became foster parents, which led to adopting our son, we knew he would not be an only child. Carl entered our home in August 1982 and six months later Helen announced she was pregnant. Tests were done to discern what went wrong in her previous pregnancies and she was diagnosed with an "incompetent cervix," as her cervix was not sufficiently strong to hold a pregnancy. At twelve weeks along a procedure called a "cerclage" was performed, inserting a tie around the cervix to help hold the weight of her pregnancy.

As her pregnancy was "high risk," Helen needed frequent appointments with her doctor, and she was instructed to stay off her feet as much as possible and to not lift anything weighing more than five pounds. Her doctor warned her that she must follow these guidelines carefully, as the risk of losing this child was high. It was a humorous challenge for Helen to care for an almost-two-year-old without lifting him. She learned to stand right behind Carl to protect him from falling while he climbed.

If God had not promised us a daughter we might have been nervous, but instead we had much joy throughout her pregnancy. Carl had already brought joy to us, and now we were expecting a little girl too! From the beginning we only discussed girl's names, finally settling on Amy Joy. *Amy* means "love" or "beloved," so Amy Joy expresses the first two fruits of the Spirit (Galatians 5:22), which is the character of God. We believed our daughter's name would reflect her character, for the glory of God. When the day came for our baby to be born, everything went smoothly and, you guessed it! We had a blond-haired baby girl!

Amy Joy was our miracle child, a child of God's promise. We knew it and she knows it. So are we all! Each of us is a miracle child, known and loved by God before we were ever conceived or born (Psalm 139:13-16). The Bible says He chose us *before the creation of the world to be holy and blameless in his sight. In love he predestined us for adoption to sonship through Jesus Christ, in accordance with his pleasure and will–to the praise of His glorious grace, which he has freely given us in the One he loves* (Ephesians 1:4-6).

Life Application Questions:

1. How is it affecting you to know that you are a child of God's promise?

2. How does the truth of Ephesians 1:4-6 affect the way you see children?

3. What response is the Holy Spirit asking of you now?

48

God Desires His Children

*Take delight in the LORD, and he will give
you the desires of your heart* (Psalm 37:4)

God created us with longings that He wants to fill. What are we to do with the longings we yearn for? God taught me to pray and leave them with Him. If our desire is of Him, He will surely fulfill it as we trust in Him. I have learned this lesson quite often, seeing God move in amazing ways to strengthen my faith and remove all doubt, showing again that His promise in Psalm 37:4 is entirely true.

This was certainly true in our having children. In 1983, Helen and I added two little ones to our family. In July we adopted Carl and in November Amy was born. With two children now we were content. Carl and Amy were gifts of God and we loved them dearly, but by the time they were six and four years old I longed to add one more child. Helen and I grew up in families of different sizes. Her parents had two children and mine had six, so our ideas of the optimal family size were not the same.

Because we already had a son and daughter and our family was the size of her family of origin, Helen was less inclined to think we should add another child. She had been pregnant three times, and it was difficult for her. Her last pregnancy was high risk, and she wasn't eager to do it again. We both trusted the Lord, and agreed it was only His will we wanted, but for the reasons already stated Helen was predisposed to conclude that our family was complete.

I prayed about this, believing God had given me a desire for another child. I understood that being pregnant was hard for Helen, but I also knew if God wanted to give us another child He would watch over Helen and the baby she carried. I was willing for our family to be already

PART VI ~ WALKING WITH GOD AS A PARENT

complete if this was God's will, but I longed for one more child so I wrestled about it in prayer for many weeks.

God heard my prayer. One Sunday following a sweet service of Holy Communion John Bandilli, a friend and leader in our congregation, approached me. He is the same man who seven years earlier was given a prophetic vision of Helen and me with a blond-haired girl. To my knowledge he had received no other visions since.

> *God created us with longings that He wants to fill.*

When he approached me that Sunday John was moved in the Spirit. He said, "God showed me a vision today during the communion service, and I must share it with you."

"Certainly John," I said. "What did He show you?"

"Pastor Steve, I saw you and Helen with a blond-haired little boy!" My heart leapt with gladness and I urged him to share with Helen what he had seen.

Very shortly thereafter Helen was pregnant again. Now we were both so excited we could hardly stand it! From the beginning we told Carl and Amy in a few months they would have a baby brother. Because her diagnosis of an incompetent cervix remained, at twelve weeks along in her pregnancy a cerclage was again performed, inserting a tie around her cervix to hold the weight of her pregnancy. We were reminded this was a high-risk pregnancy, so Helen had to be exceptionally careful. It also meant she had to see her doctor more frequently, and I generally went with her to her appointments. On one appointment when she was not yet five months along, after examining her the doctor said, "Uh-oh."

Those are not the kind of words a patient likes to hear! We asked, "What do you mean by 'Uh-oh'?"

The reply was, "The cerclage is effacing. It is coming off."

"What does that mean?" we asked.

"It means chances are high you will lose this baby."

"Will complete bed rest help?" we asked.

"No. If the cerclage fails there isn't anything we can do." We knew otherwise. We could pray and ask others to pray with us, standing on the promises of God.

It was surreal really. Every couple of weeks when Helen visited her doctor we heard the same thing. "The cerclage is effacing; the pregnancy could end anytime." Week after week went by. At one point late in the pregnancy her doctor said, "I don't know what is keeping that baby in there!"

We provided the answer. "God is!"

On one visit as the doctor prepared to do an ultrasound we heard, "In a moment we'll know if it's a boy or a girl. Do you want to know?"

We replied, "We already know it's a boy."

"How do you know?"

"God told us," was our answer.

Surprising her doctors, Helen carried to full term, delivering a son. What a joyful day that was! It had been my heart's desire to have this child, and there was no doubt God protected and gave life to him. We gave God all the praise that day, and we still do. We named him Jonathan from the Hebrew *Yehonatan*, which means "Yahweh has given." At birth he had dark, fuzzy hair, but in a short time the color changed and, you guessed it, he was a blond-haired little boy.

God desires you. He desires every one of His children. As we walk with Him He puts within us desires that honor Him. Whatever your heart's desires are, keep seeking the One who can do more than you can ask or imagine (Ephesians 3:20). When He grants you the desire of your heart, remember to give Him the praise.

Life Application Questions:

1. Do you know that almighty God deeply desires you and your children?

2. Reflecting on your heart's desire, what does it mean for you to know that with God nothing is impossible?

3. What response is the Holy Spirit asking of you now?

49

Our Children Belong to God, Not to Us

The promise is for you and your children and for all who are far off—for all whom the Lord our God will call (Acts 2:39)

As parents we must know we cannot forever hold on to our daughters and sons but must prepare them for the life God intends for them. They will not always be little children living under our roof, but they can always be in His presence and under His care. They must learn themselves to trust and obey and lean on Him.

This conviction caused me to want to give my children a foundation for life that will not fail; a foundation of personal faith and obedience to Jesus (Luke 6:46-49). Launching children is never easy. For me it was a difficult challenge. This process works best when as parents we put our trust in Him.

God used our daughter, Amy, to help me learn this. When she was fourteen years old she came to me one day with a question. Speaking a mile a minute and with much excitement she said, "Dad, I want to go to Africa next summer on a missions trip with a group called Teen Mania. We will travel and present the gospel to people. I want to share Jesus with boys and girls there. God wants me to go! Will you let me go, Dad? Please?"

My mind sifted quickly through what I had just heard. I asked Amy to sit down so we could discuss it. I began by asking questions. "Where did you learn about this missions trip, Amy?" She said the opportunity was presented at an "Acquire the Fire" rally she attended in Worcester, Massachusetts. She said they challenged teenagers to serve God on short-term missions trips, promising if they did this they would discover the joy of serving Jesus and want to serve Him the rest of their life.

"Where are they going?" I asked.

"To several countries in southern Africa," she replied.

I asked, "How long is this trip you want to go on?"

She replied, "Two months." By now I was very sure I did not want my little girl to do this. After all, she was just fourteen years old and would be fifteen years old by the time summer came. I thought, *I love Amy's passion, but there is plenty of time for such adventures when she gets older.* I looked for a way to bring her down gently.

"How much does it cost, Amy?" I asked.

"Five thousand dollars," was her reply. My mind went to the balance in my checkbook, and I thought here was an irrefutable reason for denying her request.

As tenderly as I could I said, "Now honey, that's a lot of money."

Her reply was immediate, her face reflecting surprise and disappointment. Amy's words echoed in my soul like reverberations from a gong solidly struck, as God opened my eyes to her faith and to know He was doing something magnificent here. She said, "But Dad! Is ANYTHING too hard for God?"

> God assured us that when we release our children and trust Him with their care we can know in faith that He will hold them close always.

She had me there. Actually, God had me! How could I splash the waters of my reluctance and limited faith on the fire of this girl's devotion? After all, the Holy Spirit reminded me, my daughter did not belong to me anyway. She was His! He is the One who created her and who has had a plan for her from before the foundation of the world (Ephesians 1:4-5; Psalm 139:13-16), the One who has promised to be with her all the days of her life. Realizing these truths again that day, I knew my not-so-little girl would be serving the Lord that summer in Africa, and I knew God would do great things through her and in her – which is precisely what happened.

By God's provision the funds were raised, and Amy experienced a life-changing summer of service to the Lord. Helen and I choked up when we prayed over her and said our good-byes, but we knew God would do great things in and through our daughter. God assured us that when we release our children and trust Him with their care we can know in faith that He will hold them close always.

Life Application Questions:

1. How might the belief that our children belong to God and not to us affect the way Christian parents raise their children?

2. At whatever age our children are, why is it important to pray for them and be ready to release them to God for whatever His plan for them may be?

3. What response is the Holy Spirit asking of you now?

5 0

The Best Thing That Can Happen to Our Children

For I am convinced that neither death nor life, neither angels nor demons, neither the present nor the future, nor any powers, neither height nor depth, nor anything else in all creation, will be able to separate us from the love of God that is in Christ Jesus our Lord (Romans 8:38-39)

On Amy's mission trip were teenagers ages fourteen to nineteen. They were discipled to trust Jesus completely, believe His Word, listen to the Spirit, and step out in obedience to God. Bathed in prayer, the group used music, mime, testimonies, preaching, and witnessing to share the good news of Jesus with many, including some who had never heard the gospel. Working alongside indigenous churches, the goal was to lead people to faith in Christ so churches could be planted. Teen Mania leaders divided the teens into teams, appointing a member of each group as team leader. Although she was among the youngest who were there, Amy was appointed a team leader, as she demonstrated a close relationship with Jesus and gifts of faith, discernment, and leadership.

On the few occasions Amy could make a phone call or send an email message home, she described some of the great things God was doing in and through the group. Each time we heard from Amy we rejoiced in how God was using her in His service, all the while growing her up in relationship with Him. She was especially thrilled when she witnessed people, sometimes crowds of people, coming to faith in Christ. She was overjoyed to be a part of such miracles!

She also told of the Lord performing miracles of healing, in the process stretching her faith and providing people confirmations of the truth of the gospel. One occasion she described was an open-air meeting at a remote village in Namibia. The Holy Spirit was moving among them, opening spiritual eyes to the truth of Jesus Christ. As the message was preached and people came in faith and repentance for forgiveness and salvation, Amy watched miracles of grace happening around her. Tears flowed, joy was evident, and showers of blessing descended upon the crowd as God brought people into relationship with Himself through Jesus.

Watching and praying as the Holy Spirit moved among the people that day, Amy felt God drawing her attention to a man sitting on the ground who had come to the meeting without the use of his legs. He had waddled in using his arms for movement and dragging his body along. His legs were shriveled and twisted, but he came eager and ready. By God's grace, when that man heard the good news of Jesus he responded in faith. Amy saw it happening as he confessed his sins, professed his faith, and asked Jesus to be his Savior and Lord. She witnessed the joy of the Lord settling upon him because of his newfound relationship with God through Jesus.

While observing this she heard the Lord say, "Amy, do you believe I can heal that man?"

"Yes, Lord!"

"Will you step out in faith and pray over him for his healing?" Amy gathered her ministry team and with an interpreter they approached the man who sat on the ground with twisted legs. They were filled with joy because he and many others had come to Christ that day.

Through the interpreter Amy asked the man, "Do you believe in Jesus, and have you confessed to Him your sins and asked Him to be your Savior?"

"Yes," he replied.

"Do you believe Jesus has forgiven you and is with you now and will be forever?"

"Yes, I believe," he said.

"Do you believe the same Lord Jesus who died for you and has forgiven your sins is also able to heal you so you can walk?"

Looking intently at Amy and the others, and with faith and joy in his heart he said, "Yes, I believe." Reminiscent of the way the apostle Paul addressed a crippled man in Lystra (Acts 14:8-10), they saw he had faith to be healed so Amy and her team of teenagers stepped out in faith. They laid hands upon the man and prayed over him in Jesus' name, asking God to touch him and restore his legs for His praise and glory. Then she said, "In the name of Jesus Christ rise up and walk."

Like the story told in Acts 3, the man's legs filled in with flesh and became strong. Then *He jumped to his feet ... walking and jumping, and praising God* (Acts 3:8). As happened one day in Jerusalem when Peter and John trusted Christ to heal a crippled beggar, now in a Namibian village the crowd was astounded and God was glorified! *When all the people saw him walking and praising God, they recognized him as the same man who used to sit begging ... and they were filled with wonder and amazement at what had happened to him* (Acts 3:9). By God's grace He visited that remote village that day, bringing salvation and confirmation of the truth of the gospel of Jesus. Amy was blessed to be used of God that day.

She also described an occasion in another village when they were going house to house sharing the good news of Jesus. With her team and interpreter she entered a dimly lit home. Receiving the family's warm hospitality, they explained the reason they had come so far was to tell them about Jesus and His love and power to save. The family listened intently.

Because the lighting was dim it took some time before they noticed there was a man there who was blind. His eyes were white, as though covered with wax paper. The teens agreed God could restore sight to this man, so they asked about his blindness and learned he had been blind from birth. They asked the man if he believed in Jesus and that Jesus could restore his sight. He replied, "I believe."

They laid their hands on the man and prayed, asking Jesus to restore his sight. When they finished praying the man was still blind, so they discussed among themselves what to do next. They reasoned that sometimes God's answer is no, so perhaps that was true in this case. As they reflected on this, all the while asking God to lead them, they concluded they should keep asking, as Jesus taught that God honors persistence in prayer (Luke 11:5-10).

One of the teens recalled the story of when Jesus made mud and put it on a blind man's eyes and then told him to wash in the pool of Siloam, after which his sight was restored (John 9:6-7). In childlike faith they did as Jesus did. They made mud and put it on the man's eyes and told him to wash. When he did so the appearance of the man's eyes changed. The clouds of white disappeared, pupils appeared, and then eye color. The man blinked and said, "I can see! I can see!"

After the joy of being used by God, Amy came home from her summer of ministry in southern Africa. At age fifteen she announced that God had revealed His plan for her future, that she would serve Him as a medical doctor. At that time I was senior pastor of Trinity Evangelical Church in Peterborough, New Hampshire. We sent out many people on short-term mission trips, and upon their return we gave them an opportunity to share with the congregation highlights of their ministry.

> *I can forever testify that the best thing that could happen to any of us and to our children is that we and they should fall in love with Jesus.*

The first Sunday after her return Amy came forward to share her story of God's faithfulness. After describing some of the amazing things she witnessed, including the miracle of seeing people come to saving faith in Jesus, with tears streaming down her face she concluded with these words, "But the best thing that happened to me this summer is – I fell in love with Jesus!" With these sweet words hanging in the room, I knew God had given us a glimpse of what He desires of us all. When faith and love become the center of our priorities and treasures, the rest of life comes into balance. This is the best thing that can happen to us and to our children!

Fast forwarding a few years I had the joy of walking my daughter down a church aisle to offer her in marriage to Joey Hatcher. Helen and I rejoiced greatly because Amy and Joey were making a covenant to each other and before God to have a Christ-centered marriage. Loving each other and loving Jesus, they committed to a lifetime of serving Him together. God loves to bless such devotion! Amy is now Dr. Amy Hatcher, a board-certified pediatrician, and Amy and Joey have made me a grandfather. I can forever testify that the best thing that could happen to any of us and to our children is that we and they should fall in love with Jesus.

Life Application Questions:

1. Has the "best thing that can happen to our children" happened to you?

2. How is childlike faith connected to obedience and ministering in His name?

3. What response is the Holy Spirit asking of you now?

51

Tough Love is Tough

My son, do not despise the LORD's discipline, and do not resent his rebuke, because the LORD disciplines those he loves, as a father the son he delights in (Proverbs 3:11-12)

Parenting is not easy, and some children are harder to parent than others. Some are by nature compliant and others are strong-willed to the point of stubbornness. Some respond more easily to correction while others fight it as though it were a frontal assault on their personhood. No matter our children's temperament, all are born with a sin nature, so at times they must be corrected. God instructs us to discipline our children, teaching them to honor and respect their parents and to obey. Learning these lessons is important in spiritual development, because obedience is part of living in right relationship with God. This is why honoring one's parents is included among the Ten Commandments (Exodus 20:12).

The apostle Paul reminded Christians of this commandment, for those who obey it inherit a promise: *Children, obey your parents in the Lord, for this is right. "Honor your father and mother"—which is the first commandment with a promise—"so that it may go well with you and that you may enjoy long life on the earth"* (Ephesians 6:1-3). Loving parents must teach their children obedience.

A battle rages within all of us, a tug of war between stubbornness and obedience (Jeremiah 16:12). In the Scriptures we see that whenever God's children choose disobedience He allows them to experience the painful consequences of their choices (Ezekiel 44:12; Deuteronomy 28). This is "tough love" by God, intended to bring His children to repentance and restoration (Deuteronomy 30). God disciplines us because

He loves us. *My son, do not despise the LORD's discipline, and do not resent his rebuke, because the LORD disciplines those he loves, as a father the son he delights in* (Proverbs 3:11-12). For the same reasons parents must discipline their children, even when it is tough.

James Dobson's 1978 bestseller *The Strong-Willed Child* offered helpful advice for raising and shaping the will of strong-willed children. Helen and I appreciated insights from that book, as at times our children demonstrated stubbornness. We were comforted by the assurance that if a strong-willed temperament is inherent in a child, the challenges of parenting will be increased no matter who the parents are. In his original classic and in his 2005 rewrite, *The New Strong-Willed Child*, Dr. Dobson includes humorous and serious accounts of raising strong-willed children.

Helen and I discovered early on that God had given us a strong-willed child. When our oldest son, Carl, was a little boy he left no doubts that he had such a temperament. A couple of incidents will illustrate this, which I share with his permission. We taught our son to pick up after himself, putting his toys back where they belong. We had to patiently remind him to do this, explaining why it was important, and guiding him to clean up whatever messes he had spread across the floor. We explained, "Carl, since you made the mess you must clean it up." Though he often let us know he didn't think he should have to do it, he did as he was told.

One Saturday when he was not yet four years old I took Carl with me to a regional church meeting at which activities were offered for children. Arriving early I conversed with other attendees while Carl explored. Discovering the refreshments table he found an apple and asked me to peel it for him. While continuing my adult conversation I peeled his apple over a trash can, and a piece of apple peel fell onto the floor. At this I paused in my conversation, turned to my son and said, "Carl, would you please pick up that apple peel for Daddy and put it in the trash?"

My strong-willed son had been saving up for this moment. With hands on his hips, Carl looked up at me and declared as emphatically as

PART VI ~ WALKING WITH GOD AS A PARENT

he could, "He who makes the mess cleans up the mess!" I didn't mean to laugh, but I couldn't help it! There was no way that boy was going to willingly pick up that apple peel.

As a boy he was bright, a quick learner, and a chatterbox. In his preschool Sunday school class the children were learning to recite the books of the Bible in order. Carl proudly showed that he could recite them from beginning to end. In those days I was also working on a doctor of ministry program, for which in one assignment I needed a video camera. As I did not own such a camera I rented one for a couple of days, during which time I decided to record our children.

For Carl's part I thought it would be cute to record him reciting the books of the Bible. Without pausing for a breath he began, "Genesis, Exodus, Leviticus, Numbers." He kept going all the way to the Prophets, "Isaiah, Jeremiah, Lamentations, Ezekiel, Daniel, Hosea, Joel." Then he paused for a moment. He started again, "Obadiah, Jonah, Micah." He had skipped over Amos. I knew it and I was quite sure he knew it. When he was learning the books of the Bible someone suggested a way for him to remember this name by saying, "Amos sounds something like Amy." That was a mistake. In Carl's mind if there was no Bible book sounding like his name there could not be one that sounds like his sister's name either.

In the Scriptures we see that whenever God's children choose disobedience He allows them to experience the painful consequences of their choices.

On the video recording that day I am heard asking, "Carl, did you miss a name?"

"No!" he replied.

"Let's try it again, Carl."

"Hosea, Joel."

"Then what?" I asked.

"Obadiah," was his reply.

"What about Amos?" I asked.

He then declared emphatically, "There is no Amos!"

Our son was an adorable strong-willed child! He gave us many reasons to laugh, and we saw his determination as a strong suit, but parenting him was at times challenging, especially when he reached adolescence and pushed back hard against authority. We did not always get it right, nor do any parents always get it right, but Helen and I did our best to be united in teaching respect and showing love. Along the way, as God commands, sometimes we had to show tough love.

This was required when Carl was eighteen years old. One day in January of his senior year, I received a phone call from a friend who said his teenage daughter was found with marijuana, and when asked how she obtained it she said Carl gave it to her. At this Helen and I looked in one of his bags and discovered evidence confirming what we had heard. Being grieved we prayed, asking God to grant us His wisdom so we might show His love and ours to Carl.

When Carl arrived home that day we told him what we had learned. He did not deny any of it, but he informed us he would live his life the way he wanted to live it and there was nothing we could do about it. Helen and I knew we must show our son tough love. We told him we loved him and that he was free to live his life the way he wanted, but as long as he lived under our roof there were limits within which he and everyone in the family must abide. These included respecting us and all members of the family, attending worship together, living within the law, and zero tolerance for illegal substances.

Carl's reply was that these were our rules, not his, and he would not abide by them. We told him he faced two choices – to abide by these rules and continue living under our roof or to move out. He replied that he would do whatever he wanted, when he wanted, and that was that! I explained that every decision in life brings consequences, and the consequence of his decision was he must now move out of our home. I told him I would help him pack his things and would take him wherever he wanted me to take him. He called friends who had an apartment and they agreed to let him stay with them for a while. I then got out his suitcase and some boxes and began helping him pack. My heart was broken. Helen and I were scared for our son but knew we had to do this.

While packing Carl's things I said through my tears, "Son, always remember you have two fathers who love you. You have me, your earthly father. I have not always loved you perfectly and for that I am sorry, but I have always loved you and I always will love you. You also have a heavenly Father who has loved you perfectly and always will. You can call both of us at any time. If ever you should call me, if I can possibly help you I will. If ever you call your heavenly Father He will hear you and He will come every time." When Carl's things were boxed up and in my car, I drove him to his friend's apartment. That was painful. It was tough love.

Life Application Questions:

1. In what ways has God shown tough love to you, and what has been the result?

2. In what ways did your parents show you tough love or how have you shown it to your own children, and what has been the result?

3. What response is the Holy Spirit asking of you now?

52

Praying for Children Is a Lifelong Assignment

But while he was still a long way off, his father saw him and was filled with compassion for him; he ran to his son, threw his arms around him and kissed him (Luke 15:20)

The Sunday after Carl moved out of our home was difficult. I was heartbroken and struggling with how to preach and what to say. As Helen and I discussed this matter, we agreed I must tell our church family what we were going through so they could pray with us. That Sunday I described our heartache as our oldest son moved out of our home. The congregation assured us we were not alone in this, and the elders gathered around and prayed. Helen and I were touched after the service when so many approached to offer assurances they would pray for us and our son.

One person who was especially encouraging was Sheri Fleming. Sheri and her husband, Bill, were good friends of ours, part of a small group fellowship that met in our home. Sheri was a seminary graduate and director of our counseling ministry, and she was a prayer warrior. Recognizing our heartache, Sheri expressed confidence that God would answer our prayers for Carl.

She said, "Pastor Steve, as I prayed for you and for Carl, God laid on my heart a phrase from Jesus' parable of the prodigal son. The phrase is, *When he came to his senses* [Luke 15:17]. Keep praying, Pastor Steve. Your son will come to his senses and will come home." In the weeks that followed, every time I saw Sheri she reminded me of this promise. We continued praying.

In February Sheri began feeling sick. She thought she would shake it off, but medication and rest didn't help. In March she was hospitalized for tests, and after a biopsy Sheri and Bill received the unexpected news that she had a progressive form of lung cancer. When I received a call informing me of this diagnosis, I immediately went to the hospital to see Sheri and Bill.

When I arrived I hugged them both and listened as they shared their story and expressed their faith that God would yet bring glory to His name. The plan was for Sheri to be released from the hospital and then begin treatments, but a decision must be made about where she would go. She must be on oxygen and have wheelchair accessibility, which their home lacked. Before I prayed with them, Sheri reminded me yet again of God's promise for Carl, claiming in faith that soon he would come to his senses and return home. When we prayed that day for Sheri and Bill we also prayed for my son.

> One of the lifetime joys and responsibilities of parenting is to pray for our children, and as God grants them, our grandchildren.

Arriving home I filled Helen in on Sheri's diagnosis, as well as the lack of wheelchair accessibility in their home. Helen immediately suggested we invite them into our home. We had a first-floor bedroom we could make available, bringing in a hospital bed and oxygen, and this way they would not have to worry about meals. I agreed with Helen's suggestion and called Bill to extend our offer. Bill said he liked the idea and would discuss it with Sheri and then call us back.

On Wednesday Bill called from Sheri's hospital room expressing appreciation for our offer, but he said Sheri would not accept because she did not want to impose on us. At this I asked Bill if I might please speak directly with Sheri. When Sheri got on the phone I asked her if she would have made a similar offer to Helen or me if either of us were in her situation. She insisted that of course she would. I said, "I know you would because you love us." Then I said, "Sheri, we love you. Please let us do this for you and Bill." She agreed. Soon after we received a phone call from the hospital to arrange deliveries the next day of a hospital bed and oxygen tanks, and we discussed visiting nurses coming to our home. We learned that an ambulance would bring Sheri the next afternoon.

The next day the deliveries were made and we made preparations for Sheri's arrival. Oxygen tanks, a hospital bed, and other supplies were carried into our home and organized in the bedroom Sheri would occupy. As all of this was happening the phone rang. When I answered I heard words I had longed to hear, "Dad, this is Carl. Can I come home?" Turning over to Helen the remaining preparations for Sheri's arrival, I found a quiet place to speak with our son.

"Carl, it is wonderful to hear your voice and I want to say yes, but I must first ask you some questions and hear your replies." I went through the requirements I had previously laid out for living under our roof. Two months earlier he refused to accept them, but now to each one he said, "I agree."

I said, "Carl, absolutely you can come home! We cannot wait to see you, but first I must tell you what is happening in our home." I then explained about Sheri's illness and her imminent arrival. Carl was concerned to hear this in part because he was a friend of Bill and Sheri's son Ryan. Our son was coming home.

Soon after I hung up the telephone the ambulance arrived with Sheri, and shortly thereafter Carl arrived to a family overjoyed to see him. As Sheri entered our home we welcomed her warmly. She was weak and exhausted but when I told her the good news that Carl was home she beamed and said, "I told you, Pastor Steve. He came to his senses! God answered our prayer!" He surely did!

I have never forgotten this lesson. One of the lifetime joys and responsibilities of parenting is to pray for our children, and as God grants them, our grandchildren. I have witnessed the reward of that. Like many of us, our son Carl has faced challenges through the years that would defeat some, but God has guarded and strengthened him with endurance, a sharp mind, intuitive insights, and a generous heart. He beautifully displays the love and grace of God.

I have continued in prayer for my sons, daughter, son-in-law, and grandson, and for any daughters-in-law or grandchildren who may join our family in the future. I will do this until my final breath. My parents set this example for me. On the day I write this paragraph I called my aged parents, and their concluding words were to again let me know they are praying for me. Praying for our children is a lifelong assignment.

Life Application Questions:

1. Why is praying for children a lifelong assignment, and how are you doing at it?

2. What blessings have you known because you were prayed for, or what blessings have you witnessed for other children who were prayed for?

3. What response is the Holy Spirit asking of you now?

53

Let Children See That Death Is Part of Life

*Precious in the sight of the LORD is the death
of his faithful servants* (Psalm 116:15)

Sheri moved into our home on a Thursday afternoon. Friday morning she made her way to our kitchen and had tea and toast for breakfast. We chatted and prayed for a few minutes before I went to work and she returned to bed. I was to depart that afternoon and return the next day, as our church elders' retreat would be held at a nearby retreat facility.

That evening Helen called to tell me Sheri had slipped into a coma. Helen was a hospice social worker, so she was accustomed to working with dying people and their families, but as Sheri was her dear friend and as this diagnosis came so suddenly Helen was taking it hard. She assured me hospice nurses were present and Bill and Sheri's son was on his way. Helen said she had the support she needed, but she asked us to pray. We discussed how our children were doing as they were watching everything and this was their home too. We agreed to pray for them, and I assured her we would cut the elders' retreat short if needed.

On Saturday Helen reported nothing had changed; Sheri was still in a coma and was expected to die within days. Cutting our elders' retreat short, we all went to our home and gathered around Sheri's bed. At that point Sheri had been comatose for more than twenty-four hours. We began reading Scripture and singing worship songs and hymns. At one point as we sang a song of worship Sheri raised both arms heavenward in worship, as though she could see Jesus beckoning. At the conclusion of the worship song her arms returned to her sides. God was tangibly with us, and we knew Sheri would soon be welcomed into His presence.

We talked with our children about grief and death and dying, and about the joy and heavenly reward that is ours in Christ.

Hosting Sheri's passing into glory was a gift to our family, reminding us all of the fragility of life. She was promoted to heaven on Sunday morning, less than a week after receiving her diagnosis and just three days after moving into our home. Sheri taught our family to keep praying, and in the peace and anticipation of her death she demonstrated the good news that in Christ *"Death has been swallowed up in victory"* (1 Corinthians 15:54). We know with certainty that our children will confront mortality. People they know will die, people they love will die, and so will they. Helping them grieve, and teaching them God's truth is our privilege and responsibility as parents.

> *Helping them grieve, and teaching them God's truth is our privilege and responsibility as parents.*

Life Application Questions:

1. How would you explain death and dying to children using biblical truth?

2. What is your level of comfort with your mortality and that of people you love?

3. What response is the Holy Spirit asking of you now?

Part VII

WALKING WITH GOD IN CHRISTIAN LEADERSHIP

When God calls us to lead His people our first priority is to follow Him. We can only lead people in following Christ to the extent we are doing so ourselves. The apostle Paul, who had responsibility for planting and leading many churches said, *Follow my example, as I follow the example of Christ* (1 Corinthians 11:1).

54

Shepherd Christ's Church on His Behalf

"Simon son of John, do you love me?" He answered, "Yes, Lord, you know that I love you." Jesus said, "Take care of my sheep" (John 21:16)

Being a pastor was not something I aspired to. Like Peter I heard the Lord's call to care for His sheep after becoming aware of the depths of His love for me. I then determined that the aim of my life would be to love Him above all and serve Him however He led me. These are prerequisites for a pastoral call: Believe Christ loves you, love Him above all, and stand by for orders to feed His sheep. Jesus told Peter to *Feed my lambs*, *Take care of my sheep*, and *Feed my sheep*. Whose sheep are they? They are His. In more than thirty years of serving as a pastor, God has consistently reminded me that the people I serve are His flock not mine.

Shepherds have two primary responsibilities: to feed and protect the sheep. These things we do on behalf of Jesus. Pastors must therefore teach His truth, all of it without fear (Jeremiah 26:2). Knowing Christ is the Bread of Life (John 6:35) who alone can satisfy and bring strength to the flock, we must feed them spiritual food that can strengthen and satisfy. We are also called to guard the flock, interceding for them and protecting them from the powers of darkness. Paul instructed the elders of Ephesus to *guard [keep watch over] what has been entrusted to your care*. What are we to guard them from? We are to guard them from false teaching and evil influences in this world that could steal or wound or destroy them.

Jesus says the good shepherd protects and cares for every lamb in His flock (Luke 15:3-7). He calls them by name and notices when any are wounded or lost. The good shepherd searches for the lost sheep, finds and brings it home, then has a party to celebrate! This is what His under-shepherds do. Faithful pastors must grasp that every person in our flock is precious to the Lord Jesus – even the ones we might not particularly like or haven't noticed. He calls the shepherds of our congregation to care for every lamb and on His behalf to feed and guard them.

> *Faithful pastors must grasp that every person in our flock is precious to the Lord Jesus.*

To do this we must know what food is needed and give it to them in Christ's name. We must also know what threats come against them so we can come to their aid to protect them. If we confess that we have lost sight of the high calling Christ has given us, but now repent and reaffirm our love for Him and desire to love the flock of God, He will enable us afresh for this calling. Pastors, we must never forget that we are called to shepherd His church on His behalf. This requires speaking His words and revealing His character to people so precious to Him.

Life Application Questions:

1. What qualities does Jesus want in church leaders?

2. How does it affect you to know that everyone you see is precious to Jesus?

3. What response is the Holy Spirit asking of you now?

55

Job #1 is to Love the Lord

Jesus replied: "'Love the Lord your God with all your heart and with all your soul and with all your mind.' This is the first and greatest commandment" (Matthew 22:37-38)

Having been around the church my entire life I presumed I had a good grasp on what is required of a pastor. Though cultural contexts and church polities vary, a wide diversity of responsibilities always comes with the pastoral job description. Pastors must at various times be prophet, evangelist, teacher and preacher, parent and brother, social worker, project supervisor, motivational leader, financial officer, visionary, counselor, comforter, prayer warrior, community organizer, consoler, encourager, leadership developer, and servant to all.

Through my years as a local church pastor and later as a denominational leader I have enjoyed some good laughs after reading job descriptions written by pastoral search committees. Sometimes the only thing missing is "walks on water" and "raises the dead." But God taught me that the first important aim of every person in spiritual leadership is not to excel in everything. Rather, it is to love God.

Before Jesus gave Peter his post-resurrection leadership assignment he asked, *"Do you love me?"* Though Peter was very eager to serve his Lord, Jesus knew that for Peter to effectively serve the flock of God he must love Jesus most. This prerequisite is ours too. Jesus asked Peter this question three times. Now He asks you and me.

We might, like Peter, be prone to quickly say, "Yes Lord, you know I love you" (John 21:15-17). He wants us to carefully consider the implications of our answer. Loving Jesus most means our relationship with Him will be so important to us that whenever the Holy Spirit convicts of sin in our life, without delay we repent of it (Hosea 14:1-2). Loving Him most means that pleasing Him is the joy of our heart.

Loving Jesus most requires taking time to meet often with God, as Moses did when entering the "tent of meeting" (Exodus 33:11). Moses knew that without God guiding him, he and the people of Israel would die. Loving God most means doing as Moses did, accepting God's invitation to enter His presence often, to be silent before Him (Habakkuk 2:20). Christian leadership requires such discipline.

Loving Jesus most means longing for Him (Matthew 5:6), because He alone satisfies our deepest longings. As with any personal relationship, growing closer to Jesus requires prioritizing that relationship. Saying we love Him is insufficient. We must take time to enjoy His presence, worship Him, listen carefully as He speaks through His Word, and show our love in the way we live.

> *Loving Jesus most means longing for Him (Matthew 5:6), because He alone satisfies our deepest longings.*

For Christians, priority one is to love Jesus. If you serve in a place of spiritual authority, it was most likely your love for Jesus that brought you to accept His call to ministry. If so, celebrate His love for you and do what He requires you to do. Reflect on what you have been doing lately. Has your focus been more on what you do or on Jesus Himself? He still calls us to love Him most, and thus to intentionally seek Him in the "tent of meeting." He still invites us to treasure our relationship with Him above all else. When we make our relationship with Jesus our first priority, He meets us and gives us all we need and more.

Life Application Questions:

1. Jesus is asking you what He once asked Peter: "Do you love me [most]?" What is your answer?

2. Why is this priority so important for Christian leaders?

3. What response is the Holy Spirit asking of you now?

56

Job #2 Is to Love the People

And the second is like it: 'Love your neighbor as yourself' (Matthew 22:39)

When Jesus was asked what the greatest commandment was, He gave two answers, like opposite sides of a coin that cannot be separated. The face side of the coin is to love God above all else, *with all your heart and with all your soul and with all your mind. This is the first and greatest commandment,* Jesus said. Without pausing to allow anyone to conclude loving God is the end of the matter He then added, *And the second is like it: 'Love your neighbor as yourself.'* For Christians, job two is to love people. If we fail to love people we fail to love Jesus. Though most Christians are cognitively aware of this principle, the test of whether we get it will be seen in our daily life, the extent to which we demonstrate love in action.

In Luke 10 we read about an expert in the law who came to Jesus to ask what he must do to inherit eternal life, a profoundly important question. Jesus asked what he understood the Scriptures to teach concerning God's requirements, whereupon the man quoted the two greatest commandments: to love God wholly and to love our neighbor as ourselves. When Jesus said he had replied correctly, the man asked Jesus a follow-up question: *"And who is my neighbor?"*

Along the way of our life journey we too need a clear vision of this. It is one thing to say we love people; but it's quite another to love them in ways that please God. Jesus answered that man's question in the parable of the good Samaritan.

In this parable two religious men pass by a man lying on the road who has been beaten and robbed. First a priest and then a Levite pass by. Both men would have been esteemed by others and regarded themselves as men who sincerely loved God and others. But their actions did not reflect this, as they walked by without offering aid. Then along came a Samaritan, one who would have received disdain from the religious people of the day. He demonstrated God's compassion through sacrificial action, giving of his time and personal resources to care for the injured stranger.

After telling this parable Jesus dialogued with the man and offered a clear imperative for all. *"Which of these three do you think was a neighbor to the man who fell into the hands of robbers?" The expert in the law replied, "The one who had mercy on him." Jesus told him, "Go and do likewise"* (Luke 10:36-37). Jesus used the Samaritan's sacrificial love as an illustration of loving our neighbors; then he commanded us all to do likewise.

In my early years as a pastor, when I prayed for my congregation and community asking God for His priorities, I kept hearing Him say, "Love them and show them how to love each other." There was some tension in our church family then. I saw some folks being selective in whom they would greet or be friendly toward. In my preaching I emphasized loving one another as Christ has loved us. This went on so long that some asked why I kept repeating this theme. I replied that I would stay on it until I saw it happening and love became the character of the church. Although my message was biblical and my words true, it takes more than words to communicate love. Perhaps that is why God brought Brownie to us.

It was a cold Wednesday night in February. At Darlington Congregational Church in Pawtucket, Rhode Island, a group was gathered for our midweek service of worship, Bible study, and prayer. That night a stranger entered. He was bearded, his hair more gray than brown, his clothes unkempt, and when I came close I could tell it had been a little while since he had bathed. He introduced himself as Irving Brown and said, "Folks call me Brownie."

We had refreshments which Brownie enjoyed. He was attentive to the Bible study and participated in discussions. He seemed moved by our prayer time and at one point I saw tears in his eyes. When the meeting concluded folks greeted Brownie warmly on their way out. I asked Brownie to stay behind for a moment so we might speak privately.

I learned he had worked for many years as a construction project engineer, living in California with his wife, but the previous year she died. He became so grief-stricken he could not stay where he was, so he quit his job and left everything behind, driving cross-country to New England to revisit places where he enjoyed precious memories of time with his wife. He had been doing this for several months until he used up all his resources. Now he was trying to figure out what to do next.

> *It is one thing to say we love people; but it's quite another to love them in ways that please God.*

When I asked where he was staying he hesitated, so I asked again. He did not want to tell me so I said, "Brownie, God led you here tonight because He loves you and wants to help you. Where are you sleeping tonight?"

He replied, "In my car." I knew Jesus wanted me to show His love to Brownie. There were homeless shelters I could bring him to, but I knew this time I must do more. I called Helen to let her know my intention, which she blessed, and then I brought him home. We gave him the use of a shower and a warm bed. We put his clothes in the washer and as it was late and we were tired we called it a night. I prayed with him and assured him in the morning we would talk about next steps for him.

I had no idea how God would bless our family and congregation! Brownie needed tender loving care and the Lord brought him to our home and congregation to give it to him. Brownie began to heal. He received the love of Christ and he loved God back by loving all of us. He shared our home for ten months, during which time he became as family to us. He was great with hand tools and he liked repairing things, so wherever he saw a project needing attention, he tackled it.

About this time a vacancy opened for a church custodian and the job was offered to Brownie. This provided him some income and plenty of interaction with people in the congregation and community. He loved the people and they loved him. A couple of years later God led Brownie back to California to be near family, and we remained in contact until a few years later when God welcomed him home to heaven.

God used Brownie as a catalyst to remind us to love each other, even those who are wounded, broken, or different. Jesus taught that for the church to reflect Him in this world we must love one another. *"A new command I give you: Love one another. As I have loved you, so you must love one another. By this everyone will know that you are my disciples, if you love one another"* (John 13:34-35). May we ever remember that for Christians, loving people is job two!

Life Application Questions:

1. Why are loving God and loving people both essential for Christian leaders?

2. How have you recently reflected or witnessed the kind of love demonstrated by the Good Samaritan?

3. What response is the Holy Spirit asking of you now?

57

Prioritize Family

*He must manage his own family well and see that his
children obey him, and he must do so in a manner
worthy of full respect* (1 Timothy 3:4)

Being called into His service is not an excuse for neglecting family. I have known far too many Christian leaders whose families experienced the consequences of neglect. At times I too wrestled with this issue. As a young pastor there were so many demands on my time. My schedule required study time for sermon preparations and Bible studies, administrative duties, counseling appointments, visitations to the sick and shut-ins, attending leadership and committee meetings, weddings and funerals, area clergy meetings, community events, and denominational activities. Sometimes it seemed these responsibilities required more time than I had, which required choosing one priority above another. When it seemed something had to be shortchanged, sometimes my family was neglected. Thankfully, I had a wife, friends, and church leaders who did not let me get away with it. God used them to remind me to prioritize my family. The Scriptures have much to say about this. For married leaders, our relationship priorities begin there.

When Helen and I married I was twenty-one and she was twenty-two years of age. We loved each other and intended to remain married until death separated us. Because of the security of our promise, in my early years of pastoral ministry I sometimes took her for granted and neglected to give her and our relationship the priority it deserved.

When that happened Helen let me know, and God reminded me to make changes. A key instruction is Ephesians 5:25 which says as a husband I must love my wife in the same way Christ loved the church and gave Himself for her. If prioritizing my marriage with Helen was to be that important and to reflect His love to her, then I was compelled to make some adjustments.

Specific changes included scheduling what we called "mini-moons," or mini honeymoons away together. We attempted to do this at least twice yearly, giving us precious time to look back upon and look forward to. We also scheduled dates regularly, including going out to breakfast every Monday. We agreed to read at least one book together per year that helped us focus on marriage enrichment. In these and other ways we re-prioritized our marriage.

> *If God has given you a family, love them as Christ has loved you.*

When children arrived they became a new high priority. On several occasions God reminded me that others could serve in the various places I was called to serve, but I was the only person who could serve as father to my children. It was my assignment to love and teach and nurture them, to prepare them for life.

When Paul instructed Pastor Timothy about choosing elders (1 Timothy 3:12), he made it clear that evidence of prioritizing family was a firm prerequisite for Christian leaders. If God has given you a family, loving them as Christ has loved you and giving of yourself to them is a key part of His calling as you walk with Him.

Life Application Questions:

1. What challenges have you faced in prioritizing family relationships?

2. Why is this a priority for Christian leaders and what can happen if it is ignored?

3. What response is the Holy Spirit asking of you now?

58

Make Disciples Along the Way

> *"Therefore go and make disciples of all nations, baptizing them in the name of the Father and of the Son and of the Holy Spirit, and teaching them to obey everything I have commanded you. And surely I am with you always, to the very end of the age"* (Matthew 28:19-20)

Before ascending into heaven Jesus gave orders to His disciples, standing orders that remain in effect today. He instructed us to go in His name to all peoples of this world to make disciples. If you are a Christian these orders are for you. We are to introduce people to Jesus, extending His invitation to follow Him. Making disciples includes baptizing them and teaching them to obey everything He has commanded. To Christians who accept this mission Jesus is with us until the end.

Calling people to discipleship includes teaching them God's Word and showing them how to be His devoted followers, loving Him most, obeying Him willingly, and serving Him entirely. There are always more people interested in knowing about Jesus from a distance than there are those who truly want to be His disciples. A major reason for this is the cost of discipleship. Yielding to His authority will cost us time, treasure, reputation, and maybe even our lives. Jesus' disciples gladly do this, for we have discovered that knowing Him is of greater value than anything else this world offers. No matter what we do for a living, no matter where we live or serve, if we are disciples of Jesus we share a common purpose. We are called by the Lord Jesus to make disciples. This is not a distinctive or command only for an elite few. This is our Lord's command for all His disciples.

As a pastor I understood that this was my assignment. Through preaching, teaching, and developing leaders I was to help people of my flock grow in spiritual maturity. Such teaching includes calls to holiness and repentance, to self-sacrifice and obedience, and to loving service. I have rejoiced to see people take their relationship with Jesus seriously and therefore mature in faith and witness.

At times as a young pastor I became frustrated when some were clearly not getting it! I heard grumbling and found in some an unwillingness to allow God to change them. They did not want to be challenged or to repent and be changed. They listened but did not want to obey. As I wrestled about this in prayer I heard the Lord say, "Lead those who want to follow." Through the years this has been my emphasis. Jesus said God draws people to Himself: *No one can come to me unless the Father who sent me draws him* (John 6:44). When God draws someone to Himself, He places in their heart a desire to know and love and serve Him, to be His disciple. You and I are not capable of imparting this desire to anyone.

> *We are called to be His followers, to be His disciples, and to make disciples.*

The Gospels tell of people who gathered around Jesus because He was compelling in word and deed. But when His teaching called for sacrifice they left. We also read of disciples who gladly left everything to follow Jesus, whose life purpose became to love, follow, and serve Him until their dying breath. Our task is not to be fans of Jesus. We are called to be His followers, to be His disciples, and to make disciples. There is no higher calling than this!

Life Application Questions:

1. Are you taking time for prayer, God's Word, Christian fellowship, and serving?

2. Are you available to speak of Jesus to people who do not yet know Him?

3. What response is the Holy Spirit asking of you now?

59

Aim for Biblical Unity

I will remain in the world no longer, but they are still in the world, and I am coming to you. Holy Father, protect them by the power of your name, the name you gave me, so that they may be one as we are one (John 17:11)

I have learned that biblical unity requires considerable effort and prayer. Sadly, Christians can become so accustomed to disunity in the church that they regard it as normal and so lose all motivation to pursue biblical unity. We must return to Jesus' vision for unity in His church.

As a pastor I experienced much grief when biblical unity was lacking. At times I ached from it, which brought me to His Word. This led me to see three essential ingredients for pursuing unity in the church: prayer, effort, and humility.

(1) Prayer – Because Jesus prayed for unity in the church so must we. His prayer recorded in John 17 was offered on the day before His crucifixion. We can be very certain the things Jesus prayed that day were extremely important to Him, so they must also be to us. He prayed for unity among His followers. He prayed, *Holy Father, protect them by the power of your name, the name you gave me, so that they may be one as we are one* (John 17:11). Realizing the impact disunity would have on the witness of the church, He prayed, *May they be brought to complete unity to let the world know that you sent me and have loved them even as you have loved me* (John 17:23). Since Jesus saw the importance of praying for unity in the church, how much more should we! We are engaged in a great spiritual battle, and our enemy the Devil will do all he can to divide and conquer the church, so we must fight back in prayer, seeking our Lord's help to bring us to *complete unity*.

(2) Effort – Aiming for biblical unity requires effort. It will not happen otherwise. If ever we take it for granted, or allow grievances to

fester, unity will be overcome by disunity. Paul encouraged the church of Ephesus to *Make every effort to keep the unity of the Spirit through the bond of peace* (Ephesians 4:3). What does it mean to *Make every effort*? It means to go the extra mile to reconcile. It means to love people even when we do not agree. It means to lay aside our own desires and agendas, agreeing with brothers and sisters to pursue only what honors Jesus. It means if ever we are not of one mind, we more fervently pray, asking the Lord to bring us to one mind.

(3) Humility – Recognizing that Christ is head of the church, attaining biblical unity requires leaders who will humble themselves to pursue unity of the Spirit. This means that when it comes to congregational meetings or meetings of church leaders, we all lay aside our own egos, prayerfully agreeing with all present that it is only His will that matters. As a pastor and denominational leader I have had the privilege of working with leaders who understood this concept, and who were thus instruments to effect Christian unity in the church. I have also experienced the heartache of working with leaders who had no desire to fulfill their responsibility to humble themselves and pray to seek the unity of the Spirit. The church is instructed to *Live in harmony with one another* and *If it is possible, as far as it depends on you, live at peace with everyone* (Romans 12:16, 18). The church, beginning with its leaders, is called to *Make every effort to keep the unity of the Spirit through the bond of peace* (Ephesians 4:3).

One of my great joys in life has been to witness the Holy Spirit accomplish this miracle: seeing leaders respect and love each other, reaching agreement regarding the mind of Christ; seeing congregations who before were accustomed to division and tension, now experience love and peace and agreement; and seeing people who formerly despised each other, now forgive and love each other. Such victories are remarkable testimonies of God's grace and the fruit that comes from applying principles revealed in Scripture and aiming for biblical unity.

Life Application Questions:

1. What are the implications for your local church and for you of this lesson?

2. How is God calling you to make every effort for biblical unity?

3. What response is the Holy Spirit asking of you now?

60

Aim for Increased Fruitfulness

"I am the true vine, and my Father is the gardener. He cuts off every branch in me that bears no fruit, while every branch that does bear fruit he prunes so that it will be even more fruitful" (John 15:1-2)

Like a gardener with a "green thumb," God pays careful attention to our fruitfulness, cutting off branches that no longer bear fruit, and pruning other branches so we can produce even more. This idea became real to me as a young minister when I experienced God's painful intervention in my life. God began impressing upon me that as increased fruitfulness was His desire for me it was good for me to aim for it too. Settling for mediocrity is not an option with God, so neither should it be for me.

> *Until we cross the finish line into heaven, may our aim be fruitfulness for Him.*

This revelation dawned on me in a time of anguish because of marriage and family conflicts in our church family and community. I cared and counseled as best as I could, but my frustration grew because I did not know how to help them.

As I shared these concerns with mentors and with Helen and church leaders, I heard God calling me to aim for increased ministry effectiveness. When I made this determination, He revealed His direction. I found a doctor of ministry program that focused on marriage and family counseling and enrichment, the skill sets I wanted to strengthen in ministry. I shared what I learned with Helen and our church leaders, all of whom gave their blessing to pursue it. The church even voted to provide some financial support and study time for this, thus giving added confirmation that this was God's direction for me. From 1984 to 1987 I pursued this program of study, increasing my fruitfulness in various ways.

God taught me to apply this principle in other areas of life too. In my marriage, for example, He reminded me to not be satisfied with just being married. Rather, I was to aim for the best marriage I could have with Helen until death separates us. Until we cross the finish line into heaven, may our aim be fruitfulness for Him.

Life Application Questions:

1. How has God "pruned" you to make you more fruitful?

2. In what ways might God call you to aim for increased fruitfulness?

3. What response is the Holy Spirit asking of you now?

61

See the Church as One

*There is one body and one Spirit – just as you were called
to one hope when you were called – one Lord, one faith,
one baptism; one God and Father of all, who is over all
and through all and in all* (Ephesians 4:4-6)

Christ sees His church as one (Galatians 3:26-28; Ephesians 4:4-6; 1 Corinthians 12:12-13). Just as various parts of our physical bodies look and function very differently yet are the same body, so do various parts of the church, though different, comprise one body with Christ as its head. In God's eyes we are one, and this is how He wants us to see it. This is true in local churches and between churches and denominations. We are too prone to see ourselves as disconnected from one another, but Jesus wants us to see His church as one.

I began learning this as a college student interacting with students and faculty from so many theological traditions. To the extent we loved and trusted Christ as Savior and Lord we discovered we were brothers and sisters. In my early years of pastoral ministry God continued teaching me this lesson. There was much to do within my local church and such ministry required so much of my attention, but God also reminded me that He wanted me to serve in unity with other ministers and congregations who loved Him.

Many such opportunities opened for me. Within my denominational group, I became active in our New England Fellowship, serving on the executive committee. From 1988 to 1989 I was asked to serve as central New England area representative for the CCCC, which I did with the blessing of Helen and our church leaders. I also worked with pastors and lay leaders from churches of various evangelical denominations, allowing us to sponsor evangelistic ministries together. Within walking distance of the church I served, I also established friendships with pastors of Methodist, Episcopal, and Roman Catholic congregations, which allowed us to pray together and find ways to make a shared impact on our community.

Later, when God led me into navy chaplaincy, I brought a vision of biblical unity, seeing the church as Jesus sees it, with a capital "C." When Christians go to our respective corners and only fellowship with people with whom we agree on everything, we fail to convey to the world the spiritual unity Jesus brings. Too many have discounted the gospel message because instead of seeing unity in the church, they see disunity and distrust. This grieves the Lord and should also grieve us.

> *This is not a suggestion. It is His command.*

When we are welcomed into heaven we will no longer see disunity in the body of Christ. We will be one! This is the way Christ sees His church. He calls us to see what He sees, not only in some future day but now. He calls us to see His church as one and to demonstrate this vision in the way we meet and work with Christian brothers and sisters. This is not a suggestion. It is His command.

Life Application Questions:

1. In what ways might a local church show that it sees His church as one?

2. In what ways might God call you to reflect His vision of a church that is one?

3. What response is the Holy Spirit asking of you now?

6 2

Shine as a Light in This World

> Jesus said: *"You are the light of the world. A city on a hill cannot be hidden. Neither do people light a lamp and put it under a bowl. Instead they put it on its stand, and it gives light to everyone in the house. In the same way, let your light shine before men, that they may see your good deeds and praise your Father in heaven"* (Matthew 5:14-16)

Jesus does not intend for His people to remain in a holy huddle, interacting only with people who love Him. He does not want us to hide our light *under a bowl*. He wants us to let our light so shine in this world that people who do not yet know Him will see the light and be drawn to Him. God taught me this early in ministry. One way I learned this was by conducting funerals for unchurched people in my community. A local funeral home director who was a member of our congregation asked if I would be willing to assist by officiating at funerals for families with no church connection. At first I said no, as I had much on my plate. But as I prayed about this God made it clear I must change my answer to yes.

This decision provided opportunities to enter homes of unchurched people and to share with them the love and gospel of Jesus Christ. This allowed me to establish relationships with people who were on the outside looking in concerning Christ. They were able to see that I knew the Lord and I cared for them, which caused them to feel safe enough to contact me in times of crisis.

One contact I cannot forget. I was awakened at 2:00 a.m. by someone banging on my front door. I went to the door and found two people I previously met at a funeral. They were terrified. Inviting them in I heard their story. They told of moving into an apartment in which they later learned a previous occupant was involved in the occult. They reported sensing evil in their home. Both of them described seeing knives flying across the room, barely missing them! They pleaded for help.

> *The only way many may come to see this truth is if we live the faith in an attractive way.*

I assured them the power of Christ was greater than all powers of darkness, including what they were experiencing. I promised them if they would trust fully in Christ He would remove their fear and replace it with peace. I prayed with them and promised to come the next day with another church leader when we would pray over their home for deliverance. When they departed my home they seemed relieved to know help was on the way.

The next afternoon, I went with another prayer warrior to their apartment. We offered prayers of deliverance over the couple and their apartment, commanding the powers of darkness to depart, and claiming the territory as holy ground for Christ. Peace entered that home. Later, the couple reported that they never again felt the pervasive evil and fear they had known. Too easily Christians can forget that the people around us who do not know Jesus Christ are lost in their sin. He died to make a way for their salvation, but the only way many may come to see this truth is if we live the faith in an attractive way.

Life Application Questions:

1. Why does Jesus command us to let your light shine before men, and how might this have an impact on a local church's strategy for outreach?

2. In what ways might God be calling you to shine your light before men?

3. What response is the Holy Spirit asking of you now?

Part VIII

WALKING WITH GOD IN SACRIFICIAL SERVICE

Obedience requires letting go of our presumptions and saying yes to Him. I experienced this when He called me as a navy chaplain. I had been a local church pastor for nine years and presumed I would always serve in this way, but when God made His will known I obeyed. Twenty-five years of military service followed, some active duty and some reserves. The ministry opportunities were tremendous. What follows are lessons I learned while serving as a navy chaplain.

63

Taking Orders Is Mandatory!

Hear, O Israel, and be careful to obey so that it may go well with you and that you may increase greatly in a land flowing with milk and honey, just as the LORD, the God of your fathers, promised you (Deuteronomy 6:3)

Everyone who serves in the military understands obeying orders. We swear such allegiance when joining the military, but taking an oath is only the beginning. We must then make good on our commitment. If anyone in uniform refuses to obey a direct order there are painful consequences. The same is true of God's people. Moses told about the Israelites whom God called to be His people and who promised, *"We will do everything the LORD has said; we will obey"* (Exodus 24:7). But they didn't do it; their heart was not in it. Nearing the end of life Moses presented the choice to them and the corresponding results of their decision. He said obeying God would bring blessing and disobeying would bring disaster. Becoming a Christian means determining to take our orders from Christ even if He gives an order we do not like or understand, or that we think must be a mistake.

When God called me into the military, the process was a test of my willingness to obey. Military life was not something I aspired to. I was a local church pastor. Why would I want to do something else? By 1989, I had been pastor of Darlington Congregational Church for nine years. Helen and I had welcomed three children into our family. We loved where we were and had no desire to move. A few times during those years I was contacted by churches looking for a pastor to see if I might be interested, but my answer was always no.

One of my clergy friends was Reverend Jim Cravens, rector of St. Martins Episcopal Church, a short walk from where I served in

Pawtucket. Besides serving his church Jim served as a chaplain in the Navy Reserves. For years Jim encouraged me to do what he was doing, to become a Navy Reserves chaplain. Each time he brought it up my answer was no, because I was too busy to add anything else.

One lesson God was teaching me then is to remember that He is Lord and I am not. Therefore I must avoid being presumptuous and assuming whatever I was called to in life would be forever. Except for the covenant of marriage which is until death separates us, in every other calling I must never refuse His orders should He call me to move on. When God told Abraham to leave his home in Ur he had no idea where he was going, but in faith he left, determined to follow wherever God would lead. In the spring of 1989, I expressed that commitment to God. I did not want to leave where I was, but I wanted to be very sure I was taking orders from God.

I generally took a personal retreat three or four times per year to fast and pray, putting my ear on the Lord's chest to hear His heartbeat. For anyone God calls to spiritual leadership, it is imperative that we carefully listen to God so we can speak to others what He gives us to say, and to lead as He leads us.

In May 1989 I was preparing for my tenth year of pastoral service. While on spiritual retreat I consecrated myself once again to God, asking Him to confirm in that year if I was to continue serving in Pawtucket or if He would be issuing me new orders. I would not look for another place to go, but if anyone approached me I would prayerfully listen in order to discern if this was God's leading.

Then my friend Jim Cravens encouraged me yet again to consider navy chaplaincy. This was not something I had ever considered, but remembering the promise I made to God, this time I determined to listen carefully to see if this was His leading. I think Jim was surprised when I asked him for the phone number. I expected one quick phone call would bring assurance that this was not for me. When the chaplain recruiter answered my call I told him who referred me and that I was inquiring about Navy Reserve chaplaincy. He said they had enough reserve chaplains at that time but there still were some slots for active duty chaplains. He then asked me a series of questions, after which he said I exceeded the criteria and he encouraged me to apply for an active duty commission. I did not want to, but because of my promise I determined to consider it.

Knowing nothing about navy chaplaincy I asked the recruiter many questions, all of which he answered satisfactorily. He assured me I could remain faithful to my biblical convictions and the tenets of my faith while ministering in the military. I asked how long it took from beginning the process of applying for a commission until entering the navy as a chaplain. He said it could be eight to twelve months. Assured that a quick decision was not required, I asked for an application. The timeline he gave would put me near the end of my tenth year at the church, and I reasoned there was plenty of time for God to close this door. The application arrived on May 15. On June 15 I put the completed package in the mail.

On July 15 I received a call from the navy chaplain recruiter offering me an active duty commission as a chaplain. I replied, "But you said it would take eight to twelve months! I applied just one month ago!"

He replied, "The timing of your application was just right."

I then asked, "For how long would I have to serve?"

He said, "You would sign a contract for a total of eight years active and reserve, with a minimum of three years on active duty."

"How long before you need my answer?" I asked.

He said, "How about a week?"

I agreed to give an answer the next week and then I hung up the phone and prayed, "Lord, you don't want me to do this, do you? You know I like it where I am!" Then I took a deep breath. "But you are Lord and I will take my orders from you."

I was scheduled to get on a plane the next day for Chicago, as the annual meeting of the CCCC would be held at Wheaton College in Wheaton, Illinois. Helen and our children were in North Carolina visiting her parents. I called to tell her about the call from the navy. We agreed we only wanted God's will. We would keep praying and compare notes the next week, trusting God to lead us.

On my flight to Chicago I wrestled with the idea of signing a contract that committed me to three years on active duty. I prayed, "Lord, do you really want me to sign this contract, making a commitment to serve for three years doing something I never imagined doing?" I asked this question presuming the answer would be no, but trusting God to show me.

Wheaton College offered various housing options for people attending the CCCC annual meeting. As I was traveling alone I chose the least-expensive option, a single dormitory room with a bathroom shared with another single dormitory room. Upon arrival I opened the door to the bathroom and who was there but a military chaplain. The next morning at the Bible hour in the auditorium, who sat next to me but a navy chaplain in his summer-white uniform. No one in attendance except God knew the question I was wrestling with that day.

> We do not know precisely when, but the Lord will return and we shall forever be with Him.

The Bible teacher was Dr. David Mains, pastor of a prominent Chicago church and teacher of a nationally broadcast radio program called *Chapel of the Air*. In his message that day, David Mains amplified a point by using an illustration from Hong Kong, a place where he frequently ministered. He said, "Everyone who lives in Hong Kong realizes they are living in a window in time. Though currently under British rule, people who live there know in 1997 Hong Kong returns to Chinese rule. Every decision they make is made with this awareness. Personal decisions, business decisions, relationship decisions, and financial decisions – every decision is made with the awareness that in 1997 this window in time will close and Hong Kong will return to Chinese rule."

He then made his point. "Christians, we too are living in a window in time. Jesus is coming again. We do not know precisely when, but the Lord will return and we shall forever be with Him. In the same way that citizens of Hong Kong would be foolish to ignore that their present window in time will soon close, so is it foolish for citizens of heaven to ignore that soon Christ will return. Every decision should be made in light of this reality."

Agreeing with his point, I asked God to help me apply this truth in my life. Then David Mains raised his hand and opened his mouth as though to speak further. He paused for a moment as though listening. He then stretched out his arm and pointed in the direction where I was sitting and said something that startled me to the core. He said, "And God wants to know, are you willing to look at the next three years of your life as a window in time? Are you willing to do something for God that you never considered doing?" I was astounded! Only God knew this was the question I was wrestling with. I was now open to the possibility that navy chaplaincy could be something God wanted me to do.

Life Application Questions:

1. If God has ever ordered you to do something you had never considered and at first did not want to do, how did you respond and what did you learn?

2. How have you experienced blessings of obedience or disasters of disobedience?

3. What response is the Holy Spirit asking of you now?

64

Our Surprises Are Not Surprises to God

All the days ordained for me were written in your book before one of them came to be (Psalm 139:16)

Sometimes we find ourselves in places we never imagined, doing things we never thought we would do. Unexpected events happen that change the trajectory of life. When this occurs it may well be a surprise to us, but it is never a surprise to God. Since He ordains all our days we can be sure of His presence as we face the changes ahead.

I was committed to obey God. If He wanted me in the navy I would go, but I was reeling from shock. I loved local church ministry, and the prospect of leaving it was hard to swallow. I liked coming home to family every night, and the thought of deployments scared me. I asked God to convince me beyond all doubt if this was His will, and I promised that if He did I would obey.

For the first time in my life I did something like what Gideon did. His story is told in Judges 6 when he asked God to confirm His will beyond all doubt. Gideon placed a wool fleece on the ground and asked God to leave the ground dry and leave morning dew on the fleece. When that request was granted, he prayed the next day for the ground to be wet with dew and the fleece to be dry. When it happened as he asked, Gideon was surprised by God's answer but he knew beyond all doubt this was the Lord's will, and he gladly stepped out in obedience.

As the ripple effects of my decision weighed upon me, including the impact upon my congregation and family, I had to get this right so I asked God to remove all doubts from my mind. Returning from my travels, I compared notes with Helen as she too had been praying. She said God had given her peace that this was His will. I reminded her this would mean time apart, potentially with long deployments for me at sea or overseas and that I might have to go in harm's way while she raised our children alone. She said she understood this but nowhere in Scripture does it say God will only call us to easy things. She said He would enable us to do what He called us to do. I respected her for this but I still was not convinced.

On Tuesday, July 25, the chaplain recruiter called. He asked if I had made my decision. I promised to do so by the end of the week but said I had a few questions. I said, "This has happened so fast. Is an active duty commission guaranteed if I accept it?"

He replied, "Not yet."

"Why not?" I asked.

He said, "The person who makes the final approval on your selection is away for the next two weeks."

I then asked, "If I accept a commission when would I need to report?"

"Two possibilities," he said. "You might be ordered to report to chaplain school in Newport on October 2, but you could be delayed until January."

I asked, "Could I have a choice?"

He replied, "No, you would be required to report when ordered."

I summarized what I had heard. "What I hear you saying is there is no guarantee I am offered a commission, but if I am offered one I will most likely be required to report October 2, but it might not be until January. You also said I won't know for certain about any of this for two weeks, but you want me to tell you this week if I will accept a commission if it is offered."

"That is right," he replied. I agreed to give him my answer in two days.

Hanging up the phone I prayed, "Lord, I am confused, but I know you have a plan. Let me know your will and I will obey."

The first thing I did was pull out our church bylaws to see what time requirements were established for pastoral resignations. The bylaws required sixty days' notice. As I had made a covenant with the church in this matter I did not feel free to disregard this requirement, so I then pulled out the calendar. The next week our family would be on our annual vacation in Maine. As October 2 was the most likely start

PART VIII ~ WALKING WITH GOD IN SACRIFICIAL SERVICE

date for Navy Chaplaincy School, I counted backward from there by sixty days, which brought me to the first week of August. As I would be on vacation then, I realized that to attend Navy Chaplaincy School on October 2 I would have to resign this Sunday – five days hence.

As there was no way I could stand before the congregation that I loved to resign unless God had given me a clear call to do so, and considering the things I had just been told, I thought it unlikely I would be resigning on Sunday. Either way I must prepare a sermon for Sunday. I would either be preparing a message like others, expecting to remain for many years to come, or I would be preparing a message after which I would submit my resignation. I had to know by Thursday morning which it would be. So on Tuesday I prayed my Gideon prayer.

I had no idea how God would answer my prayer, but I knew He would.

"Lord, let me know your will on this matter by Thursday morning. If by then you have convinced me beyond all doubt you want me to do this, I will resign on Sunday, but if clear confirmation has not come by then, I will refuse this commission and continue serving here. It is your will I desire." I had no idea how God would answer my prayer, but I knew He would. I told no one what I had prayed.

Wednesday evening I met some men at the church who were rehearsing to sing on Sunday morning. Afterward, John Bandilli, the deacon board chair, took me aside and asked how I was doing. I told him I was offered a navy commission and was praying for God's answer. John invited me to a nearby diner so we could talk and pray. I told him I was not sleeping well. I also told him Helen believed this was God's leading but I had questions yet unanswered. I did not tell him what my questions were, nor that I had laid out a fleece asking for an answer by Thursday morning.

As we parted John promised to continue praying. About 10:00 p.m. my phone rang and I heard John's voice. He said, "Pastor Steve, I prayed for you while driving home and God gave me a message for you. He wants you to be at peace and sleep well tonight, because the questions you are wrestling with will be answered tomorrow." I was astonished, as only God knew I had prayed for an answer by the next morning. I thanked John for his call and went to bed with heightened expectancy about the next day. I wish I could say I slept well, but I did not.

Thursday morning I was in prayer. This was the day I must know His answer, but how would He answer? I thought, If God is to answer my questions today I must speak with the chaplain recruiter again, but just two days ago he said it would be two weeks before he had any definite answers. I sat at my desk praying, with one hand on the phone receiver, wrestling with whether to call the chaplain recruiter. Then the phone rang. Before the first ring was ended I answered and immediately recognized the chaplain recruiter's voice. He said, "Lieutenant Gammon, this is to inform you your name is on the list for Navy Chaplaincy School in Newport, Rhode Island, beginning October 2. I did not know how this was possible so I called Washington, D.C. to confirm, and it is confirmed. I have no explanation."

When I heard his words the Holy Spirit flooded my soul with peace. I replied, "You have no explanation, but I do. This was God's way of letting me know beyond all doubt that this is His will for me."

"Will you accept this commission?" I was asked.

"Yes, I will," was my reply. Though my call into the navy was a surprise to me, it was not to God. That Sunday I resigned, announcing that my last day as their pastor would be Sunday, October 1. Leaving the church family I loved and led for nine years was very hard and I grieved the loss. In my last week there God used one more way to give me peace that this was all part of His plan.

Packing up my office I looked once again at a framed photo taken on the day of my ordination when hands were laid upon me as I was set apart for gospel ministry. I remembered my father and grandfather and other ministers laying hands on me that day. Then, thumbing once more through my grandfather's written testimonies of grace my eyes fell upon his description of the conclusion of his first pastorate.

I noticed three things that were the same for me as for my grandfather: (1) his first pastorate ended only when God clearly directed him, (2) his first pastorate was nine years in length, and (3) the final day of his first pastorate was Sunday, October 1. All these were true of me also.

God allowed me to laugh heartily that day, with peace that none of this was a surprise to Him. I was where He ordained me to be.

In Isaiah 55:8 God says, *"For my thoughts are not your thoughts, neither are your ways my ways," declares the LORD.* We will from time to time face uncertainties and unforeseen challenges, but when we put our trust in God we can approach every change with peace and confidence because He is on His throne and is ever faithful. He is with us until the end of the age (Matthew 28:20)!

Life Application Questions:

1. What surprises have you faced that were part of God's plan for you?

2. How does God want you to approach decision making and change when you face something you have not done before?

3. What response is the Holy Spirit asking of you now?

65

God Goes Wherever His Service Members Go

If I rise on the wings of the dawn, if I settle on the far side of the sea, even there your hand will guide me, your right hand will hold me fast (Psalm 139:9-10)

In Christ we have one who goes before us and with us wherever we go, even if it is into harm's way. God's promise to watch over all who trust in Him has brought comfort, hope, and peace to many, and it will for us too until we reach the end of our journey and see Him face to face. I know He keeps His promises.

The idea of leaving my comfort zone to go who knows where and do who knows what, all without the support of a local church was a lonely prospect for me. I could not conceive of how God would take care of me in the navy or how He would care for my family. I only hoped and prayed and believed that He would. God showed me right away that He watches over me and I have no reason to fear.

Soon after I announced my decision to enter the navy Helen informed her sister Carol who then lived with her family in Atlanta, Georgia. Helen said to Carol, "You won't believe what Steve is doing. On October 2 he begins Navy Chaplaincy School in Newport, Rhode Island, to become an active duty navy chaplain."

Carol and her husband, Gary, are followers of Jesus and are actively involved in their local church. Carol's reply was, "A friend who was recently in our home is also going to Navy Chaplaincy School beginning October 2." When Helen told me of this conversation with her sister I was very comforted, as God assured me He would provide me with fellowship and family.

On Sunday, October 1, 1989, I preached my last sermon as pastor of

PART VIII ~ WALKING WITH GOD IN SACRIFICIAL SERVICE

Darlington Congregational Church. Though confident God was leading in this move, saying good-bye to church family was tough. That afternoon I kissed Helen and our children good-bye, loaded up my car, and drove to Newport, Rhode Island, where Navy Chaplaincy School would begin the next morning.

On the drive to Newport I had mixed feelings. I was excited about the adventure yet apprehensive, as I had to do this without the support I was accustomed to from church and family. I reminded God of His promises, but I did not need to remind Him as He had already gone before me.

> *God watched over me that day and every day since.*

Arriving at Naval Station Newport, my first stop was the base pass office to present my orders and obtain windshield decals for driving aboard base. Standing at the counter in one of two customer service lines I overheard the person in front of the other line say he was there to attend Navy Chaplaincy School. At this I turned to express my welcome and introduce myself. I asked his name and where he was from. He said he was Sam Larson from Atlanta.

Hearing this I had to ask, "Do you know Gary and Carol Pardun?"

He said, "Yes!" I could hardly believe it! The very first person I met in the United States Navy was a friend of the family, and even more, a brother in Christ! After obtaining windshield decals Sam and I talked in the parking lot a few moments, marveling at how God had connected us. We then made our way to the chaplaincy school where we checked in. When that process was finished we went to the building where we would live while attending the school. We were directed to the floor we would live on and informed that two chaplains were pre-assigned to each room.

They told us to walk down the hall and look for a room with our name posted on the door. You guessed it! Sam and I found our names on the same door! We were roommates! From my first moments in the navy God provided what I needed – a brother and prayer partner. God watched over me that day and every day since.

While God was taking care of me in Newport, He was also taking care of Helen and my family. An immediate need was to sell our home.

In the weeks I would be at chaplaincy school we needed our house in Pawtucket to sell and to find a home in Virginia. We asked God to accomplish this. In a short time we had an offer on our home, the buyer's financing was approved, and a closing date was set. I then went to navy legal services to obtain a power of attorney allowing Helen to sell our home and another power of attorney so she could buy a home. We discussed the limits of what we could afford and what we needed; she arranged for someone to watch our children while she was away; then she contacted a realtor and booked a flight to Norfolk.

The wife of a friend at chaplaincy school who lived in Virginia offered a place for her to stay while house-hunting and even picked her up at the airport. In the few days Helen was there she found a great home in Virginia Beach in a good school system. She made an offer that was accepted and she made all the arrangements. The first time I saw that house was the day we moved in.

We lived there less than two years before I was unexpectedly given new orders. My next set of orders was to another "operational assignment," which meant I would be deployed. For this reason we wanted to move as a family so we could share as much time together as possible, but Helen and I agreed that she and the children would not join me until our house was sold. We decided to put a "For Sale by Owner" sign on our front yard and agreed that if we had not sold it by a certain date we would list it with a realtor and take a loss, as we had lived in it less than two years. We believed God could bring a buyer quickly and we asked Him to do so.

It was the last day we were going to list it for sale by owner. Our doorbell rang and when we answered it a woman identifying herself as a real estate agent said she was showing homes to a couple now sitting in her car in the driveway. She had just shown them a home on our street and driving by they asked if they could look at our home. She inquired if she might bring them in to show our house and if they made an offer if we would agree to give her a 3 percent commission for bringing a buyer. We agreed, then handed her a copy of our sheet listing the specifics of our home, including our asking price. The couple entered and toured our home for a few minutes, then spoke privately for a moment and said, "We will buy your home for your asking price if you can be out in three weeks." We agreed, and within an hour we had signed a purchase and sales agreement.

As we walk with God through life and ministry He continually demonstrates His faithfulness. Have surprises come to me in the navy? Yes, as they do in all of life. Have I gone to places I had never been and done things I never imagined doing? Yes, and I have faced many challenges! This is part of life for Jesus' disciples, but His lordship extends to all our circumstances. There are no situations we ever confront that God cannot address, and no places we will ever go where God is not there too. He watches over His children, reminding us that we are not alone.

Life Application Questions:

1. Have you ever felt alone and then God let you know you were not alone after all?

2. How have you approached decision making when faced with changes?

3. What response is the Holy Spirit asking of you now?

66

God Places Us Where We Are Needed

After Paul had seen the vision, we got ready at once to leave for Macedonia, concluding that God had called us to preach the gospel to them (Acts 16:10)

Everything God does is for His purpose, including where He places us. When Paul went into Macedonia he knew God led him there. God places us too. I have had many conversations with service members who were not where they wished to be, so they spent much energy dreaming about being elsewhere. I can relate to that.

Reporting to my first command, USS Emory S. Land (AS-39), I was out of my comfort zone. I did not know port from starboard or bow from stern. Being six feet five inches tall, I was forever bumping my head on the bulkhead. I felt like a freshwater fish in a saltwater pond. The ship was a submarine tender with a crew of sixteen hundred men and women and I was the junior of two chaplains aboard. Sights and sounds of shipboard life were all strange to me. It was an unfamiliar culture with a language of its own. The crew ranged from young sailors on their first orders to old salts who had been in the navy for more than twenty years. From the first day I reported aboard people lined up to see me because of stresses they were facing. This was a hard work environment for me.

I often found myself longing for the familiar world I once knew, for the Christian community I loved, for more personal time with family and friends, and other perks of pastoral life I missed, including blocks of time in my schedule for Bible study and prayer. It was especially hard when the ship lifted anchor to go underway and I kissed Helen and our children good-bye for a while. There were times when I wondered why God placed me there. I wondered if a mistake was made.

But as time went on I saw I was needed where God placed me.

Opportunities for ministry were plentiful. Soon after I reported aboard President George H. W. Bush launched Operation Desert Storm to liberate Kuwait from the Iraqi invasion. We were in wartime mode. On a submarine tender we serviced, repaired, and supported nineteen submarines and every requirement had to be finished yesterday. Our crew worked long days and stress was very high.

On one horrible day after I had been aboard just three months, two members of our crew committed suicide on the same day without any connection to the other. Suddenly the chaplains' office was swamped with grieving crew members, some reeling from the pain of guilt and regret for not noticing the warning signs of their coworker, or for not acting upon them. In the following days I cried and prayed with many, and we offered a memorial service that allowed the crew to grieve.

This hurting crew was my flock now and it was my privilege to be with them and love them with the love of Christ. The Holy Spirit orchestrated many opportunities for me to share Christ with people who were ready. Though the ship's operational tempo often precluded the crew from getting off ship to take adequate care of themselves and their families, I was available and talked at length with many.

Whether counseling in my office or in "deck-plate" conversations throughout the ship, it was evident that many divine appointments were being orchestrated by God. For some sailors who had neither inclination nor opportunity to enter a church, God allowed me to show them His love and be His instrument to *bind up the brokenhearted, to proclaim freedom for the captives and release from darkness for the prisoners* (Isaiah 61:1, Luke 4:18).

Through twenty-five years of military ministry that followed, whether serving aboard ship, or with infantry marines, or forward deployed, or in shore-based commands, I have been privileged to represent the Lord, caring for people He brought across my path. I will describe a couple of very memorable encounters.

A twenty-nine-year-old sailor who grew up in Boston admitted to me that no one had ever told him about Jesus and not once in his life had he been invited to attend a church service. He had never been in a church, and he knew absolutely nothing of Jesus. I met with that sailor a few times and as I spoke the truth to Him the Holy Spirit opened his heart to believe, as he came to faith in the Lord Jesus.

I will also never forget a sailor whose life was completely out of control. He had been referred to me by his supervisor because of his self-destructive behavior. The day I met him he could not express himself clearly or give eye contact. I knew if something was not done to help this young man that day he would be referred for a mental health evaluation and most likely hospitalized and recommended for a medical discharge.

From the moment he entered my office I prayed, asking God for discernment. Sensing a demonic presence I asked the young man if he had ever had experience in the occult. He admitted he had. Praying in the Spirit I was able to sense three specific demons, and I heard the Holy Spirit direct me to name them and cast them out in Jesus' name. This was not something I had done before as a chaplain, and I did not want to do it, but remembering the authority given by Jesus (Matthew 10:1) and recalling Peter and John's words (Acts 4:19), I obeyed.

I told the young man I was going to address the demons present in him. I named them and commanded them in Jesus' name to leave this man and not return. Immediately his countenance changed. His head lifted, his eyes cleared, he was no longer agitated, and he knew something wonderful had just happened. I then opened the Bible and introduced him to Jesus, who accomplished a miracle of grace that day. I followed up several times in the following days and saw him growing in faith while no longer demonstrating the previous destructive symptoms.

We must trust God to direct us. He does not promise it will be easy for us or that He will only send us to pleasant places, but He does promise to be with us and to put us where we are needed in His service. Our part is not to complain or run away from our orders. Our part is to be yielded, available, and faithful, and to bloom where He plants us. In so doing we will find satisfaction, blessing, and joy!

Life Application Questions:

1. Have you ever been somewhere you did not want to be but found God teaching you and using you in His service?

2. Are you willing to step out in obedience, even if it means doing something you never imagined doing?

3. What response is the Holy Spirit asking of you now?

God Superintends Our Unexpected Changes

Many are the plans in a person's heart, but it is the LORD'S purpose that prevails (Proverbs 19:21)

Life doesn't always go as we expect it. We make plans and proceed accordingly; then something happens to change our course. In such times God's children can learn not to fear, for we can be sure God remains in control over all things and He superintends our unexpected changes.

My brother-in-law, Rick Colpitts, is a superintendent of schools. He oversees, presides over, administers, manages, and is responsible for that school district. He has assumed responsibility for its oversight. That is what our Father in heaven does for us. He is always on the job. When something comes up we did not expect, He knows what to do. God has taught me this lesson so many times, including when I received unexpected orders to a new assignment.

When I entered the navy I fully expected to serve on active duty for three years, the required minimum of my contract. I then hoped to return to a local church and serve in the Navy Reserves. As my orders to USS Emory S. Land were for three years I thought it would be my only active duty assignment. God had other plans.

One day in October 1991 I attended Norfolk area chaplains' training. The chaplain corps detailer who was also in attendance that day approached me. Navy detailers are the ones who select people for specific jobs and then initiate order writing for those assignments. That day the detailer said, "Chaplain Gammon, I am going to move you. Where do you want to go?"

I was dumbfounded, as I had been at my current assignment less than two years. I had presumed this would be my only active duty assignment, after which I would return to local church life. For this reason I had given no thought to future orders, yet here I was being told I was about to move. "Why are you moving me?" I asked.

"There are few ships to which I can send women chaplains, and I have a woman chaplain who needs to go to sea. I have already written her orders as your relief. Where do you want to go?"

I asked, "Can you please give me a list of options I can discuss with my wife?"

"No," was his reply. "I know all the possibilities so we will make a decision now."

My pulse increased, as I would have no opportunity to pray about this or discuss it with Helen. We were going to decide here and now where my family and I would move to. In that moment the Holy Spirit gave me calm, reminding me my Father in heaven is sovereign. I offered a quick prayer of faith and then heard myself say, "Send me to the green side" (that is, to the marines).

He said, "To the marines you will go. Now the question is, Where?"

I heard myself say, "Send me to the other side of the pond" (that is, across the ocean).

He said, "We have two choices: Okinawa or Hawaii."

Of these I knew which one Helen would prefer so I said, "Hawaii."

The detailer said, "You will receive orders to 1st Marine Expeditionary Brigade in Kaneohe, Hawaii."

It was fun that night telling Helen and our children we would be moving to Hawaii. We had not expected this, but God did. Sometimes unexpected changes are exciting and sometimes they are troubling. In every unexpected change God wants us to know He is our Father, He loves us, He is with us, and He watches over us for our good.

Life Application Questions:

1. What lessons have you learned in unexpected change, about God and yourself?

2. In a season of unexpected change what does trusting God look like?

3. What response is the Holy Spirit asking of you now?

68

There Is a Cost of Discipleship

Then Jesus said to his disciples, "Whoever wants to be my disciple must deny themselves and take up their cross and follow me" (Matthew 16:24)

When He lived and ministered in Israel Jesus drew large crowds. They came because nobody ever spoke with such wisdom and authority, and nobody ever performed miracles as He did. Jesus turned water into wine, filled boats full of fish, healed people of diseases and ailments including leprosy, blindness, deafness, and paralysis, fed thousands with a little boy's lunch, stilled raging storms, cast out demons, and raised people from the dead. No wonder people came to Him! He was the most compelling, anointed, and powerful person to ever walk on earth! Yet when Jesus told His followers there was a cost to discipleship they left Him in droves. They were glad to be around when it was convenient, but when He confronted them about sin or challenged them to sacrifice, they left. This still happens.

Jesus said when we find the "treasure hidden in a field" and the pearl "of great value" (Matthew 13:44-45), we will give everything for such treasure. Living as His disciples will cost us. Jesus described the cost in ways that many rejected. He said if we do not love Him more than all other relationships in life we are not worthy to be His disciples (Matthew 10:37-38). He also said we must take up our cross daily and follow him (Luke 9:23). Jesus' hearers understood that a cross is an instrument of suffering and death, so "taking up a cross" meant major sacrifice. Jesus was drawing a line to distinguish onlookers from followers. Only those who treasure Jesus above all else are willing to make sacrifices no matter the cost.

Though I knew this cognitively, I began to understand it experientially.

The lifestyle I was now called to live was hard, as it required prolonged time away from family and local church. Though at times my heart ached terribly because of these sacrifices, God reminded me He was my greatest treasure and I had chosen well.

The church largely omits the cost of discipleship from our message today. We prefer marketing that promotes the cheap price and great benefits of our "product," enticing people to take advantage of this sweet deal. By failing to mention the sacrifice Jesus spoke of, we do a great disservice to the gospel and the people we serve. The good news of Jesus is so priceless it is worth sacrificing everything! God taught me this lesson when He called me into the navy, reinforcing it in later years when I had opportunities to meet brothers and sisters who had experienced much persecution for their faith in Christ.

> *Their faith and willingness to give all for the cause of Christ stirred me to the core.*

In 1997 I was invited by my brother-in-law, evangelist Dr. Philip Eyster, of Eagle Projects International, to join him to minister in Nepal. Though the church in the predominantly Hindu nation of Nepal has always experienced persecution, the Holy Spirit was moving in that land drawing people to Christ. Phil invited me and Pastor Bob Burnock (Burni) of Darlington Congregational Church in Pawtucket, Rhode Island, to be teachers at a pastors' conference in Kathmandu. When we arrived we learned the meetings were being moved to a remote mountain village to avoid the threat of violence. News of this change had been carried on foot to church leaders across the country.

Our journey was not easy. We traversed several hours on a crowded bus along narrow winding roads. As we traveled passengers were moving in and out of the bus, crawling through windows between the roof and interior. Some Christians rode with us on their way to the conference. A few spoke some English so Burni and I heard their stories. They had all suffered much loss for the sake of Christ. Most had been disowned by family, and some had experienced torture. Still they all expressed joy and determination to serve the Lord and keep telling the good news. Their faith and willingness to give all for the cause of Christ stirred me to the core.

When our bus journey concluded we spent the next five hours climbing higher and higher along narrow mountain paths. Well past sunset we reached the village. The word quickly spread and soon about two hundred believers who had preceded us on foot, some having walked as long as a week to get there, all gathered at the dirt-floored, mud-walled church building for a time of worship. Those days were a taste of heaven!

The privilege of worshiping with these Christian brothers and sisters, the joy of opening God's Word for them, the excellence of breaking bread and celebrating with them the wonders of God's love and grace was all priceless! It was in the best sense of the phrase, a mountain-top experience. I was especially blessed in testimony times as they gave praise to God and shared with one another what the Lord had done. Sitting in the back next to an interpreter who whispered the testimonies as they were told, I heard Christians count it all joy for having been imprisoned or beaten or disowned or left for dead for the cause of Christ. Every one of them reflected joy because they knew in Jesus they had the greatest treasure of all. Through such people God was building His church.

This idea of the cost of discipleship began dawning on me in my early days in the navy. My later experiences in Nepal and the joy I have known of following Jesus through the years has confirmed that personal Christianity without a willingness to sacrifice is a hollowed-out faith that lacks awareness of God's glory and greatness. To know Him is to gladly give anything and everything for His sake.

Life Application Questions:

1. How does Jesus' teaching to take up a cross to follow Him apply to you?

2. What example(s) of sacrifice for the cause of Christ have inspired you?

3. What response is the Holy Spirit asking of you now?

69

God Continually Watches Over Our Loved Ones

"May the LORD keep watch between you and me when we are away from each other" (Genesis 31:49)

We have all struggled saying good-bye to someone we love. It's hard. We want to be with them but cannot and it hurts. It happens as children when we go to school the first time, or when our parents leave us with somebody else as they go away for a while. It happens when parents divorce and we don't see one of our parents as much anymore. It happens when we move or graduate or leave home for college or the military. For parents it happens as our children grow up and when they leave home to make their way in this world. Being apart from people we love is hard.

God reminds us that although we cannot always be with our loved ones, He can and He is. He invites us to rest in this certainty and to trust Him to hold and care for our loved ones when we cannot. A biblical example of this is found in Genesis 31. Jacob and his family were on their way to Canaan. Laban was saying good-bye to his son-in-law, daughters, and grandchildren. Though there were family conflicts, they loved each other and were aware they would not see each other again for a long time and perhaps never again. I imagine tears were shed that day, but this family knew who to lean on. Though they would be geographically separated, they knew God would watch over them and in that they took comfort saying, "May the LORD keep watch between you and me when we are away from each other." That is what God does; He never stops watching over us and over our loved ones.

The New Testament offers the same assurance. God promises: *"Never will I leave you; never will I forsake you"* (Hebrews 13:5). This is for us and the people we love. Before ascending to heaven Jesus promised His disciples: *"And surely I am with you always, to the very end of the age"* (Matthew 28:20). When the apostle Paul and the Ephesian elders said good-bye to each other (Acts 20) there were tears, and when Paul wrote to Timothy, who was like a son to him (2 Timothy 1), he recalled Timothy's tears when they previously parted. They prayed with confidence that the Lord watches over each of us while we are apart.

> *He reminded me that my family is His family.*

This lesson became very important to me in the years our family lived in Hawaii and I was assigned with the marines as a battalion chaplain. Though stationed there a total of two years and eight months, I was away from home about sixty percent of the time, including two six-month deployments plus a number of field training exercises lasting from a few days to several weeks in duration.

Though I knew I was where God wanted me, being away from family was difficult. I missed birthdays and holidays and family mealtimes and helping with homework. I missed holding my children and the embrace of my wife. I treasured the notes and artwork my children made and mailed to me, and every phone call home when I heard Helen's voice and the voices of my children. I was proud of Helen and the way she juggled everything, but when I called sometimes I could tell she was weary or frustrated. It was not easy for her either. While separated from family I was reminded that God heard my prayers and He was with them even as He was with me. He reminded me that my family is His family, and He would use others in His family to care for mine.

Helen and I had prayed for God to lead us to a church who would be our family in Hawaii. Arriving a month before Helen and our children, I asked God to lead me to the church He intended for us so my family could quickly connect. My first Sunday morning there I asked God to lead me to the church He would have be our home. I was staying in a motel in Kaneohe and did not know where churches were located, so I opened the Yellow Pages and found pages of listings.

Asking God, "Which one?" my eyes fell first on a listing for First Baptist Church Windward in Kailua. I determined to go there so I called to confirm service times. From the moment I arrived I felt welcomed.

Pastor Dave and Phyllis Thomsen welcomed me. They had two sons about the same age as our oldest two. They too loved Jesus, declared His truth, and exuded His love. God's presence was evident in the congregation. It felt like family to me.

Later, when I was far from my family and interceding for them, God reminded me He was hearing my prayers and caring for Helen, Carl, Amy, and Jonathan. I was often encouraged when I spoke with Helen and she described how people in the church had helped her in some way, or taken the children for a while, or provided a meal. One friend, Ken Harnett, was especially generous with time caring for our children so Helen could do what she needed to do. Kip, the church worship leader, took our son Carl under his wing, encouraging him and giving him opportunities to use his musical gifts in worship. Through His family God was caring for my family.

Standing watch is a concept military people understand well. It is being on duty, alert and on guard. Navy retirement ceremonies often include a poem called *The Watch* that recalls how that sailor stood the watch for twenty-plus years "so that we, our families and our fellow countrymen could sleep soundly in safety, each and every night knowing that a sailor stood the watch." Every time I have heard that poem my mind immediately turns toward God, rejoicing that He always stands watch over me, my loved ones, and all of us. Knowing He is ever on watch, even over the family I love, has helped me sleep soundly.

Life Application Questions:

1. Reflecting on times when you struggled with being apart from someone you love, how did you handle it?

2. How does believing God is always on watch over your loved ones affect you?

3. What response is the Holy Spirit asking of you now?

70

Marriage Is Worth the Sacrifice

Each one of you also must love his wife as he loves himself, and the wife must respect her husband (Ephesians 5:33)

In God's definition, marriage is a lifetime covenant between a man and a woman. It begins with a promise before God and witnesses to love, honor, and cherish one another until death separates us. Biblical marriage is living out this commitment day by day and year by year. Although God's Word shows that this is His intention for marriage (Genesis 2:24-25; Mark 10:9; 1 Corinthians 7:10-11), many couples fall short, lacking in intimacy, faithfulness, and trust. Their marriage becomes unsatisfying and over time they grow apart, sometimes leading to divorce.

When such heartache comes to people who once began marriage with hope and promise, long-lasting scars come to children, extended families, and future generations. Broken promises and failed dreams have brought us to a place in America where fewer than half of our children grow up in an intact family. Defining an intact family as "a biological mother and father who remain legally married to one another from the time of their child's birth," Dr. Pat Fagan of the Family Research Council's Marriage and Religion Research Institute reported in a 2010 survey that just forty-five percent of American children were growing up in intact families.

In several years of counseling young adults, I have met many who have never witnessed a healthy marriage and are clueless about how to experience one. Addressing groups of servicemen and women from a cross section of our culture, when mentioning how long I have been married I have often seen jaws drop and heard them say they have never met anyone who has been married as long as me.

The ultimate cause of marriage dysfunction is sin, and the ultimate hope for marital health is Jesus Christ who won for us the victory over sin and enters every relationship where He is invited. When we lean on Him together, marriage can be wonderful! Having His presence with us and character in us, we are enabled to love and forgive and give of ourselves in ways we would otherwise be incapable of. Christian marriage requires love-inspired sacrifice and Jesus equips us for it.

Through our years of marriage Helen and I have often sacrificed for each other, she especially so. She has moved with me many times, leaving family and friends and jobs behind. She has trusted, followed, and supported me, allowing me to travel in His service, without ever complaining about how hard it was for her. She has demonstrated God's love to me over and over, day after day and year after year.

God gave me an opportunity to sacrifice for her in 1992 when I was forward deployed with the marines. I entered the navy committed to just three years on active duty. I missed local church life and hoped to return to it after my three-year commitment was completed, but after moving to Hawaii and reporting to 1st Marine Expeditionary Brigade, I was assigned to 3rd Battalion 3rd Marines and we were sent forward on a six-month-long WestPac Deployment. During this time I comforted myself with the thought that this would be my last deployment and in a few months I would be home with family and could begin searching for a local church pastorate. Then I was asked to sacrifice.

> *Through our years of marriage Helen and I have often sacrificed for each other, she especially so.*

On one of my weekly calls to Helen from Japan I was unprepared for what she asked. She said she was in contact with the University of Hawaii about enrolling in a Master's of Social Work program. She said U of H offered in-state tuition to family members of active-duty service members, the cost was affordable, and she had a plan for childcare. Then she asked something requiring me to sacrifice: "Steve, would you commit to remain here for two more years so I can do this?"

I wanted her to fulfill her dreams and was proud of her for wanting to do it while raising our children and holding down the home front while I was away, but this would affect my dreams. Remaining on active duty for two more years meant I would have to deploy again a year after returning from my current deployment. It also meant delaying a return to a local church. If I made this decision based on my own desires my answer would be "No," but I realized how much this meant to Helen. Recalling the ways she sacrificed for me I knew what my answer must be.

I am not sure how she accomplished it all, but she completed a full-time graduate program in two years, earning an MSW degree. She did it with me away more than half the time. I missed attending her graduation but cheered loudly from a distance. I cannot begin to describe how proud of her I was and am.

Being married in any context is a challenge, and being married in the military is especially so, but God has shown me many times that Christian marriage is worth the sacrifices. In Ephesians 5:25 husbands are urged to *love your wives, just as Christ loved the church and gave himself up for her.* Our ultimate example for marriage is the love of Jesus. No one ever loved or sacrificed like Jesus did. We who are recipients of His love are to pass it on in marriage. I am here to tell you, the long-term joy and intimacy of this kind of marriage is worth the sacrifice!

Life Application Questions:

1. What examples have you witnessed of sacrificial love in Christian marriage, and how has this affected you?

2. What is the connection between receiving and giving Christ's love?

3. What response is the Holy Spirit asking of you now?

God Keeps Reminding Us of His Love

I will sing of the LORD'S great love forever; with my mouth I will make your faithfulness known through all generations (Psalm 89:1)

God loves us with a deep and never-ending love, and He keeps telling us so. He wants us to never tire of hearing it. He wants us to recognize His love and receive it gratefully day by day. He wants us to reciprocate and never tire of showing Him we adore Him. There are times in all close relationships, especially when we are troubled or stressed, that we are so grateful to receive a hug or hear again, "I love you." The same is true in our relationship with God. He knows what we need and He never tires of telling and showing us that He loves us.

God showed me this again in 1994 while on my second deployment with the marines. The first few months were very difficult. The previous year I returned to Hawaii following a six-month deployment and immediately began preparations for the next. Though home for some of 1993, there were a number of field training exercises throughout the year which took me away for weeks at a time. When it came time to deploy again in January 1994 it was hard on my family. Our daughter Amy's reaction expressed our collective pain when on the night of my departure she tearfully begged me not to go. I had to tear myself away.

While struggling on deployment in 1994 God expressed His love in two surprising ways. The first concerned my next orders. Being in the western Pacific meant it was implausible to have conversations with churches about pastoral openings, especially since I wanted to move to the Northeast. Also, after back-to-back operational assignments, if I stayed in the navy my next tour would be shore duty, so Helen and I determined to accept another set of orders.

In early January when I learned the chaplain corps detailer was in

PART VIII ~ WALKING WITH GOD IN SACRIFICIAL SERVICE

Pearl Harbor for a quick visit I made an appointment, as my current orders were to end immediately after my deployment. I wanted to discuss options for where I might go next. My appointment was on the day before I was to leave on deployment. As this matter affected Helen too, I took her with me. The detailer welcomed us warmly, thanked me for serving back-to-back operational tours, and thanked Helen for her sacrifice. He said I had earned a shore assignment next and asked what I desired. I told him as all of our family was on the East Coast I preferred assignment on that coast. I said I would like to be in New England if any billets were available there.

> *God loves us with a deep and never-ending love, and He keeps telling us so.*

He said he could get me orders to the East Coast but no billets were open in New England. He said he would keep me in mind should anything change. The next day I left on deployment and soon after received orders directing me to detach in July and report in August to Naval Air Station Key West, Florida. Though technically on the East Coast, Key West was far from New England, so I kept praying, asking God to give me His peace about this move or to intervene.

Several weeks later and very early one morning in Okinawa I was in my office aboard Camp Hanson. I had been in prayer awhile when my desk phone rang. Answering it I was surprised to hear the chaplain corps detailer identify himself. He was calling from Washington, D.C., where across the dateline and distance between us it was 5:00 p.m. the previous day. I was amazed he was calling and even more that he called when I was in my office.

He said, "Chaplain Gammon, how does Groton, Connecticut sound?"

I said, "Sir, that sounds great! What's the assignment and how did it become available?"

He replied, "Staff Chaplain at Naval Submarine School. The billet is available because the chaplain currently there is leaving early. I remembered my conversation with you! Does it sound good?"

I said, "Yes sir, it does!" Within days I received a change of orders, directing me to detach after returning from deployment in July and to report in August. Helen and our children were happy when they heard we were moving back to New England, as we would be near family. I was excited as I sensed God might lead me from there to a local church.

The fact that a chaplain billet became available in New England for the very time I was scheduled to move and that the detailer remembered me from afar and reached me by phone on his first try was amazing to me. My wife and children and family and I were all thrilled at this turn of events. This was an expression of God's love.

Helen and I received another expression of God's love midway through my deployment. I was stressed from having been apart from family so long, and it was even more stressful for Helen. While managing our home and children's schedules she was working hard on graduate studies and field work assignments. Because I was to return from deployment just before we would depart for Connecticut, Helen carried the added responsibilities of making all preparations for our move. Both of us were tired and stressed, missing each other terribly. As we prayed for each other from a distance God gave us an unexpected gift.

A friend in Helen's MSW program offered her enough frequent-flyer miles to buy round-trip airfare to Japan so we could spend a few days together. Helen's parents were already scheduled to visit Hawaii for a few weeks to assist with the children and they offered to do it alone if Helen could get away. When Helen saw on the U of H school calendar that spring break would be the week before Holy Week, she asked if I could get a few days away to meet her in Tokyo. I loved the idea but encouraged her not to get her hopes up as I could not leave my troops without chaplain support. I told her I would look into it and get back to her.

Our battalion with additional troops was scheduled for a few weeks of training aboard Camp Fuji on mainland Japan. About fifteen hundred marines would be there, and I was the only chaplain. Because our stay would include Holy Week, I had initiated a request up the chain of command for an augmented Catholic priest to join us to offer Holy Week services for Catholic marines. The week Helen called me I learned that our request for Catholic support was approved. A chaplain was to arrive a few days before Holy Week and remain through Easter.

After receiving this news I approached the battalion commander to ask if I might take a few days of leave the week before Holy Week to join Helen in Tokyo. He gave his blessing so long as another chaplain could be aboard Camp Fuji the entire time I was away. I then contacted the Catholic chaplain who would be joining us to ask if he might come a few days earlier. He agreed to do so, as this would allow time for him to get acquainted with the troops before offering Holy Week services.

So it was in the middle of my second deployment within a year and a half that Helen and I met in Tokyo for a week together. I took the 120-miles-per-hour bullet train to meet her at Narita International Airport in Tokyo. We saw the city, held each other tight, and talked and prayed and made plans together. We were both blessed beyond words!

We realized this was a gift of love from our Father in heaven, and we thanked Him for it. After those days I returned to my deployment with renewed focus and Helen returned to our children and to her studies with new energy, both of us more ready for what God had called us to do.

Life Application Questions:

1. When has God intervened to remind you of His personal love for you?

2. When God has demonstrated His love for you, how have you responded?

3. What response is the Holy Spirit asking of you now?

Part IX

WALKING WITH GOD WHILE AWAITING ORDERS

Sometimes as we walk with God we enter what feels like a holding pattern. We are anxious for answers, but must wait for clear direction to come. Sometimes the temptation is to jump the gun and get ahead of God. At other times the temptation is to despair and conclude we are on our own, having to figure out this dilemma ourselves. What follows are some lessons God taught me when walking with Him while awaiting orders.

7 2

Decision Times Mandate Prayerful Listening

One of those days Jesus went out to a mountainside to pray, and spent the night praying to God. When morning came, he called his disciples to him and chose twelve of them, whom he also designated apostles (Luke 6:12-13)

How often in life do we face life-changing decisions? We stand at a crossroads and face a choice, aware there will be long-term consequences to that decision, and we want to get it right. Decision times mandate prayerful listening. This is the example Jesus set for us. Though divine He was also fully human, and He too faced decisions that would have long-term consequences. An example is seen in Luke 6 when it was time to choose twelve apostles. What did He do? The Bible says He *went out to a mountainside to pray, and spent the night praying to God*. In the morning He was ready and chose His apostles. If Jesus needed to pray when facing major decisions, how much more do we! When we do so He gives His peace.

Helen and I faced such a decision in 1996. We wanted His will about remaining in the navy long term or returning to local church life. We knew this was His call not ours, so we determined to pray and carefully listen. The navy was downsizing and the chaplain corps was too. Chaplains not selected for promotion to lieutenant commander were not allowed to remain on active duty. I had friends who wanted to stay but were sent home. In 1995 I was promoted, which meant staying in the navy was an option. Many told me I had a very bright future in the navy, and soon after my promotion I was called by the detailer about my next set of orders. I was to return to sea, this time aboard an aircraft carrier.

I was troubled because I knew about the operational tempo of aircraft carriers and that I could expect to be away from home as much as two-thirds of the time. The potential effect of this upon my family weighed heavily on me. I also longed to return to local church life. I understood God does not always call us to do the easy things, and taking up our cross to follow Him is required of every Christian disciple, so I was determined to obey no matter the cost.

As 1996 began Helen and I knew this was our decision year. This was the year we must hear clearly from God about staying in the navy for a career on active duty or returning to local church life. On January 1 Helen and I joined hands and prayed, "Lord, our lives are in your hands. We ask you to show us this year what your will is for us. If you call us to remain in the navy we will obey and serve you gladly. If you lead us back to local church life we will follow you there. It is your will we want, so lead us that we might glorify you." As we prayed God's peace settled upon us. We knew He heard us and would show us His will.

> *Decision times always mandate prayerful listening.*

Decision times always mandate prayerful listening. We realized our wisdom was limited and we could be prone to make shortsighted decisions based on expediency or what appears to be in our material best interest. Our decision to enter the navy seven years earlier was made through prayerful listening, as God convinced us this was His will. We knew this decision was also His, so we trusted Him to show us the way. He did just that for us, and He will do the same for all who acknowledge His lordship, determine to obey Him, and prayerfully listen.

Life Application Questions:

1. What lessons have you learned in making decisions without prayerfully listening?

2. For life-changing decisions you currently face, are you prayerfully listening?

3. What response is the Holy Spirit asking of you now?

7 3

God Sees Our Future as Clearly as Our Past and Present

In their hearts humans plan their course, but the LORD establishes their steps (Proverbs 16:9)

Though we live within the limits of lineal time, God is infinite and eternal and sees our future as clearly as our past and present. For His good purposes He can therefore choose from time to time to give us a glimpse of our future, perhaps to encourage us and keep us praying and faithful. After all, He determines our steps.

He taught me this lesson in 1996, the year Helen and I asked God whether I should stay on active duty or return to local church life. To describe how I learned this lesson I must go back more than a decade earlier to September 29, 1985. That day I drove from Pawtucket, Rhode Island, to Peterborough, New Hampshire, to attend the fall rally of the New England Congregational Christian Fellowship, the regional fellowship of ministers and churches in which I served. The previous day Hurricane Gloria passed over New England so we were without power and had a mess to clean up. For this reason I had determined to stay home the next day, but as I prayed that evening the Holy Spirit let me know He had a divine appointment for me, so I must go.

The meeting would be at Trinity Evangelical Church, a congregation just a few years old. God met us with anointed worship, teaching, and fellowship. As I drove home to Rhode Island that afternoon I sensed the Holy Spirit saying, "Remember this place, Steve. You will be back."

Thinking He was telling me I would be their pastor someday, I argued, "But God, they have a pastor and I don't want to leave where I am!"

He calmed me down and said, "I only want you to remember and pray for this church. Will you do that?" I agreed to do so and began praying for that church, a practice I continued in the following years.

In later years there were nights while I was forward deployed with the marines that I laid on hard ground after a challenging day in the field, looking up at the stars and conversing with the One who created them all. My prayers often went like this: "God I worship you, for you are holy and worthy! Thank you for giving me the privilege of knowing and serving you! I promised to go wherever you sent me, and I have and I will, but you know how much I miss my family and how much I miss local church life. I would love to pastor a local church again, one like that church I visited in New Hampshire." I prayed this many times.

I promised Helen I would remain on active duty long enough for her to complete her MSW studies, so when on deployment I read in the CCCC newsletter that Trinity Evangelical Church was seeking a senior pastor, all I could do for them was pray, so that is what I did. In a subsequent newsletter issue I saw they had called a pastor.

Whenever we are uncertain about our future course God offers strength for today and bright hope for tomorrow.

So on January 4, 1996, God surprised me. It was three days after Helen and I asked God to show us that year what His will was for us, whether to remain on active duty for twenty years or return to local church life. I was in my office at Naval Submarine School around noon eating a sandwich for lunch. My door was closed, my chair reclined, and my feet propped up on my desk. As I leaned back flipping the pages of the latest issue of *Christianity Today*, a notice jumped off the page. It read, "Trinity Evangelical Church in Peterborough, NH is seeking spirit-filled senior pastor." I read it a dozen times!

This was the church I had been praying for all these years. This was the church that came to my mind when I was forward deployed and telling God I would love to pastor a church like that someday. This was the church God urged me eleven years earlier to remember and intercede for. I was surprised to read what I was reading, because not long ago I read they had called a senior pastor, yet here it was!

I turned in my chair and typed a brief letter to the address listed in *Christianity Today*, stating who I was and that I would be glad to dialogue if they were interested. Dropping it in the mail later that day I determined that I would not mention what I had heard God say to me in 1985, nor would I tell them I had been praying for them for many years, lest it seem manipulating in any way. I trusted God to make His will clear. In a few days I was contacted by the pastoral search committee and the process began that ultimately brought me to that congregation.

My heart has been encouraged through the years by reflecting on this truth that God sees our future as clearly as our past and present. For all who trust Him this assurance melts away our worries. In the years that followed I held to this truth when the way became hard. As I came to know beyond all doubt that God brought me there, I could trust Him to see me through. Whenever we are uncertain about our future course God offers strength for today and bright hope for tomorrow.

Life Application Questions:

1. How have you realized that God saw your future and prepared you for it?

2. How does this lesson affect your prayer life and confidence for the future?

3. What response is the Holy Spirit asking of you now?

74

God Gives His Orders in His Good Time

This is what the LORD says—your Redeemer, the Holy One of Israel: "I Am the LORD your God, who teaches you what is best for you, who directs you in the way should go" (Isaiah 48:17)

We like quick answers and instant gratification. We have restaurants that give us food fast the way we like it. We receive instant downloads, text messages, and push text notifications, and immediate access through the Internet to an infinite supply of information. Our smartphones answer questions audibly with an instant answer. We become so conditioned to immediate gratification that we expect God to do the same for us and we become impatient when He does not. But it is when we are waiting that God teaches us to trust; He answers our inquiries and gives us His orders, always in His time not ours. God wants us to know that when we cannot see around the corner and do not know what lies ahead, we can be at peace because we know that He knows and He will direct us in the way we are to go.

The psalms offer many reminders of this truth. With faith the psalmist waits in expectation. *In the morning, LORD, you hear my voice; in the morning I lay my requests before you and wait expectantly* (Psalm 5:3). Psalm 62:5 has a similar theme as the psalmist expresses his resolve to seek the Lord and to find rest and hope in Him even in times of uncertainty or trouble. Such faith flows from confidence in the character of God who keeps every promise, even to give His answers in His time. Until He does we are to be patient and trust.

In 1996 God taught me this lesson again. The pastoral search team of Trinity Evangelical Church (TEC) was very deliberate. Their previous senior pastors had experienced forced exits because of sin, so they were now determined to find the right shepherd, one who would be a unifier and whom they could trust. Considering their painful history with pastors I knew I would be perceived skeptically by some. I felt like a baseball player called off the bench inheriting a two-strike count.

Helen and I kept bathing the process in prayer, asking God to make His will known. After a few months of correspondence they let me know I was on their short list. This led to two trips by search committee members to hear me preach. This was followed by more than one visit to Peterborough and days of dialogue and prayer. The nature and length of our conversations revealed insights into the struggles the church had and would yet have regarding trust. When it seemed we were making little progress I wrestled with whether to discontinue the conversation, but as I prayed I heard God reminding me to be patient and trust Him. I said, "Okay Lord, but if you want me to come here you will need to convince me beyond all doubt."

> We can be at peace because we know that He knows and He will direct us in the way we are to go.

On an overnight visit to Peterborough to meet with the search team, I awoke early and was in prayer and the Word when the Holy Spirit took me to John 21. I read the story of Jesus' resurrection appearance by the Sea of Galilee when his disciples fished all night and caught nothing. From the shore Jesus called out asking if they had caught anything. Being too far from shore to see clearly, they did not know it was Jesus. When they yelled that they had caught no fish, Jesus told them to pull in their nets and cast them on the other side of the boat. When they did so their nets were suddenly filled with fish. It was Jesus! Peter dove in and swam to shore while the others rowed to shore, dragging the full net behind them.

I noticed specific details in John's narrative. The net was full but did not break. There were 153 large fish. When the disciples came ashore Jesus had a fire prepared with fish already cooked and ready to serve, yet He told them to bring some of the fish they had caught. Two things jumped off the pages into my heart.

First, I saw that Jesus intended to feed them with what was already prepared but that this was not enough; freshly caught fish were needed too. Second, I reflected on the number 153, wondering why this specific number was included. I realized John was most likely the one who counted the fish that day, so he remembered this detail. Reflecting on the text I prayed, "How does this apply, Lord? Are you saying you will feed this church through leaders already here and through new leadership you will put in their net?" I discerned the answer to this was yes and that I was part of His provision for feeding this congregation. I then asked, "What about the number John used, one hundred fifty-three? Is there something you want me to see in this detail?" I had a sense He was going to answer that question.

When I joined the search team that morning, they informed me they were prepared to recommend me to the board of elders as their unanimous choice to be their next senior pastor. I was humbled by this news, but as the process had taken so long I wanted to discern if they were in complete unity so I said, "I want to hear how you came to the conclusion that I am God's choice to be your next senior pastor."

The chairperson's answer caused my jaw to drop. He said, "We have looked at one hundred fifty-three profiles of potential candidates and you are the only person we have all agreed on. This must be of God!"

After my devotional time that morning I was startled by what I had just heard so I asked, "Can you repeat that please?" Again he included this number; not 152 or 154, but 153. The details were in God's purview.

I agreed to go forward, which meant being examined by the TEC board of elders. Their process included a pastoral search team finding a candidate who must be unanimously selected and then reviewed by the elders who must also unanimously agree before the candidate would be presented to the congregation. Considering the church's history, I understood their reasons for caution but I was unprepared for how long the process would take.

It became quickly obvious that various elders had differing visions of what kind of leadership was needed. I prayed that God would bring them to unity. After a long meeting in which they were still not united about the way forward, as I began my drive home to Connecticut I pulled over to the side of the road just south of town. There I prayed over Peterborough and the church, expressing my frustration. "Lord, what's wrong with this picture? You brought me here, so why can't they come to unity? Please bring them to unity or release me from this process." Peace settled upon me that God was answering my prayer.

The next weekend I returned to meet again with the elders. We prayed together more than we talked with each other. This time the board unanimously affirmed their support for me as their pastoral candidate. Knowing the congregation would now need to be convinced, they asked if I would agree to candidate and preach on two weekends. I discussed it with Helen and we agreed. At this point we let our children know what was happening so they could pray too. We wanted them to learn the importance of asking God for His leading in life decisions. Helen and I were encouraged when after the first weekend of candidating, as we drove back to Connecticut we heard our children's voices in the back seat saying, "That was fun! Wouldn't it be great if we could go to church there every Sunday?"

In late June 1996 the congregation voted to call me as their senior pastor. It was not a unanimous call, but it was an overwhelming majority, which was a remarkable affirmation of God's favor. Helen and I agreed this was His will, so I accepted the call and requested release from active duty in the navy. In late September I began my new responsibilities. In walking with God through many years of life and ministry I have learned that God has all we need and He will guide us when we need Him to. Until He shows us the way, we must trust and hold on.

Life Application Questions:

1. When you have had to wait and trust, what did God teach you while waiting?

2. What surprising ways has God used to confirm His will for your life?

3. What response is the Holy Spirit asking of you right now?

Part X

WALKING WITH GOD IN SPIRITUAL BATTLE

Since sin entered the world warfare has been part of life. The apostle Paul reminded Christians, *For our struggle is not against flesh and blood, but against the rulers, against the authorities, against the powers of this dark world and against the spiritual forces of evil in the heavenly realms* (Ephesians 6:12). We are engaged in spiritual warfare. If we are oblivious to this reality we remain unguarded and vulnerable and are little threat to the forces of evil. But as we walk with God, when we find ourselves in spiritual battle He shows us what to do and how to win for His glory. What follows are lessons He taught me in spiritual battle.

7 5

Peace and Strength Are Available in the Battle

> David said to the Philistine army: *"All those gathered here will know that it is not by sword or spear that the LORD saves; for the battle is the LORD'S, and he will give all of you into our hands"* (1 Samuel 17:47)

First Samuel 17 tells about the boy David facing the giant. The armies of Israel stood opposite the Philistine armies. The warrior Goliath stood in a valley between the armies daring Israel to send out its strongest warrior so the two could fight to the death, determining which nation would serve the other. King Saul and the Israelite army heard Goliath's threats, saw his towering strength, and trembled with fear. They felt powerless to win. Then young David arrived. He was not big or strong but he knew the One who was, so he was unafraid. When David volunteered to take on this giant in the name of the Lord, King Saul said, "You are only a boy."

David was young but he had walked with the Lord long enough to know what He could do. He replied to the king: *"Your servant has been keeping his father's sheep. When a lion or a bear came and carried off a sheep from the flock, I went after it, struck it and rescued the sheep from its mouth. When it turned on me, I seized it by its hair, struck it and killed it. Your servant has killed both the lion and the bear; this uncircumcised Philistine will be like one of them, because he has defied the armies of the living God"* (1 Samuel 17:34-37).

Rightly discerning that God was with David, Saul sent the boy into battle. David had confidence and faith because God was with him. The giant fell, the battle was won, and God received the glory! God wants us to know that as we trust in Him and step out in faith, peace and strength are available for every battle. He taught me this when facing battles in the church.

Though I knew God was able, at times I heard "giants" calling. I saw the size and strength of what we were up against, and I felt small and weak. In such times, God reminds us of who He is and of His mighty power, of all He has done and yet can do. As I prayed with brothers and sisters who also had faith in the greatness of God my faith was strengthened and my heart was at peace – even when "Goliath" was ranting.

> *Being in God's will does not imply our way will be smooth.*

Being in God's will does not imply our way will be smooth. For me the waters were choppy for a while. Some in the church let me know they did not trust me. I observed factions and heard opinions about who was to blame. God kept reminding me this was His flock, He loved them, and I was to love them too. When we face battles in life, God wants us to know ultimately these are His battles not ours. Let our confidence be in Him (Deuteronomy 20:1-4).

After I was there a number of months a man visited my office to inform me he had not voted to call me as pastor, and thus far he had not changed his opinion. He was not alone in his point of view, but I told him I loved him anyway as God had brought me to pastor the whole flock. I kept praying, keeping my eyes on the One who conquers giants and heals the broken. In time God showed me what He showed David and the Israelites. When God is for us He supplies strength and peace for every battle, and by His power the giants fall.

Life Application Questions:

1. If you have ever faced a "giant" that challenged your faith, what did you learn?

2. What "giants" are you currently facing, and how does David's example apply?

3. What response is the Holy Spirit asking of you now?

76

We Are Never in This Alone

Then Caleb silenced the people before Moses and said, "We should go up and take possession of the land, for we can certainly do it" (Numbers 13:30)

God's people have always faced obstacles, and you and I will not be exceptions. The key question we face is, where is our faith? If our faith is in our own abilities we will look at challenges before us, then at our resources, and conclude we will lose this battle. But we are not in this alone and God wants us to trust Him.

Numbers 13-14 illustrate this. At the edge of the Promised Land Moses sent twelve spies to scout out the territory, one from each tribe. Forty days later they returned with glowing reports of the beauty and richness of the land, but ten of the twelve saw the opposition as invincible and the task undoable. Comparing themselves to the strength of the adversary they said, *"We seemed like grasshoppers in our own eyes, and we looked the same to them"* (Numbers 13:33). They concluded this was a battle they could not win.

Joshua and Caleb came to a very different conclusion. *Joshua son of Nun and Caleb son of Jephunneh, who were among those who had explored the land, tore their clothes and said to the entire Israelite assembly, "The land we passed through and explored is exceedingly good. If the LORD is pleased with us, He will lead us into that land, a land flowing with milk and honey, and will give it to us. Only do not rebel against the LORD. And do not be afraid of the people of the land, because we will devour them. Their protection is gone, but the LORD is with us. Do not be afraid of them"* (Numbers 14:6-9).

The rest of the story reminds us that those whose focus is on the strength of the obstacles or on their inability to defeat those obstacles may be in the majority, and such attitudes will inevitably preclude them from entering the land of promise. Those whose focus is on the strength of the Lord who is with us, these are the ones who will enter the land of promise.

God said through His prophet Isaiah: *"Do not fear, for I have redeemed you; I have summoned you by name; you are mine. When you pass through the waters, I will be with you; and when you pass through the rivers, they will not sweep over you. When you walk through the fire, you will not be burned; the flames will not set you ablaze"* (Isaiah 43:1b-2). No matter what our circumstances are, our Father in heaven wants us to know we are not alone, for He is with us.

God reinforced this lesson to me as a pastor in time of conflict. I knew I lacked the wherewithal to accomplish the changes He intended for our congregation. I needed Him more than the air I breathed. The good news is I had people around me who shared this conviction. One of my pastoral joys has been the privilege of seeking His face with godly leadership teams, together laying at His feet the burdens and needs of our community and church, and believing God for the victory.

God taught me to lean on Him in these ways: First, He called me to a personal lifestyle of prayer, taking blocks of time away from busyness to listen and pray. Second, He called our church elders to seek His face together. We prayed at each of our meetings and scheduled meetings where this was our sole agenda. In time we established a prayer room that was continually open for prayer, and gathered there ourselves early on Sunday mornings and invited others to come. Third, He called area clergy together to pray for each other and our community. In time we scheduled joint prayer and worship events to seek His face together. In these ways we expressed faith that our God is with us and by His power we are victorious.

As we prayed God revealed the importance of humility and repentance. Whenever we fall short of His glory and we sin in thought, word, or deed, God convicts us and calls us to acknowledge it and repent. Doing so allows Him to show mercy and restore us. Exemplifying such praying Daniel *turned to the LORD God and pleaded with him in prayer and petition, in fasting, and in sackcloth and ashes* (Daniel 9:3).

Daniel's prayer focused on confession and repentance for his own sin and the corporate sins of the people, after which he prayed for mercy and pardon. He was in foreign exile facing extraordinary obstacles and the people were in disarray, facing the consequences of their sins and those of generations preceding them. But Daniel knew God was with them and He could deliver them, so in humility he prayed.

> *In every generation God's people have faced obstacles, and we will not be exceptions.*

From prison Paul wrote to Timothy, expressing confidence in God. *But the Lord stood at my side and gave me strength, so that through me the message might be fully proclaimed and all the Gentiles might hear it. And I was delivered from the lion's mouth. The Lord will rescue me from every evil attack and will bring me safely to his heavenly kingdom. To him be glory for ever and ever. Amen* (2 Timothy 4:17-18).

In every generation God's people have faced obstacles, and we will not be exceptions. The question we face is, where is our faith? If we are self-reliant we have reason to fear. If we are God-reliant we will humble ourselves and pray and know that He will accomplish great things for us to the glory of His name.

Life Application Questions:

1. Has there been a time when you felt like a grasshopper in your own eyes? If so, what did you learn?

2. How has God's promise to be with you in the waters and in the fire applied in your circumstances?

3. What response is the Holy Spirit asking of you now?

77

There Are Reasons for the Chaos in the Land

The sins of some are obvious, reaching the place of judgment ahead of them; the sins of others trail behind them (1 Timothy 5:24)

Sin always brings consequences. Sometimes consequences are immediate and sometimes delayed, but there are always consequences to sin. This is true individually and corporately. God says all individuals are culpable for their own sins. *Parents are not be put to death for their children, nor children put to death for their parents; each will die for their own sin* (Deuteronomy 24:16). Consequences of a person's sins may also ravage their children and later generations, as every marriage and family counselor can attest; *"for I, the LORD your God, am a jealous God, punishing the children for the sin of the parents to the third and fourth generation of those who hate me"* (Exodus 20:5).

King David's sin with Bathsheba demonstrates this, as the impact of his sin was seen in his children. The consequences of sin can have far-reaching effects on family and community. This is especially true when leaders sin. It can be debated whether a leader's sins are a reflection of the people's sins, or if the people's sins are a reflection of the leader's sins. Both may be true. There are many biblical examples of sinful leaders painfully affecting the people they were entrusted to lead.

Many accounts of leaders and their sins are recorded in 1 and 2 Kings and 1 and 2 Chronicles. King Jotham tried to bring reforms. *He did what was right in the sight of the LORD* (2 Chronicles 27:2), but despite his best efforts the corporate sin of Israel was unaffected. When Jotham's son Ahaz came into power as the next ruler, Ahaz's sinfulness allowed an increase in Israel's sin. While the corporate sins of a group can often be seen in its leaders, leaders need only to lower their moral standards for the sins of the people to increase.

Leaders of groups, cities, and nations do represent the whole. Leviticus 4:15 instructs elders to represent the people in an offering for their corporate sins. Another example of representative leadership is seen in the ruler of Nineveh in the days of Jonah. The king saw the pending judgment of God upon his city's sin and he personally repented; then he instituted national decrees of repentance (Jonah 3:7). The king understood that the sins of the people were not separate from his own sins, so repentance must begin with himself and then in his people.

I knew my predecessors had sinned and the church was still dealing with the consequences. I prayed for God's mercy on me personally and upon our congregation. I asked the Holy Spirit to bring us to repentance for our corporate sins in what occurred. The elders of the church prayed with me toward this end, and on behalf of the congregation they owned the church's responsibility for sins previously committed. This led to a season of repentance followed by steps toward extending forgiveness and reconciliation with a former pastor, setting us free to move forward.

God then caused me to wonder if there might be other sins in the church or community for which we still experienced consequences. There were a number of troubling indicators. A very small percentage of the area population attended worship services of any kind. There was real suspicion among non-churched people toward the church. The predominant view among local clergy was truth is relative and suggestions that faith in Christ is the only way to heaven were seen as bigoted.

The degree of resistance toward the gospel in that area was so strong I wondered if there might be sin in the community's history that contributed to the development of this malaise. If this was true God might want us to acknowledge and repent of such sins, perhaps to set us free from lingering consequences. Determined to find the answer to this question I visited the local historical society to see what records I could find on the history of the church in our town.

I learned that the first matter voted on by the town founders was to set aside funds to call a minister and build a church "to propagate the gospel of the Lord Jesus Christ." I then read about the sins of two early ministers. In the days of the Revolutionary War, while locals joined the militia to fight for independence, the local minister left his flock to fight with British Loyalists, causing the congregation to feel betrayed. Another early minister was chased out of town for beating his wife. My heart ached when I realized that so early in our community's history the sins of the clergy marred the witness of the church, causing people to regard the gospel with suspicion. I then learned that the first church in town that was established to "propagate the gospel of the Lord Jesus Christ" morphed into the Unitarian Church, which teaches that truth is relative and all religions are equal. The consequences of early sins remained in our community.

I then discovered the effect of false teaching propagated among three gospel-preaching churches in the town. William Miller, a Baptist lay preacher and Bible student, had gained a regional and then a national following with a message announcing the imminent return and then an actual date of the second coming of Jesus Christ. Disregarding Jesus' teaching in Matthew 24:36-44 that no one could know when the Lord will return so we must always be ready, and using a convoluted hermeneutic, Miller announced a specific time frame within which Jesus would return. Prophetic charts were promulgated showing 1843 was the year. Miller defined the date as sometime between March 21, 1843, and March 21, 1844. Then a specific date was targeted: April 18, 1844. When these prophecies did not happen, a disciple of William Miller by the name of Samuel Snow announced the actual date would be October 22, 1844. Many people, especially in the northeastern U.S., believed and proclaimed these various dates as truth.

In Peterborough the Baptist, Methodist, and Congregational churches all joined for a combined New Year's Eve "Watch Night Service" to start in 1843. The theme of the service was the imminent return of Christ and the preacher declared this was the year of His coming. Signs of spiritual fervor were evident in the three churches, and members of these churches proclaimed this message to friends and family throughout the region. Years later the editor of the local newspaper wrote an article reminiscing about his childhood experience on the expected date of Christ's return. He described sitting on his father's lap with family and friends gathered around, listening to the tick-tock of his father's timepiece, all expecting at any moment Jesus would part the heavens and take them home to heaven.

When it became apparent the message proclaimed by these churches was wrong, their credibility was gone. Though ministers and members of these churches believed and proclaimed the gospel of Jesus and the authority of Scripture, the lingering consequence of accepting and proclaiming a false message was that nonbelievers could not trust their message. Ripple effects of that sin also remained.

I then learned that the following year Mormon messengers came to town proclaiming their false teaching. I read of an evening meeting in Peterborough that took place in late June 1844. The speaker was Brigham Young and the venue was the largest hall in town. The crowd was so large people could not squeeze in, so windows were left open and people gathered around windows to hear what was being said.

At one point during the meeting a messenger ran into the hall and announced a newsflash that Joseph Smith, the founder of Mormonism, who was a candidate for president of the United States that year, had been assassinated. This caused a great deal of commotion in the meeting. Upon hearing this news Brigham Young's first words were, "I wonder if he took the keys to the kingdom with him." After a pause he pounded the table and proclaimed, "No! The keys of the kingdom are still here!" Soon thereafter it was reported that Brigham Young packed up his entourage to begin a trek toward his ultimate destination in Utah. The report I read said when he left he took with him a local girl as his fourteenth wife.

Sin brings consequences, whether immediately or eventually, for short duration or long.

Though I was amazed at the gullibility of the people and their inability to discern truth from false teaching, reasons became clearer considering the hoopla and loss of esteem that happened toward local churches for proclaiming a false message the previous year. I sensed that here too the ripple effects still lingered in prevailing suspicion toward Christians and churches who proclaim the gospel, and in the predominant opinion within local faith communities that truth is relative.

The point I learned when walking with God through times of spiritual battle is that wherever there is spiritual chaos there are inevitably reasons for the chaos. Sin brings consequences, whether immediately or eventually, for short duration or long. Because we are engaged in spiritual warfare the reasons may not always be obvious to us at first glance, so we must pray for God to show us what is going on so we can know how to pray and how to proceed. Daniel 10 offers an example of this. It was a time of great confusion and malaise. Daniel prayed for understanding so he would know what to do. In time God sent His messenger to allow Daniel to see what was taking place in the spiritual realm. The angel said, *"Do not be afraid, Daniel. Since the first day that you set your mind to gain understanding and to humble yourself before your God, your words were heard, and I have come in response to them"* (Daniel 10:12).

As spiritual leaders our first responsibility is to pray, then as God reveals reasons for the chaos around us we must humble ourselves and pray more. When there is chaos in the land inevitably there are reasons. If we do not know what the reasons are it is wise to ask God to open our eyes to see whatever we must see. If we discover the church or previous leaders sinned, we may need to confess the corporate sins and repent to God and to whomever was wronged, taking whatever steps the Lord shows us to allow healing. In all of this we must be united with brothers and sisters in Christ, trusting together that God is merciful, He forgives, and He restores.

Life Application Questions:

1. In what ways have you observed that sin brings consequences, whether immediately or over time?

2. When is repentance required, and what can be the consequences when it is lacking and the effect when it is real?

3. What response is the Holy Spirit asking of you now?

78

Hidden Sin Will Be Disclosed

For there is nothing hidden that will not be disclosed, and nothing concealed that will not be known or brought out into the open (Luke 8:17)

When teaching about giving and about prayer and fasting Jesus taught us to do them quietly without drawing attention to ourselves. He concluded each point with *Then your Father, who sees what is done in secret, will reward you* (Matthew 6:4, 6, 18). When we honor God in secret He sees what we have done and rewards us. God also sees the sin we commit in secret (Luke 8:17).

I thought we were making good progress in the church. Substantial healing had occurred and our focus was shifting outward toward our mission. The elders were spending more time in prayer and there appeared to be increased unity, but we were still dealing with trust issues. I could not readily identify what the remaining obstacles were so I prayed, "Lord, please reveal what is hidden so we might glorify you."

Joel prophesied what Peter declared as fulfilled on Pentecost: *I will pour out my Spirit on all people. Your sons and daughters will prophesy, your old men will dream dreams, your young men will see visions. Even on my servants, both men and women, I will pour out my Spirit in those days* (Joel 2:28-29; Acts 2:17-18).

God gave me a dream in which I knew He was showing me what He was about to do. I saw lights from heaven penetrating the darkness revealing hidden things. When I awoke I went to my knees, asking God to show me what this meant. I discerned the Holy Spirit was showing me that He would soon bring to light hidden sin affecting our church family. He wanted me to know this beforehand so when it happened I would not be afraid, but would know God was bringing it to light.

A few days later it happened. An allegation was brought to me about a church leader. The accuser was visibly distraught. I approached the accused who denied wrongdoing. Because it was one person's word against another and since I knew and trusted him as a brother and friend, he urged me to discount the accuser as a liar. I replied, "I do not yet know what the truth is, but God does and He will show us, so if you are telling me the truth you have nothing to worry about."

He said, "I told you what the truth is!"

I said, "Then be at peace, for God has assured me the truth will come out." I discerned that this was not the answer he wanted.

Taking with me two elders with gifts of discernment I visited the accuser again, so they too could hear what I had heard. Comparing notes with these elders afterward we all sensed the accuser was being truthful. Realizing it was one person's word against another, we reminded each other of God's guidance in 1 Timothy 5:19: *Do not entertain an accusation against an elder unless it is brought by two or three witnesses.* We would continue praying.

Over the next few days I spoke with various people to see if anyone observed anything to corroborate the story told by the accuser. Though I heard some troubling observations no one offered specific information regarding the allegation. After a week of investigating we still had one person's word against another's but still the assurance that God knew the truth. Referencing 1 Timothy 5:19 we informed both the accused and accuser of where we stood.

When the elders met to confidentially consider this matter we considered an offer from the accused leader to resign and go away quietly. What disturbed us the most was a disturbing threat that if we should ever make anything public "there will be hell to pay." We were very disturbed by this warning, but as we had only one accuser and could not prove the allegation we agreed to accept the resignation offer. On Sunday we would announce the resignation of this leader for personal reasons.

On Saturday evening as I prayerfully prepared for Sunday I found myself greatly troubled by the decision the elders had made. Our practice was in every decision as a leadership team we must pursue complete unity, based on the premise that the Holy Spirit is a Spirit of unity. We were also agreed that if ever we were not united, if possible we would delay our decision in order to devote more time to prayer for God to bring us to one mind concerning His will. As I was now troubled by what we were planning to do the next day I called one of our elders to inquire whether they remained at peace with the decision we had made. When I did so I learned that this elder too was troubled. We therefore agreed to change course. We called the other elders and our accused brother to inform them we would be announcing a continued leave of absence, as we remained in prayer for God's leading.

On Monday morning light penetrated the darkness when someone else came forward with a confession and allegation involving the same accused leader. Along with this member two elders approached the accused leader, who tearfully confessed. Later I recalled that well before the sins of this leader became known my son Carl rightly discerned that this leader was not all he professed to be. God says that hidden sin will be disclosed.

Though all of this happened many years ago I still grieve to write about it. I throw stones at no one, for we are all sinners fallen short of God's glory and in need of His grace and mercy. I am reminded of the holiness of God and how seriously He regards our sin. He takes it so seriously it required Jesus to suffer and die in judgment for us. He offers forgiveness and mercy to all who will believe and repent.

As we walk with God through life and ministry He invites us to righteousness and holiness. If ever we pretend righteousness on the outside while on the inside we hide sin and live in rebellion, we cannot know the joy and intimacy with God that only comes through obedience. Nothing is ever hidden from God. He is not impressed by outward appearance. He longs for people who love Him and want to be real and fully yielded to Him.

Life Application Questions:

1. How have you learned that hidden sin will be brought into the light?

2. How are these connected: prayer, rejecting sin, and being real with God?

3. What response is the Holy Spirit asking of you now?

79

When Battles Rage, Satan Tempts Us to Run

The hired hand is not the shepherd and does not own the sheep. So when he sees the wolf coming, he abandons the sheep and runs away. Then the wolf attacks the flock and scatters it. The man runs away because he is a hired hand and cares nothing for the sheep (John 10:12-13)

Have you ever been in such a hard battle you would have given anything to be transported elsewhere? Warfare by its nature is dangerous, destructive, and hard. When fighting is intense, warriors become exhausted and long to get away from it all. The same happens in spiritual warfare. Satan tempts God's warriors to leave their post, run away, and stop fighting.

I have had many conversations with battle-scarred troopers who were so overloaded with stress all they could think about was getting out. Though I have not been in such a place in military warfare, I have been there in spiritual warfare. I was tempted to run away and abandon my post, and I almost did. For me it happened during a time of intense conflict in the church when powers of darkness were unleashing a full assault. It came about after church elders confronted sin in a church leader. After showing some initial humility and brokenness, the person we confronted vehemently lashed out. He went house to house to convince people of his innocence and to accuse me and all the church elders of lying and deceit.

In part because seeds of mistrust lingered because of earlier sins by church leaders, a number of people accepted the deception told by this man who was now under church discipline, including the allegation that I and all the church elders were lying and in collusion. It was horrible. It felt to me like shrapnel was tearing holes in my soul and in our church family. I was angry, heartbroken, and depressed. I pressed on because I had to, but I was despondent. I asked God to strengthen me and enable our elders to reflect His character in the way we led. I was wounded but determined to press on.

Then an arrow pierced me on a day when I was exhausted in every way. I had tried hard to protect my family from attacks coming my way and I thought I had been successful, but that day I learned otherwise. We had a Christian school at the church then and our daughter Amy attended the school. When she came home from school that day she was very distraught. The reason for her distress was some of her friends said, "Your father is a liar!" She did her best to defend me to them but she felt she had lost the battle.

> "What I hear you saying is you are prepared to say to Satan, 'You win!'"

As I heard my daughter's story I attempted to comfort and calm her, but inside I was distraught and defeated. It was one thing for people to attack me, but to see this effect on my child was too much to handle. Rage and self-pity whirled in my soul, bringing me to a resolve that for my sake and the sake of my family I would quit. The enemy wanted me out of this battle and I would yield. With my decision made I announced it to Helen.

She immediately discerned what was happening and responded with the exact words I needed to hear. She said, "What I hear you saying is you are prepared to say to Satan, 'You win!'" Her words were like a slap across my face.

"NO!" I replied. "Satan does not win! Christ wins!" At this we picked up our offensive weapon, the *sword of the Spirit, which is the word of God* (Ephesians 6:17), and we began to pray. By grace God strengthened me again, reminding me that we must remain fervent in prayer, wearing the full armor of God described in Ephesians 6. The temptation to quit vanished and I was resolved to press on. As God had not abandoned me and as He called me to shepherd His flock, I would not abandon them now.

Although I and the elders did our best to guard the flock entrusted to our care, we were unable to prevent a number of people from leaving the church. We knew we were incapable of bringing healing to this situation, and that we were engaged in a spiritual battle. We also knew that walking with the Lord together through this time of spiritual warfare meant we must fervently pray, humbly repent, and join forces in biblical unity. We asked God to intervene, believing Him for the answer He gave to Daniel (Daniel 10:12): *"Do not be afraid, Daniel. Since the first day that you set your mind to gain understanding and to humble yourself before your God, your words were heard and I have come in response to them."*

On this side of heaven followers of Jesus Christ will often engage in spiritual battles, and our enemy the Devil may well attack us in our most vulnerable moments, tempting us to abandon the fight. In such times we face a clear choice: to take what seems to be the easier way or to lean in faith upon the strong arms of Jesus, using the weapons and armor He offers, being fervent in intercession, and united with other warriors who press on with us for the glory of His name.

Life Application Questions:

1. If you have ever been in a battle and been tempted to quit, what did you learn?

2. Read Ephesians 6:10-18 which describes the armor of God available to you. How have these resources helped in your spiritual battles?

3. What response is the Holy Spirit asking of you now?

80

No Circumstance Is Too Difficult for God

I prayed to the LORD: "Ah, Sovereign LORD, you have made the heavens and the earth by your great power and outstretched arm. Nothing is too hard for you" (Jeremiah 32:16b-17)

When we find ourselves in seemingly impossible circumstances, what do we do? Jeremiah shows us. Jerusalem was under siege by Babylon. The people were terrified, sensing soon the siege would lead to death or captivity. The situation felt impossible. While others panicked Jeremiah turned to God. The prayer he prayed is a moving expression of unconquerable faith. Looking past the hard circumstances and praying with confidence in almighty God he said, *"Ah, Sovereign LORD, you have made the heavens and the earth by your great power and outstretched arm. Nothing is too hard for you."* This sort of prayer God answers, for it is the conclusion He wants us to live by. In mercy God answered, reaffirming what Jeremiah already knew: *"I am the LORD, the God of all mankind. Is anything too hard for me?"* (Jeremiah 32:27)

Having walked with God through many years of life and ministry my life experience bears witness to this truth, that God reveals Himself to us when we call upon Him in our seemingly impossible situations. Jeremiah's testimony glorifies God for this truth: *They tried to end my life in a pit and threw stones at me; the waters closed over my head and I thought I was about to perish. I called on your name, LORD, from the depths of the pit. You heard my plea: "Do not close your ears to my cry for relief." You came near when I called you, and you said, "Do not fear." You, Lord, took up my case; you redeemed my life* (Lamentations 3:53-58).

When I was tempted to quit God strengthened me with hope and resolve to press on. My difficulty did not end overnight though. Other things happened that were painful to deal with, including facing a lawsuit against the church and against me and our church elders. Though it was frivolous we still had to deal with it, along with rumors and innuendos. Though confident in the outcome I was nervous over the potential of Satan to disparage the message of Christ in our community.

> *God intervenes when we are helpless to effect change, and when He does we must give Him glory.*

What do we do when a situation seems unfair or impossible, or when we are up to our necks in mud? We do what Jeremiah did and call upon the Lord. We declare: *Nothing is too hard for you.* This is what I and our elders did and God answered our cries. He used a wonderful Christian attorney who prayed with us and argued for dismissal on First Amendment grounds that the court has no jurisdiction over matters of church discipline. The judge agreed and the case was dismissed.

God intervenes when we are helpless to effect change, and when He does we must give Him glory. He wants us to learn that He can make a way when there seems to be no way, that we can trust Him in every circumstance (Philippians 4:11-12).

Life Application Questions:

1. Have you ever been in a "mud pit" with no conceivable way of getting out, but you called to God and He delivered you?

2. When God intervenes to deliver us from a seemingly impossible situation, what conclusions are we left with?

3. What response is the Holy Spirit asking of you now?

81

Pray with Availability for Divine Appointments

For we are God's handiwork, created in Christ Jesus to do good works, which God prepared in advance for us to do (Ephesians 2:10)

God has prepared good works for us to do. We must be prayerfully available to recognize and respond to every divine appointment. Great examples are revealed in Scripture of God's people showing up at the right time and place to accomplish what He prepared for them to do. To spiritually untrained eyes such things can appear to be coincidences, but they are divine appointments. Biblical examples include Abraham's servant and Rebekah meeting at the well (Genesis 24), Abigail's kindness to David (1 Samuel 25), Elisha's meeting the woman from Shunem (2 Kings 4), and Philip's encounter with the Ethiopian eunuch (Acts 8).

This principle has been confirmed to me many times through the years and I have often marveled at the divine appointments He has brought me to. There are many examples I could tell but I will describe a memorable few that occurred on Monday and Tuesday of President's Day weekend in February 2003, when God reminded me again to pray with availability and to respond to every opportunity.

The previous week Helen flew to North Carolina to visit her parents. While there her father gave her his Toyota Camry which she intended to drive home to New Hampshire by herself. Because it was winter and a long way to drive alone I asked her to remain a few more days, promising to make my way to North Carolina to drive home with her. I determined to travel by Amtrak rather than air, so I booked a ticket to depart Monday, February 17. I would arrive in North Carolina on Tuesday, have a quick visit with Helen's parents, then drive home with Helen and arrive on Wednesday; or that was my plan.

Sunday it began snowing but I had no idea the size of the coming storm. My friend Kurt agreed to pick me up at 4:00 a.m. Monday morning to drive me to Springfield, Massachusetts, where I would catch an Amtrak train to New York City. From there I would board a train to Washington, D.C., and then on to Raleigh, North Carolina. Awaking early Monday morning I prayed as is my daily custom. That day I prayed, "Lord, this stormy weather reminds me of how small I am and how powerful you are, but this snow is no surprise to you. As I begin my journey I do not know if or when I will reach Helen, but this I do know: You are God, you are on your throne, and you have a plan. I am your servant. Allow me to recognize and respond to every divine appointment you have for me along the way. In Jesus' name I pray this."

My first appointment was with Kurt who arrived on schedule. We enjoyed great fellowship on our journey to Springfield, and were both blessed as we rejoiced in the Lord. Snow was falling hard but visibility was not too bad, and the plows were keeping up with the snow. Arriving at our destination Kurt and I prayed, then he left to return to Peterborough and I boarded the train for Penn Station in New York.

The train was full of passengers and nearly every seat was full. My next divine appointment was the man who sat next to me. He was from Jaffrey, New Hampshire, the town just south of Peterborough, and we discovered we had a number of mutual friends. He loved the Lord and we had a good time of encouraging each other. I was able to offer biblical counsel concerning some personal matters in his life. When our train stopped we agreed God had put us together.

Penn Station was crowded that day. Looking up I saw why. All southbound trains were cancelled. The only destinations remaining on the board were northbound. People all around were discussing the forecast that this would be a huge blizzard, which meant trains to the south would not resume for several days. Hearing this I was not distraught but was at peace knowing God was on His throne and this was no surprise to Him. Not wanting to be stuck in Penn Station for the foreseeable future, I went to the back of a long line at the ticket window. When at last I reached the counter I bought a seat on the next train toward Springfield, Massachusetts, which would first stop in

Hartford, Connecticut. I then boarded the train where I met my next divine appointment.

The young man sitting beside me was a student at the University of Connecticut. I learned his girlfriend had recently committed her life to Jesus Christ and was now a changed person (2 Corinthians 5:17). She had shared her newfound faith with him but he did not know what to make of it. He had many questions and I fielded them one by one, opening my Bible and showing him who Jesus is, the things He did, and how to be forgiven and enter into relationship with Him. My seat mate seemed to hang onto every word as though hearing most of it for the first time. I told him God loved him and placed me next to him to address his questions. Nearing the Hartford train station which was his destination, he was not yet ready to yield his life to Jesus but he was on his way, and promised to consider further the claims of Jesus, to read the Bible, and attend church with his girlfriend. He thanked me profusely, grabbed his bag, and headed toward the exit.

Others were also grabbing bags and filling the aisle as the train approached the Hartford station. Everyone was talking about the snowstorm. Someone across the aisle asked me where I was headed and I said my destination was Peterborough, New Hampshire, but I was taking the train as far as Springfield, Massachusetts. He asked, "How will you get from Springfield to Peterborough?"

I replied, "I don't know. I am hoping there will be a motel I can walk to near the Springfield station. Tomorrow I will look for a way home."

The man standing in the aisle next to me then said, "I'm getting off the train here in Hartford. My car is parked in the lot and I will be driving to my home in Massachusetts, which is a lot closer to Peterborough than Springfield. You are welcome to come with me." I did not know what to do. The train was stopping and in one minute he would be getting off. I was not sure if he was a dangerous man and I would be foolish to go with him, or if this was another divine appointment.

I offered a prayer for immediate discernment. "Are you traveling alone?" I asked.

He replied, "No, this is my fiancée." A young woman with a cheery face stood behind him. She looked friendly enough. As I had to make an immediate decision, and recalling my prayer earlier that morning, I trusted God to go with me, grabbed my bag, and exited the train. Was this a divine appointment?

Just two minutes after meeting this couple I was traipsing with them through knee-high snow toward a parking lot where he found his car plowed in and buried. For several minutes we worked to clear a way to get his car out of the lot. With our arms we brushed off the snow and with feet and hands we pulled enough away from doors and tires so we could get in, start it up, and attempt to push it from its parking spot. While all this was going on the man was spilling out enough profanities to make most sailors blush. He cursed everything he could think of, including the weather forecasters, the snowplow operators, his car, his tires, the falling snow, and God himself! He kept up a steady stream of it the entire time we worked to free his car, until at last the car was freed from the parking lot, and we were laying new tracks on the ramp to the highway.

Pulling onto the interstate we saw few headlights. Occasionally we saw a plow but for the most part we were alone on the highway, driving through several inches of unplowed snow. From my front seat beside the driver I initiated conversation to get acquainted with the people with whom I was experiencing this blizzard.

"What took you to New York City?" I asked. "Was it business or pleasure?"

He said, "We attended a wedding yesterday."

I replied, "That's great! I don't hear about many Sunday weddings."

He said, "We're Jews."

To this I said, "Great! That explains it!"

To this he asked, "What do you do?"

I said, "I am a pastor."

I wish I could repeat for you the reply he emitted. It was not a word, but was a loud and palpable sigh, almost a sigh of despair! For the next few moments it was quiet in the car, the most noticeable sound being the swoosh-swoosh of windshield wipers. He then blurted out emphatically, "I am an atheist!" to which I replied, "Okay. I am a Christian." He was clearly troubled by my presence, and I began to wonder if he

PART X ~ WALKING WITH GOD IN SPIRITUAL BATTLE

would pull over to the side of the road and make me get out of his car. As I prayed I remembered Ephesians 5:16 and sensed the Holy Spirit was saying, "This is a divine appointment I have prepared for you; seize the opportunity."

For the next three hours as we journeyed slowly and carefully through the blizzard our conversation focused on spiritual matters. The woman initiated the dialogue and the man joined in. They asked question after question about Christianity and matters of theology, deep questions I sensed they had been contemplating for many years. Praying in the Spirit along the way I shared God's truth. Each answer prompted more questions and answers until at last we arrived at their home. I marveled. For an avowed atheist this man had an extraordinary interest in spiritual things.

> *This is a divine appointment I have prepared for you; seize the opportunity.*

By now it was well past dark and two feet of snow was piled up in their driveway with snow still falling hard. Because of the snow emergency, if he left his car in the street he feared it would be towed away, so he backed it up, then floored the accelerator, ramming the car up the driveway until it became firmly wedged in snow. He then said, "I guess you'll be staying with us tonight," whereupon we piled out of the car and crawled over snow banks until we reached and entered their home. Electrical power was out, but they had heat through a wood pellet stove, portable lanterns for light, and a gas-powered stove for cooking. Before long we were warm and preparations for dinner had begun in the kitchen.

Over dinner our conversation returned to spiritual matters. I opened my Bible and answered their questions with Scripture. The focus of our conversation was Jesus. I read Old Testament prophesies anticipating the coming Messiah. I then turned to New Testament passages and showed how Jesus fulfilled every one. They had not heard any of this before, and it was having an effect. We talked until past 1:00 a.m. when we turned in for the night, promising to talk more in the morning.

When I awoke Tuesday morning I looked outside and saw it had stopped snowing. About three feet of snow had fallen and now the sun was shining. After breakfast I asked for a shovel and spent the next couple of hours helping them shovel steps and a path to their car and the road. I called my friend Kurt in Peterborough who agreed to come that afternoon to pick me up. While waiting for his arrival and the arrival of a snowplow we resumed our conversation of the previous evening about spiritual matters.

Though not yet ready to surrender to Jesus, this couple was now considering the claims of Christ. Because questions remained I wanted to put into their hands a book that dives into the questions they were asking about Jesus. I wished to give them *The Case for Christ* by Lee Strobel, which describes Lee's story of being prompted by his wife's conversion to investigate Jesus, asking hard questions, and seeing where the facts would lead. This ultimately brought him to an unexpected conclusion, that Jesus is the Savior of the world and the Son of God.

> *The purpose of each divine appointment is determined by God not us.*

I asked my new friends if they would read such a book were I to send it to them, and they agreed that they would. As we parted I prayed for them, expressing my profound gratitude for their kindness and hospitality, and thanking God for blessing us with this divine appointment. When Kurt picked me up, as we journeyed toward Peterborough I celebrated with him the various divine appointments God had provided since we parted the previous day.

My intention now was to book a one-way flight to North Carolina to join Helen for her drive home. First I hoped to find *The Case for Christ* so I could put a copy in the mail before I left. After booking a flight to depart the next day, I wondered where I could find this book in a hurry. After cleaning up snow at my house I stopped at my church office where a box of books leaned against my office door. Opening it I rejoiced to see *The Case for Christ*. I grabbed it, wrote a personal note inside the cover, then wrapped and mailed it. The people I saw along the way that day I would not see again this side of eternity. I prayed for each one, knowing God brought them across my path for His purposes. I asked God to lead others to them who will also respond to divine appointments.

As you and I walk with God through life and ministry we may be blessed in divine appointments to witness someone's conversion as Philip did with the Ethiopian eunuch (Acts 8), and as I have experienced on a number of occasions, including once on an airplane at 35,000 feet up. In other divine appointments God brings us along to help someone on their journey toward Him, or to bring encouragement, or express love or comfort, or to bring aid. The purpose of each divine appointment is determined by God not us. Our part is to offer availability and obedience.

Life Application Questions:

1. Can you recount examples of when you recognized and responded to divine appointments or have been the recipient of one that ministered to you?

2. Why is it helpful to pray with availability for divine appointments?

3. What response is the Holy Spirit asking of you now?

8 2

Live with Heaven in Mind

"Enter through the narrow gate. For wide is the gate and broad is the road that leads to destruction, and many enter through it. But small is the gate and narrow the road that leads to life, and only a few find it" (Matthew 7:13-14)

Jesus had much to say about everlasting life and heaven, which He promised to all who come to the Father through Him (John 3:16). He told His disciples He was returning to heaven where He would prepare a place for us, and one day He will come again and take us to be with Him forever (John 14:1-6). Jesus wants us to live with an eternal perspective. He wants our values to be rooted in heaven because we believe what He taught us; that earthly things will perish but heavenly things will endure forever (Matthew 6:19-20).

There have been times when I have lived as though eternity were not real, losing sight for a while of God's priorities, and caring little about the eternal destiny of people. I have at times ignored God's truth that everyone is an eternal soul who will either be forever with Him in heaven or forever apart from Him in judgment.

God taught me this through a life-changing dream more vivid to me than any I have had before or since. It was a taste of heaven. Since then hardly a day has gone by that I have not longed to be there. God's Word says at times He speaks through visions and dreams (Joel 2:28-29; Acts 2:17-18). When God spoke to Solomon in a dream (1 Kings 3:5) it changed his life. Joseph, the earthly father of Jesus, also heard from the Lord through dreams several times (Matthew 1:20; 2:13, 19, 22), and each time he knew with certainty God had spoken.

The apostle Paul mentioned a life-changing picture of heaven he experienced, some of which was so astounding that words could not express the glory of it. Paul was not boasting, but was letting his readers know that fourteen years earlier he tasted heaven. After so many years the experience still affected him deeply. *I know a man in Christ who fourteen years ago was caught up to the third heaven. Whether it was in the body or out of the body I do not know – God knows. And I know that this man – whether in the body or apart from the body I do not know, but God knows – was caught up to paradise* (2 Corinthians 12:2-4a).

I identify with some of what Paul described as I cannot find words to describe all I experienced in my dream of heaven. After many years I am still profoundly affected by it so I will attempt to describe some of what I saw. As the written Word of God is our only infallible source of divine revelation for faith and practice I urge you to do as I have done, prayerfully examine my story or anyone else's story of heaven in light of God's Word, retaining only what is consistent with Scripture.

Suddenly I was surrounded by a large number of people from every culture and nation, people of all ages. I knew these were people who had just entered eternity. More and more people appeared, as all around the world people were dying. I presumed I had just died, but then I heard the Spirit say, "You have not yet died. I am showing you what is taking place." I was astounded at the number of people dying at that moment. I have since read that throughout the world more than 150,000 people die and enter eternity every day. Of course the percentage of people who will one day die is 100 percent; there will be no exceptions. Because of sin all will die (Romans 6:23; Hebrews 9:27).

In my dream all who died were on a sort of moving sidewalk that we could not get off, as our eternal destiny was now firmly determined. I saw the moving sidewalk split into opposite directions (see Daniel 12:2; Matthew 7:13-14). The path moving left was wide and most were on that path toward destruction and judgment. The path to the right was the path of life. It was narrow and fewer were on it, and by God's grace I was among them. This came to a narrow gate, the gate to heaven. No one could be carried in by anyone else. Each person who entered came as a child of God through faith in Jesus (see Zechariah 13:1; 1 Peter 1:18-19). Entering the gate I immediately saw the Lamb who was slain

(John 1:36; Revelation 5:6) and the blood of the Lamb. The only way in was through the blood of the Lamb.

I did not want to go any farther! All I desired was to stay there and worship the Lamb, but there was more to see. Indescribable beauty was shown me that caused my heart to overflow with wonder, but all the while the one thing I longed to do was to worship Him who alone is worthy.

I was then taken outside the gate of heaven where I saw people attempting to enter through other means. Some were trying to enter through religion, but all such attempts were futile. Others tried by good works, but that did not work. Some were trying by affiliation with people in heaven, but God's reply to them was: *'Depart from me, you who are cursed'* (Matthew 25:41). I was again reminded that the only way to enter is through the blood of Jesus, the Lamb of God (John 1:29; 14:6).

As my tour was ending I yearned to enter heaven again to worship my Lord. Returning to the gate I asked for re-entry. "Please may I enter to worship my Lord?" I was allowed entrance. Running toward the throne I became vividly aware of His holiness! God is infinite in majesty, splendor, righteousness, and purity. In His presence I saw my sinful condition and felt my unworthiness. My righteousness felt like filthy rags (Isaiah 64:6).

Unable to stand in His presence I fell prostrate before Him. I could not move. I was precisely where I wanted to be and yet I felt unworthy because of my sin. Beside me was a fountain of living water springing up to eternal life (John 4:10-11; 7:38; Revelation 7:17). The sound of it was so compelling I had an insatiable thirst to drink it, for I instinctively knew it would satisfy. But I felt unworthy to drink of it, so there I lay wanting to be in His presence, yet conscious of my sin and feeling unworthy to be there. So I cried, "I am unworthy, unworthy!"

The Bible says that in heaven God wipes away the tears from our eyes (Revelation 21:4). I heard my Lord's footsteps as He approached and I saw His nail-scarred feet. He stooped down, took me by the hand, and lifted me up (see Ezekiel 43:3-5). He then took a cup and filled it with water from the fountain, placed it in my hands, and said with glorious love, "Drink, for I have made you worthy!" With adoration, joy, and peace I drank deeply and then found myself back in my bed, awestruck and savoring His presence. My body trembled for the next several hours (see Psalm 96:9; 114:7) and an overwhelming sense of His presence endured for many days.

In the years since then I have often yearned for heaven. The apostle Paul expressed his yearning too (2 Corinthians 5:2-10). As we walk along with God He makes it clear that our life with Him is forever (1 Peter 1:3-5). We are created in the image of God, which means we are spiritual beings with an immortal nature. God so longs for us to spend eternity with Him that He paid the unfathomable price of the life and blood of His Son who became for us the perfect sacrifice. God made this way for us to enter. We are thereby offered a gift of entry into heaven forever. This priceless gift is realized only by those who receive it in faith. When the time comes and our heart stops beating, we will not be able to hit the rewind button and do a single moment over. Then our eternal destiny will already be determined.

> *This priceless gift is realized only by those who receive it in faith.*

How then are we to live? Paul said this is how heavenly minded Christians respond: *Therefore we do not lose heart. Though outwardly we are wasting away, yet inwardly we are being renewed day by day. For our light and momentary troubles are achieving for us an eternal glory that far outweighs them all. So we fix our eyes not on what is seen, but on what is unseen, since what is seen is temporary, but what is unseen is eternal* (2 Corinthians 4:16-18).

Life Application Questions:

1. Considering heaven's reality, how ought we to live?

2. How is keeping heaven in mind evident in your life?

3. What response is the Holy Spirit asking of you now?

Part XI

WALKING WITH GOD IN THE FOG OF UNCERTAINTY

None of us can see around the corner, and uncertainty is bothersome. We want to know what's coming so we can feel in control and so our anxiety will decrease, but along the way God is teaching us to trust. God wants us to walk with Him in the fog of uncertainty. What follows are lessons He taught me in such circumstances.

83

Trust Is Foundational in Following Jesus

As Scripture says, "Anyone who believes in Him will never be put to shame" (Romans 10:11)

I have learned that we will only obey God insofar as we trust Him. A key question we must answer then is, do we really trust Him? I'm referring to more than trusting Him for salvation, even though that is where it begins. God invites us to trust Him in daily life, through every season of life change. He wants us to know He is wholly trustworthy. He teaches us this truth by allowing us to face circumstances that confront us with this question, "Do you trust me now?"

One such occasion occurred for me twenty-two days after the attack against America on September 11. It was Wednesday evening, October 3, 2001. Wednesday evenings at Trinity Evangelical Church featured praise and worship services in which we worshiped God and sought His face together. In these services worshipers were invited to draw near to God's throne. We were free to worship however the Holy Spirit led us, whether sitting, standing, dancing, bowing, or lying prostrate. It was done decently and in order, but there was freedom in worship. With no responsibility for leading the service that evening I was among the worshiping congregation. As we worshiped I sensed God's tangible presence, and I could not stand in His presence so found myself on the floor, prostrate before Him.

I heard God asking this question: "Steve, do you trust me?"

Having walked with God since childhood, and finding Him ever faithful my answer was, "Yes Lord, I trust you."

He would not allow an automatic answer. I heard Him again ask, "Steve Gammon, do you really trust me?"

This question weighed heavily as I realized He intended for me to reflect upon its meaning before giving my answer. I reflected on His faithfulness through the years and His immutable nature throughout history, and how He has kept every promise. Then I said, "Yes Lord, you know I trust you!"

Then I heard the voice of the Lord again. "Steve, will you trust me?" By now I was deeply troubled because I presumed this question had been already answered, but He was requiring me to wrestle with it more. Through my tears I wondered, *Why are you asking me this Lord? Don't you know I trust you?* I was hurt for having been asked three times if I trusted Him, and I remembered how Simon Peter was annoyed when the Lord asked him three times if he loved Him.

> *Our part is not to worry, but to walk with Him and to trust and obey.*

This last question was future oriented: "Will you trust me?"

I knew what my answer should be, but He was asking me what it would be. In those moments I gave my heartfelt reply: "Yes Lord, I will trust you fully. No matter what happens, no matter what crisis or challenge or change comes, I will trust in you!"

As I drove home that evening I knew something significant had just happened, but I had no idea what it was about. One hour after I arrived home I found out. At 10:15 p.m. I received an unexpected phone call which went like this: "LCDR Gammon?"

"Speaking," I replied.

"You are recalled to active duty for three hundred and sixty-five days unless released sooner or extended to a maximum of twenty-four months. You are required to report within twenty-four hours. Failure to report is a violation of the Uniform Code of Military Justice. You are now subject to the Uniform Code of Military Justice. Do you understand what I have told you?"

I was stunned! I was being recalled to active duty for one year, was required to leave my congregation and family for a year, and I had to leave tomorrow! NO! I did not understand what he just told me! As the consequences of this news unfolded in my mind I became agitated and angry. Then God whispered, "Steve, remember what I asked you, and remember your reply."

How could I have forgotten so quickly? His question had been, "Will you trust me?" My reply had been, "No matter what, I will trust you Lord." Suddenly I was at peace. My burdens were laid at His feet and I knew beyond all doubt He was with me and would take care of me and my family and congregation.

Hanging up the phone I told Helen what had just happened and about the Lord's personal challenge to me that evening to fully trust Him. Helen and I prayed for God to guide us through this transition and then I called Skip Iltis, chair of our board of elders. I informed him of what had just transpired and asked him to arrange a meeting of the elders at our home the next afternoon so we could pray over each other and discuss next steps for the church, after which I would be on my way.

We would trust the Lord. What a great way to live! Through Christ we have a personal relationship with God who is never surprised and is always faithful. Our part is not to worry, but to walk with Him and to trust and obey. God asks each of His children, "Do you trust me? Do you really trust me? Will you trust me?" What is your answer?

Life Application Questions:

1. How have you answered the Lord's questions about trust?

2. What will trusting Jesus look like in your current circumstances and as you look to the future?

3. What response is the Holy Spirit asking of you now?

8 4

Make the Most of Every Opportunity to Serve Him

Be very careful, then, how you live – not as unwise but as wise, making the most of every opportunity, because the days are evil (Ephesians 5:15-16)

God wants us to adjust the lenses of our worldview until we can see what He sees. As we do this our difficult circumstances become divine opportunities and our challenges bring great rewards. I recall the Lord impressing this upon me when I was in high school through the example of my mother when she was hospitalized. She had fallen down the cellar stairs of our home and broken her leg and was in considerable pain. She was in the hospital for some time, which was not where she wanted to be, but she did not complain. She trusted God and looked for occasions to serve Him. The Lord laid such an opportunity in the bed next to hers.

The woman in that bed had a terminal condition, but did not yet know Jesus and was unprepared for eternity. From her hospital bed my mother was available to show God's love to that woman and to lead her into relationship with the Savior. That woman died soon thereafter and she is in heaven now and forever, in part because my mom made the most of the opportunity Jesus gave her.

This lesson was reinforced to me many times in the year I was recalled to active duty. I served in Groton, Connecticut, as chaplain for the Navy Mobilization Processing Site (NMPS), which processed hundreds of navy reservists on their way out and back from active duty service throughout the world. Each day I asked God to help me recognize and respond to divine appointments.

One morning I learned about a sailor who was hospitalized the previous night for suicidal ideation. I determined to visit him and made inquiries to learn what I could. I learned that his wife had recently filed for divorce and that he recently completed inpatient alcohol rehab treatment, but the previous night he was stopped at the gate for intoxication. I expected he knew this would now lead to the end of his military career, so it appeared he was losing both his wife and his job. Driving to the hospital I prayed fervently for the man I was about to meet. I asked God to show me how to reach him. As I prayed the Holy Spirit impressed upon me this thought: *He has a praying mom.*

It was a miracle of grace to be sure, as God was answering the prayers of a praying mother.

Arriving at the hospital I made my way to the ward where he was held, and then to his room. Upon entering I introduced myself and we sat down. He looked utterly dejected, his face resting in his hands and his gaze fixed on the floor. Offering a silent prayer for mercy, I called the young man by name and asked him to please lift his head and look at me. I then asked, "Son, do you have a praying mother?"

The floodgates broke. Nodding his head and weeping uncontrollably he said, "Yes, I do." I put my hand on his shoulder and told him God had sent me to him in answer to her prayers. He shared his story of being raised in a godly home, but as a young man he walked away from the faith. Through the years his mother continued praying for him, as he lived life his own way. We talked about the brokenness of his marriage and the pending end of his career; then we focused on the forgiveness and love of God that transcends all of that. We opened the Bible and looked at Jesus Christ who redeems broken lives and saves all who believe and repent and turn to Him in faith. Then we bowed in prayer and I listened with joy as this broken man turned to Jesus in faith and discovered forgiveness, life, and hope. It was a miracle of grace to be sure, as God was answering the prayers of a praying mother.

God orchestrated another memorable encounter in the year that followed the 9/11 attack. Actually it happened before, during, and after my deployment. It began on September 12, the day after the attack against America. I stopped by the hardware store in Peterborough and was greeted by Bob Peterson, a Christian man who worked there.

He appeared grief-stricken and he asked, "Pastor Steve, do you have a moment?"

"Of course," I replied.

He then told me his brother and sister-in-law, Donald and Jean Peterson, were among the passengers on United Airlines Flight 93 which was hijacked and crashed the previous day near Shanksville, Pennsylvania. I listened as he described the faith of his brother and sister-in-law who loved the Lord Jesus and taught God's Word, and who were undoubtedly praying throughout the hijacking until the plane went down. I prayed with Bob in the store that day and assured him I would continue praying for him and his family, as he expected to travel soon for memorial services.

Two weeks later I was recalled to active duty and I did not see Bob again until the next year. On September 11, 2002, the one-year anniversary of the attacks against America, services of remembrance were being held in New York City, at the Pentagon in Washington, D.C., and in the field near Shanksville. It was a busy day at the NMPS where I worked and I had not taken a lunch break, so early in the afternoon I took a break and drove to my quarters to make a sandwich. I would be there only fifteen to twenty minutes, but while making my sandwich I turned on my television to see what was going on with the September 11 anniversary observances.

I turned to CNN and heard that President and Mrs. Bush had just arrived in Shanksville, Pennsylvania, where a service was about to begin. I saw family members of Flight 93 passengers and crew lined up and President and Mrs. Bush were going up the line. Then I saw my friend Bob Peterson and President Bush greeting one another. I was astounded. My TV had been on for just two minutes and I was watching my friend and the president of the United States greeting one another. Surely God had shown me this for a reason.

About two weeks later when my mobilization was ended and I returned to Peterborough, I visited the hardware store to find Bob Peterson. I wanted him to know I had seen him on CNN. Bob described what it was like meeting the president, and then he told me something else that happened that day that impressed him far more. He said after United

Airlines Flight 93 crashed the FAA did a thorough investigation, as they do after every airline crash. Generally, he said, they pull together all that remains after the crash. In this case, because the plane was flown at full throttle into the ground, nothing survived intact larger than a dinner plate except one thing.

Now Bob's eyes filled with tears but his face expressed only joy. Leaning forward and speaking with whispered intensity he asked, "Can you guess the one thing that survived the crash intact?" I could not. "It was my brother's Bible, Pastor Steve. They returned it to our family. It smells of airplane fuel and it is charred some around the edges, but not one page of it is missing and inside it was a handwritten list of men for whom he was praying." Standing in that hardware store, Bob and I rejoiced that even through this tragedy God was reminding us and all who will listen of His timeless promise that *Heaven and earth will pass away, but my words will never pass away* (Matthew 24:35).

Bob's brother and sister-in-law made the most of many opportunities during their lifetime to point people to the Lord Jesus, likely even when Flight 93 was being hijacked. We too are given opportunities to serve wherever God sends us, even when it is in difficult or dangerous circumstances. Like early Christians we too can take His Word with us wherever we go. *Those who had been scattered preached the word wherever they went* (Acts 8:4). We too can make the most of every opportunity.

Life Application Questions:

1. What difficulties have you faced that were God-given opportunities to serve?

2. Reflecting on the Bible surviving the crash of Flight 93 intact, how precious to you is God's Word in this chaotic world in which you live?

3. What response is the Holy Spirit asking of you now?

85

Christ, the Good Shepherd for Me and Those I Love

The LORD is my shepherd, I lack nothing (Psalm 23:1)

Young David was a shepherd boy. When God sent Samuel to Jesse's family in Bethlehem to anoint the next king, seven of Jesse's sons passed in front of Samuel but the Lord said none of these was chosen. So he asked Jesse, *"Are these all the sons you have?' "There is still the youngest,"* Jesse answered. *"He is tending the sheep"* (1 Samuel 16:11). When David came in the Lord said to Samuel, *"Rise and anoint him; this is the one"* (1 Samuel 16:12).

David became the greatest king in Israel's history, and one of his descendants was Jesus, who was hailed as *the Son of David* (Matthew 21:9). God shaped David's heart when he was a young shepherd tending sheep. David took his responsibilities seriously, caring for his sheep, guarding and protecting them from dangers, and leading the flock to good pasture. As he did this God spoke to David, reminding him that what he did for his sheep, God was doing for his people (Psalm 23). If David was to be a good shepherd for Israel (2 Samuel 5:2) he must learn that the Lord was his shepherd and the shepherd of Israel (Psalm 28:8-9). Jesus described himself as *the good shepherd* who loves and cares for His sheep, even laying down His life for them (John 10).

As a shepherd of God's flock I needed to learn what David learned and Jesus taught, that the Lord is my shepherd and the good shepherd of the flock. In other words, because He took responsibility to care for us all, I could rest in Him. God reminded me that He is my shepherd. Though I believed He was with me, it was very hard to suddenly leave the family and congregation I loved. I missed them terribly. I began feeling spiritually isolated so I asked God to connect me with people who loved Him and could support me and I them. God answered my prayer.

PART XI ~ WALKING WITH GOD IN THE FOG OF UNCERTAINTY

Where I worked a steady stream of navy reservists who had been recalled to active duty arrived, and it was our job to screen, train, equip, and administratively process them so they could go forward as ordered. One important part of this process was to ensure they were medically and dentally ready. To review dental readiness the base dental clinic generally provided a dental technician to screen records and then send to the clinic anyone who needed to be seen. One day, instead of an enlisted dental tech, the senior dental officer arrived. He introduced himself as Captain Switts, director of the naval submarine base dental clinic.

After introductions the captain asked me what faith group I was from. As a chaplain I am often asked that question, but people who ask it are all over the place in their understanding of Christianity. For some who hardly know what a Christian is, denominational distinctions mean little or nothing and are confusing. Others are from a specific faith perspective and know little else, while others understand the breadth of Christianity and the distinctions among us. When asked this question I want people to know I am a follower of Christ and I do not provide more information than they can grasp. For this reason I often start with broad answers and then narrow it down as far as the understanding of the questioner allows.

"I am a follower of Jesus," I said.

"So am I," was his reply.

"I am an Evangelical Christian," I said.

"Me too," he said.

"I am Congregational," I said.

"Me too," was his reply.

I said, "I am with the Conservative Congregational Christian Conference," to which he grinned broadly, stuck out his hand to shake mine, and said, "Me too."

God connected me with a Christian brother! Bill too was a "geographic bachelor" apart from family. He was a member of the East Glenville Community Church, a CCCC congregation in Scotia, New York, where his family lived and where he intended to live when his naval service was finished. Bill was a gift to me, as God allowed us to encourage each other. God reminded me that He really is my Good Shepherd.

God also reminded me that He is the Good Shepherd of my family.

I saw them occasionally that year, as New Hampshire was close enough to travel home now and then. Helen had many people supporting her. Our daughter, Amy, who was a senior in high school, was enjoying life, excelling in school, and was already accepted in the college she wished to attend. Our son Jonathan was in eighth grade, and I missed him terribly, but he seemed well adjusted, was doing well in school, and had good friends. God was taking care of my family.

The same was true of my congregation for whom I was continually in prayer. The board of elders divided the responsibilities and used my absence as an opportunity to model the importance of every member serving in ministry, using the spiritual gifts entrusted to them by God (1 Corinthians 12-14). One of our elders, Dave Nelson, had the spiritual gift of teaching and he took on primary preaching duties for Sundays. Other elders took on other responsibilities and the focus shifted from one leader to Jesus, the chief leader and Good Shepherd.

Now and then that year I returned to Peterborough for a weekend and to worship with my congregation on Sunday mornings. Whenever I did this it was wonderful to be with family again, and each time I marveled at how God was taking such wonderful care of my flock. I was very proud of the leadership provided by our elders, and I rejoiced to see His blessing among them, hearing testimonies of God's grace, and seeing people added to the family.

Sometimes as we walk with the Lord we must go where we have not been before, leaving behind people we love. God wants us to remember we are never outside His love, He tends and cares for us, and He provides what we need. He does the same for those we love, shepherding and guarding them.

Life Application Questions:

1. In what ways has the Lord reminded you that He is your Good Shepherd?

2. How have you seen the Lord caring for your loved ones when you are apart?

3. What response is the Holy Spirit asking of you now?

86

Saying Good-bye Precedes Homecoming Joy

Jesus answered him, "Truly I tell you, today you will be with me in paradise" (Luke 23:43)

Saying good-bye is never easy, but it is easier when we anticipate seeing each other again. That is what Jesus was emphasizing to Martha when he comforted her after the death of her brother, Lazarus. He reminded her of the promise of the resurrection. Martha believed this and soon she received a foretaste of it when Jesus demonstrated His power over life and death, raising Lazarus from the grave.

In the year following the attacks on September 11, while I served again on active duty, I was energized by the promise that I would soon return to the people I loved. That day finally came. My first Sunday back was the 29th of September. I will never forget the joy in my heart that morning. I was returning to the flock of God I loved, grateful for the ways He watched over me and my family and congregation. I was looking forward to worshiping the Lord again with people I loved.

It was a festive day. Driving up the long and curving driveway of the church that morning, tears of joy came to my eyes when I made the turn and saw the church building. Hanging across the front of the building was a huge banner which said in large letters, "Welcome Home Pastor Steve!" A celebration was planned. We had balloons and noisemakers that morning and after the service a celebratory feast was planned. Homecoming joy was part of our worship that day, and it was wonderful! It was a taste of heaven, reminding me of what it might be like when God's people are welcomed home to heaven.

The best thing that happened that day had nothing to do with my return, but everything to do with a woman who through faith in Jesus

Christ was born again. Her name was Lila. Through her work as a social worker Helen met Lila and visited in her home. Lila lived alone and was wheelchair bound, but she was known around town as she made her way from place to place by way of her electrically powered wheelchair. Lila was a lonely woman who did not yet know the Lord, and God stirred Helen to love Lila and invite her to attend our church. Helen let her know she would be welcomed and she gave Lila her phone number, inviting her to call if she wished to come so a ride could be arranged.

On the Sunday of my homecoming, Lila came for the first time. The gathering place of Trinity Evangelical Church is a mile and a half west of town, uphill most of the way. With her motorized wheelchair Lila made the journey and climbed that hill. She did not call for a ride as Helen invited her to do. Instead she took the time and made the long climb, which symbolized the desire God was placing in her soul. By the time she arrived the power in her chair was running low. That day she was recharged in more ways than one.

The Holy Spirit was present as we worshiped that day, drawing us close, and opening our eyes and hearts to His truth. As I concluded my message the Holy Spirit prompted me to extend an invitation to come in faith to Jesus Christ to become a child of God. I invited anyone who would accept this invitation to make their way to the front of the sanctuary so we could pray with them and rejoice in their decision. Lila drove her wheelchair to the front of the sanctuary that day, and by faith in Jesus she was born again.

In the festivities that followed of welcoming me home, a celebration was also held in heaven welcoming Lila home to a personal relationship with God. Our family rejoiced with Lila, and with a smile I told her our party that day was really for her. She soaked in the joy of the day, finding a warm welcome from brothers and sisters. When at last it was time to leave, some men from the church gave Lila and her wheelchair a ride home and one brother, Howard Cumback, who has since been promoted to heaven, arranged to pick her up the next Sunday.

The next week Lila was again in church services, enjoying the worship, celebrating her new relationship with Christ, and reveling in the love of her new church family. She was home. It was clear God had put a new spirit within her and she was a new person in Christ (Ezekiel 36:26-27; 2 Corinthians 5:17).

The next Sunday she was not with us. Howard said he was unable to reach her on the phone, so I made a note to follow up the next day to see if she was okay. On Monday a local funeral director called to tell me Lila had died and her sister was asking if I would officiate at her funeral. I agreed.

Funeral services are an opportunity for the living to celebrate the life of the one who has died. For those who die in Christ a funeral is an opportunity for followers of Christ to hold on to the promise of everlasting life through His victory over sin and the grave. In Lila's case the funeral was a celebration of her life and of God's grace to her at the end. Jesus' words to the thief on the cross applied to Lila who was now with Him in paradise. Rarely have I led a funeral in which I knew joy as I knew it that day, because my new sister was already in heaven! After the funeral Lila's sister approached me and said, "Pastor, Lila lived a hard life, but at the end she found peace. The last two weeks of Lila's life were the happiest and best two weeks of her entire life."

> *In Christ Jesus saying good-bye anticipates and is tempered by the homecoming joy that awaits.*

Now and then we must say good-bye to people we love, and when it is because of death it is especially hard, but in Christ Jesus saying good-bye anticipates and is tempered by the homecoming joy that awaits. Knowing the sorrow His disciples would face when He went to the cross, Jesus said, *Now is your time of grief, but I will see you again and you will rejoice, and no one will take away your joy* (John 16:22). God teaches us to hold on to this perspective when we must say good-bye.

Life Application Questions:

1. When and how have you experienced the pain of saying good-bye?

2. In what ways have you also anticipated or experienced homecoming joy?

3. What response is the Holy Spirit asking of you now?

Part XII

WALKING WITH GOD INTO GREATER RESPONSIBILITY

The Bible contains inspiring stories of people whom God called to do things they never volunteered for and for which they felt inadequate; yet God used them. This pattern continues and it happened to me. When it happens, our sense of inadequacy compels us to walk closely with God, because we know we need His help. What follows are lessons I learned walking with God into greater responsibility.

87

Don't Ever Stop Listening

*My son, pay attention to what I say; turn
your ear to my words* (Proverbs 4:20)

God taught me to never stop listening, and to never presume that because I have known Him so long I know what He wants for me now. Rather, I must walk in close fellowship with Him, listening carefully to hear if He should speak new direction. I learned this lesson yet again the week I came home from my year of navy service.

The entire year I was away serving where God sent me, I was looking forward to returning to my family and congregation, so I was very excited when I arrived home. I knew that before resuming my work at the church I must get away for a few days of prayer and fasting to listen carefully to the Lord as I shifted gears. With Helen's blessing I packed a bag to leave the very next morning. I would drive to our lake cottage in Maine to be still in His presence for a few days and then to close up the cottage for the winter. I assured her when I returned I would be home to stay.

The next morning as I was leaving Helen pointed to a pile of mail addressed to me and asked me to go through it before I left so she could throw away whatever I did not want. I pulled out everything with first-class postage and read it very quickly, including a letter from the CCCC office in Minnesota, the fellowship of ministers and churches of which I am part. I read a letter from Conference Minister Reverend Clifford Christensen, in which he announced that after twenty-two years of serving in this role this would be his last year. He asked us to join him in praying for the search process and for the person God had already chosen to follow him.

It felt like a thorn pricked my side as I sensed what this could mean. After reading the letter I kissed Helen good-bye, then got in my car and began my three-hundred-mile drive. I was in turmoil. The entire year I was away I had longed to return to my family and church. With all of its challenges I loved local church life. I wanted to be a pastor and I was about to do it again. Now this letter! I determined to pray for the CCCC and for the search process that was underway to find the next conference minister. I would pray for God to bless the person He had already chosen, and for his family, and that God would prepare him for his leadership responsibilities. I determined to do that, but I knew the Holy Spirit was asking more of me. He wanted me to pray with availability. That is where I struggled. An argument ensued for most of the trip. I pleaded, "Please don't ask me to do this Lord! You know I want to be a local church pastor. I am back where I want to be now! Please don't ask me to do this!"

> As Christian disciples, we must be very careful to avoid making presumptions about His will for our future.

Our God is so gracious. He reminded me that He has never failed me yet and I can fully trust Him. He reminded me that He is Lord and sovereign over all things including the CCCC and me and my family. He reminded me of when as a young man I became aware of His lordship and made a life promise to go wherever He sent me, to do whatever He called me to do, and say whatever He called me to say. He asked me if I still meant it and I said, "Yes Lord."

He then said, "Will you trust me in this too?"

I replied, "Yes Lord. Forgive my unbelief." God met me in my car that day and His peace settled upon me, as I reaffirmed my desire to serve Him anywhere He leads me until I breathe my last.

By the time I arrived at the lake I was completely at peace and ready to prepare for resuming my responsibilities as pastor. I would begin praying for God's will for the next conference minister, but because of my love for local church life I was resolved not to express any interest in the job. If God intended for me to do this He would make His will known and the search committee would contact me.

As Christian disciples, we must be very careful to avoid making presumptions about His will for our future. Yielding to the lordship of Jesus Christ means laying down our own preferences and saying, "You are Lord and I am not. Give me ears to hear your voice so I may do your will." When we listen in this way God blesses us in ways far greater than we could have imagined.

Life Application Questions:

1. What presumptions might be holding you back from hearing God's direction?

2. What does it mean to listen to the Lord and what is necessary to do so?

3. What response is the Holy Spirit asking of you now?

8 8

Never Resist God's Will

> *The word of the LORD came to Jonah son of Amittai: "Go to the great city of Ninevah and preach against it, because its wickedness has come up before me." But Jonah ran away from the LORD and headed for Tarshish. He went down to Joppa, where he found a ship bound for that port. After paying the fare, he went aboard and sailed for Tarshish to flee from the LORD* (Jonah 1:1-3)

Jonah ran from God's will. God wanted him to go east to Ninevah to preach a message of repentance, but Jonah didn't want to do that. He ran to Joppa and booked passage on a ship headed west. He knew what God wanted of him and he wanted no part of it. Have you ever tried that? I have and I will testify to what Jonah learned the hard way. It is utmost foolishness to run from God's will! Jonah spent three days and nights in the belly of a fish, and then he repented and agreed to yield to God's will. God heard and answered Jonah's prayer and Jonah became fish vomit. Even that was God's mercy, as He could have chosen to push Jonah out the other end of the fish. Resisting God's will is never a good move, as there will be unpleasant consequences.

From the moment I read the letter from Cliff Christensen about the search for the next CCCC conference minister I had an inkling God would call me to this, and I did not want to do it. Though ultimately I did want His will, I had my own ideas about what that meant and leaving local church life was not what I had in mind. Though I resisted, ultimately God melted my resistance.

Before I was recalled to active duty service in the navy the previous year and while serving as pastor of Trinity Evangelical Church, I also served as CCCC area representative for New Hampshire. I represented the CCCC in the Granite State, interviewing individuals and churches

PART XII ~ WALKING WITH GOD INTO GREATER RESPONSIBILITY

applying for membership, offering support to CCCC ministers, and intervening in cases of conflict. When recalled to active duty I turned those responsibilities over to another New Hampshire CCCC pastor.

In my first week back in Peterborough I took the interim area representative to lunch to thank him for his service during my absence, and so he could fill me in on what had occurred during my absence. Over the course of lunch he mentioned the letter from Cliff Christensen which he too received; then he leaned forward in his chair and said, "You know Steve, you would be an excellent conference minister!" I recoiled from his words but I heard God whispering, "Are you listening?"

Resisting God's will is never a good move, as there will be unpleasant consequences.

Later when I mentioned this comment to Helen, telling her I had no interest in it, she encouraged me not to rule it out. Then I remembered something she said to me fifteen years earlier. Helen is a prayerful woman who has often discerned God's will before I have. In the mid-1980s, when I was a young pastor, Helen startled me one day when she said, "Steve, you will be conference minister someday."

Her words surprised me so I said, "Why would you say something like that?"

She replied, "Because you love the CCCC, you have administrative gifts, you know how to keep the main thing the main thing, and God uses you to effect biblical unity. Besides, like Elisha following Elijah, God has you following Cliff Christensen."

Cliff is the pastor God led us to when we moved to Minnesota to attend seminary. I then served a church in Rhode Island where Cliff previously served. I laughed at her words and discounted them, but from time to time through subsequent years Helen again mentioned that she thought one day I would serve as conference minister. As God reminded me of this my resistance began to melt, but still I did not want to pursue it.

In January 2003 I traveled to Minnesota for a meeting of CCCC area representatives. When we gathered I also served as chair of the area representatives, so I had some responsibilities for leading meetings and providing training. Though not on our agenda, a topic of discussion overheard during break times was who might be God's choice as conference minister. On a few occasions during our days together people approached me and voiced their opinion that I should be the choice. I listened but my consistent reply was I had no interest. Still I heard God whispering, "Steve, are you listening?"

I did not want to pursue it but I prayed, "Lord, if you want me to do this you, will need to convince me."

In February 2003 I traveled to New Orleans for two weeks to fulfill my Navy Reserves annual training requirement. Soon after arriving I received a call to my cellphone from the chair of the conference minister search committee. He said, "Steve, our committee has been in prayer asking God to lead us. We want to ask if you would be willing to be a candidate to serve as our next conference minister. What do you say?" For a moment I thought of Jonah, and I could not say no.

The process included submitting an extensive application questionnaire, then having a face-to-face interview with the search committee. In late April I was notified by the chair of the search committee that I was their unanimous choice. Their recommendation was then forwarded to the CCCC board of directors who also unanimously confirmed me. A mailing was then sent to CCCC membership announcing my selection to be voted on at the annual meeting in July, where again there was a unanimous vote. I am so grateful I did not run from His will.

Life Application Questions:

1. If you have ever tried running from God's will as Jonah did, what did you learn?

2. What blessings have you received in life from saying yes to God's will?

3. What response is the Holy Spirit asking of you now?

89

If You Pray, God Will Make a Way

*Let us then approach God's throne of grace with
confidence, so that we may receive mercy and find grace
to help us in our time of need* (Hebrews 4:16)

Without Him we can do nothing, but with Him we can do all He calls us to do. To experience the full measure of this truth we must be people of prayer. I learned this lesson while preparing for my duties as conference minister. After the board of directors approved my selection and after I gave my notice at the church, I called Cliff Christensen in Minnesota to ask if he would still be there upon my arrival in July. When he told me he would not be there, then we agreed I should fly to Minnesota for a couple of days so he could pass on things I must know to hit the ground running in my new job. When we agreed on some dates, Helen and I decided to also use that trip to find a place to live.

Only our youngest son, Jonathan, remained at home with us. He was fourteen years old and would be leaving good friends behind. We knew this move would be hard on him. We had prayed with him about our decision to move and he let us know he fully supported the move. Still Helen and I were concerned for him, and we wanted to do whatever we could to make things easier for him through the transition. We determined to include him in the process of selecting our new home. With this in mind we arranged for Helen and Jonathan to fly to Minnesota a few days before my arrival. They would look at possibilities and narrow the choices, and then working around my meetings with Cliff I would go with them to look at homes they wanted me to see. We asked God to guide us in the decision.

The day came for Helen and Jonathan to fly to Minnesota where I would join them a few days later. In my devotional time that day God led me to a verse I wanted to show my wife and son. I read Acts 17:26

(NIV 1984 edition): *From one man he made every nation of men, that they should inhabit the whole earth; and he determined the times set for them and the exact places where they should live.* I said to them, "You will look at a number of homes, but God has determined the exact place we should live. Let us claim this promise so we will recognize it," and so we prayed together.

By the time I arrived in St. Paul a few days later Helen and Jonathan had homes they wanted me to see. I looked with them and we ruled out some and added more to the possibilities list, as they continued looking. My primary focus was preparing for my new job. I had just two days to spend with Cliff Christensen. We talked at length and he answered my many questions.

After two days together I knew I was in over my head. Cliff had answered my questions forthrightly. I learned about the condition of our churches and the depth of apathy among many. I became aware of conflicts and the malaise of prayerlessness in churches. I learned about pastors whose passion for holiness and hunger for intimacy with Jesus had waned. Cliff was honest about the challenges we faced.

By the end of our second day when we said our good-byes I was feeling the weight of it all. Part of me wanted to do what Jonah did and board the nearest boat to Tarshish. Walking out of the CCCC office I was sending questions to the throne of God like, "Who am I to lead ministers and churches? The need is greater than my ability! How can I do this?" This was my state of mind as I left the office and climbed into the back seat of the realtor's car, where Jonathan and Helen waited to take me with them to look at homes.

They said we would first be looking again at a house we had seen the previous day and we all liked. The realtor then volunteered that she had found another house in the same town, built by the same builder, and with a similar floor plan. We would begin there so we could compare the two homes and see which one we liked better. She added that the first home we would see was for sale by owner, which meant the owner would be showing it. On the way to our first stop I overheard Helen and Jonathan and the realtor discussing homes, but my mind was fixed on only one question, *How can I possibly do this job, Lord?*

In a few minutes we pulled up in front of the first home where there was a "For Sale by Owner" sign in the front yard. On the outside it looked similar to the home we saw the previous day and were scheduled to look at again. The owner met us at the door and invited us in. The first thing I noticed was worship music was playing over the sound system. Immediately I was calmed and sensed His presence.

As I knew the floor plan I declined a tour and headed to the lowest level of the house where I immediately noticed a room with two bifold doors with etched glass. This was not in the other home we had seen. *What was this?* I wondered. Walking to the bifold doors and opening them, tears began trickling down my cheeks as God met me and answered the question I was asking. I was standing in a prayer chapel. There was an altar and a cross, and a place to kneel in prayer. I sensed God's presence and heard Him say, "Steve, if you will pray, I will make a way!" As I feasted on this promise, I felt a hand on my shoulder. It was Jonathan. He said, "Dad, this is it. This is for you!" He knew it and I knew it. When Helen joined us downstairs she knew it too. This was the home God had for us.

We lived in that home for eight years, and I began my days in that prayer chapel. There I laid many burdens at the Lord's feet, and I interceded for ministers and churches. I asked God for wisdom and He met me there. Calling churches to prayer was a theme I often emphasized as I traveled around the conference. In Luke's gospel I noticed Jesus often took time to pray (Luke 5:16). I reasoned if He needed to pray, how much more do I who am so easily distracted and struggle with sin. I encouraged pastors and leadership teams to make prayer a priority, for without it we are ill-equipped to lead His church. If we want to prosper in life and ministry, we must seek the Lord (Jeremiah 10:21). If we pray He will make a way.

Life Application Questions:

1. Do you have a "prayer closet" where you regularly pray? If you do, how has God used this to "make a way" for you? If you do not, are you ready to begin?

2. Why do you suppose God chooses to connect His equipping to our praying?

3. What response is the Holy Spirit asking of you now?

90

Following Jesus Is the Greatest Adventure

But Jesus immediately said to them: "Take courage! It is I. Don't be afraid." "Lord, if it's you," Peter replied, "tell me to come to you on the water." "Come," he said. Then Peter got down out of the boat, walked on the water and came toward Jesus (Matthew 14:27-29)

When Peter got out of the boat and walked on the water toward Jesus he shocked himself and everyone with him in the boat. With eyes fixed on Jesus he did something he never dreamed possible: he walked on water. But when he took his eyes off Jesus he began to sink. Afraid of drowning he instinctively knew what to do, as do we. He called on Jesus, and what happened? *Immediately Jesus reached out his hand and caught him. "You of little faith," he said, "why did you doubt?"* (Matthew 14:31). I so identify with Peter, for at times I too have taken my eyes off Jesus and felt like I was drowning. I too have called upon the Lord and He has come to my rescue.

I have "walked on water" with the Lord, having the great adventure of ministering in ways I never dreamed possible. Thus far I have ministered in nearly every state in America and on every continent but Antarctica. I have witnessed amazing things with Jesus and met remarkable people along the way. To illustrate, I want to introduce a woman I met in Bulgaria.

Representing the CCCC, I visited congregational churches in the Union of Evangelical Churches of Bulgaria. Since the Iron Curtain was lifted the church has enjoyed the liberty of worshiping openly and evangelizing freely. Christians are taking advantage of this freedom so churches are growing and new churches are being planted. One Sunday I had the privilege of speaking at a few Bulgarian churches, including an afternoon visit to a Gypsy church in Assenovgrad.

PART XII ~ WALKING WITH GOD INTO GREATER RESPONSIBILITY

Christians in the Gypsy communities there are very poor by American standards. The homes we passed lacked many conveniences we take for granted, including electricity and plumbing. Their church building appeared to rise as a palace from the ashes. It was magnificent! The people built the sanctuary with their own hands, giving the very best they had as a testimony of the greatness of God. I was touched by the beauty of the building and even more by the beauty of their worship. All the worshipers were financially poor but spiritually rich, beyond the dreams of many. As they sang worship songs in their language exalting the Lord Jesus, they demonstrated profound joy. I could not help but notice one woman in the congregation who was especially radiant in worship.

> *I too have called upon the Lord and He has come to my rescue.*

When testimony time came, this Gypsy woman rose to give her testimony of what the Lord had done for her. The minister sitting beside me translated as she shared her testimony. She was raised Muslim, and that was what she knew. When her adult daughter became a Christian she demanded her daughter give up this foolishness and renounce Christianity. When her daughter refused to do this she disowned her and told her she was no longer her daughter.

The woman said she became very sick. Her daughter heard about it and tried to visit and bring Christian friends to pray, but she refused to see her daughter. Then she was diagnosed with cancer. She had a tumor on her spine that paralyzed her and doctors said she was going to die. Her daughter tried again to see her mother, asking if she could please come with her pastor and Christian friends to pray over her. Reasoning at this point she had nothing to lose, she allowed her daughter to come with her pastor and friends to offer their prayers.

When they came to her bedside she was paralyzed and unable to walk. They spoke to her of Jesus Christ and then laid hands upon her and prayed over her in Jesus' name. "When they prayed," the woman said, "Jesus touched and healed me. The tumor disappeared, the paralysis was cured, and the pain was gone! He healed me and forgave my sins that day. I belong to Jesus now!"

Beaming from ear to ear this Gypsy woman then gave the first evidence of salvation: she wanted to share the good news. She said, "The first thing I wanted to do was find my sister and tell her about Jesus, what He did for me and could do for her." Then she said, "Let me introduce you to my sister!" Sitting beside her was another woman, her sister, who was also beaming with the joy of knowing Jesus.

Meeting people like this and hearing such stories of the power and grace of God, seeing evidence of changed lives because of Christ, and being part of something this amazing is a great adventure! I have known such adventure for many years now, and I will keep walking with Him until I cross the finish line into heaven.

At age ninety-three Evangelist Billy Graham wrote a great book titled *Nearing Home,* in which he talks about serving God all the way to the finish line. Billy Graham has preached the message of Jesus Christ to more people around the world than anyone else in history, but he has not quit serving the Lord. His message in the book is to continue serving the Lord until the very end. I love it!

For many years my youngest sister, Marilee Colpitts, focused her energies on raising her large family. Having largely accomplished that extraordinary feat, she then took up a new challenge – volunteering her service as sponsorship coordinator for a ministry called His Hands Support Ministries, caring for little children in Jesus' name. She loves the adventure of walking with and serving Jesus, and several of her children seem to have discovered the same joy.

We can easily think too small, presuming God would not use us to do anything of significance. He urges us to remember that the power is not from us; it is Christ in us! He calls us to fix our eyes upon Him and get out of the boat, keeping our eyes fixed on Him.

Life Application Questions:

1. Reflecting on Peter walking on the water with Jesus and the joy of the Gypsy woman who met Jesus, how are you living the adventure of walking with Jesus?

2. Applying the principle of Isaiah 54:2, how available are you for His service?

3. What response is the Holy Spirit asking of you now?

91

Remember, Hell Is Real

The angels will come and separate the wicked from the righteous and throw them into the blazing furnace, where there will be weeping and gnashing of teeth (Matthew 13:49-50)

No one who believes the Bible to be the infallible Word of God can deny Jesus believed in hell. He spoke of it as a literal and eternal place of torment and anguish, a place of agony and judgment. He warned of hell and urged His listeners in the strongest way to repent of sin to avoid it. Jesus came to save people from this awful destiny and He gave His life on a cross to do so. Though this is true, many who claim to be Jesus' followers and to believe His Word is infallible choose not to believe in the reality of hell, or like an ostrich with its head in the sand, they live as though hell was a myth. Is that wise or is it the height of foolishness?

We choose not to think about hell because the subject is too difficult to think about. To lessen the threat of it we may even diminish the term, using it as a flippant curse word. When we do this we reveal our ignorance, for if we believed in the reality of hell as the Scriptures describe it, we would shudder to tell anyone to go there. We should not be unaware of the Devil's schemes. If we adopt the lie that hell is a myth we will be prone to adopt the corollary conclusion that evangelism is not so critical after all. Rather, may God's Word be our guide, not our own preferences or the "truth-is-relative" view so prevalent in our culture today.

As we walk with the Lord He tells us to remember hell is real. Every person with whom we lock eyes will either spend eternity with God in heaven, having been saved by God's grace through faith in Jesus

Christ, or they will spend eternity separated from Him in hell. There are no other options.

Having read the Bible since I was a boy and believing it is wholly true, I had to conclude hell is real. This belief, along with the promise of heaven for those who trust in Christ, has motivated me when praying for people who remain spiritually lost, and when sharing the good news with people who do not yet know Him. I too have sometimes ignored the reality of hell because it is so painful to think about. Believing in heaven and the new life found in Christ, that is compelling enough, I have reasoned. Paying heed to eternal consequences for those who do not accept Him does not seem necessary. But a one-sided perspective of eternity is out of balance, and God does not want His children to cherry-pick which biblical truths we find acceptable. He wants us to accept His Word as truth and to live accordingly, which therefore includes the reality of hell.

Though I knew God's Word about this, He knew I was ignoring it, so by His mercy He gave me a glimpse of hell. This was not something I expected, and the experience of it was so shocking as to wake me up to the depths of my soul. It was so real I had no doubt God was showing this to me so I would never again doubt or ignore the truth of His Word that hell is a place of judgment for all who die in sin.

The ground opened before me and I was on the edge of a portal into hell. The horror was greater than any I ever imagined. A blast of heat nearly bowled me over as I stood on the edge, peering into spiritual darkness. "Agony" is too meager a word to describe the wretchedness and despair. The cries of suffering I heard were infinitely worse than any human can conceive of. Words cannot describe the horror of it.

When this window into hell had closed and I was aware again of my surroundings, I fell to my knees and cried. I cried for God's mercy and I cried in repentance for disbelieving His Word. I cried for the spiritually lost, pleading for revival in my own soul and in the church so we might more effectively share His love and compassion for the lost. I asked to be filled afresh by His Spirit, to be His instrument to declare the good news of everlasting life in Christ, and that the church might take seriously His Great Commission to make disciples. I prayed for

PART XII ~ WALKING WITH GOD INTO GREATER RESPONSIBILITY

a fresh anointing upon my life and upon our pastors and churches to proclaim the message of God's grace, offering everlasting life through faith in Christ Jesus.

It was 2006 when the Lord gave me this vision of hell. I struggled to speak of it but knew He showed it to me for a reason. He brought me back to what His Word says about eternity – offering eternal life for those who are saved through the blood of Jesus, but eternal condemnation for all who die in sin. The message of hope and life entrusted to the church is not one of several lifesaving options for this world; it is the only message that can save. *Salvation is found in no one else, for there is no other name under heaven given to mankind by which we must be saved* (Acts 4:12).

> *Like it or not, hell is real.*

In their book *Erasing Hell* (David C. Cook, 2011), Francis Chan and Preston Sprinkle do a superb job of addressing biblical teaching and contemporary struggles with the subject of hell. They point out what has perhaps been your experience as it has been mine, the tendency of reading into Scripture what we want to find. Like it or not, hell is real. It is taught by God in Scripture and as we walk with the Lord Jesus He wants His followers to live considering this reality.

Life Application Questions:

1. Where have you been concerning belief in the reality of hell, and why?

2. How does your belief about hell affect your compassion for people who are spiritually lost and your motivation to evangelize?

3. What response is the Holy Spirit asking of you now?

92

Leaders Must Lead With Faith

And without faith it is impossible to please God, because anyone who comes to him must believe that he exists and that he rewards those who earnestly seek him (Hebrews 11:6)

In the great faith chapter of the Bible (Hebrews 11) in which testimonies of heroic men and women leaders of history are recounted, a summary statement is offered in verse 6 that is descriptive of every person listed in that chapter and of every godly leader today: *And without faith it is impossible to please God.* To please God leaders must lead with faith.

Without faith, how could Abraham obey God and go to a land he did not know, and how could he look at the stars in the sky and believe that though he was old, his descendants would become as innumerable as stars? Without faith, how could Moses have led the people of Israel out of Egypt and across the Red Sea, and how could he pray and receive manna from heaven or water from a rock, and how could he receive the Word of God on Mount Sinai? Without faith, these men could not lead in a way that pleased God, and without faith, neither can you or I.

In my first years of service as conference minister I was on a sharp learning curve. My constant prayer was, "Lord, help me see what you want me to see, and give me vision and faith to respond in ways that honor you." I was privileged to represent the CCCC on the board of directors of the National Association of Evangelicals (NAE) and at meetings of the Mission America Coalition. I was blessed to meet with other Christian leaders who were also seeking His face, for God met us and spoke to us about His vision for His church. A breakthrough happened at the 2006 meeting of the Mission America Coalition. David T. Olson, director of the American Church Research Project, was a speaker that year. For many years David had done careful research tracking trends

PART XII ~ WALKING WITH GOD INTO GREATER RESPONSIBILITY

in the American church, and the trends were not looking good. His statistics were not based on poll numbers, but on hard data reflecting a declining percentage of people who were connected to a faith community and attending corporate worship.

I realized that what David Olson described was mirrored in the churches I served. I looked at our statistics and saw that most of our churches were on a plateau or were declining. Few were growing numerically and showing conversion growth. David said every local church is on an incline, recline, or decline, and the vast percentage of local churches in America were declining. He went on to describe the significant population increase happening in America through birth and immigration.

> *God did not put you there so you can take it easy and coast.*

He explained that historically, in periods of significant population growth the American church has always planted many new churches, but in the American church now more churches were closing yearly than were being planted. He said if our only goal was to keep pace with population growth, the number of new church plants must increase by about four thousand yearly, and if we did not do this the decline of the church in America would only continue.

Listening that day I saw a giant larger than Goliath. All the church leaders who were there saw it. Rather than despair we prayed. I asked God to give me clarity of vision and increase my faith so the CCCC could be part of His answer. It became clear that day that God wanted the CCCC to focus on two things: (1) church redevelopment – assisting churches in recline or decline to return to a biblical and missional focus, and (2) church multiplication – planting new churches. I had no doubt this was His will for us; now I asked for increased faith so it would happen.

If you are in a place of Christian leadership, God did not put you there so you can take it easy and coast. The time is too short for that, and the eternal destiny of many is weighed in the balance. For Christian leaders the status quo cannot be acceptable. We must get on our knees and when we have heard from the Lord, in faith we must get moving, praying continuously along the way!

God gave confirmation of this ministry vision for the CCCC later that year when we received the largest bequest ever given to the CCCC, by the Philips Church trust fund in Boston, Massachusetts. The funds were designated for outreach and church planting. Specific instructions from the trust required that the funds not be saved for a rainy day, but that they be invested now to plant churches and make disciples for Jesus Christ. With God's provision of these seed monies and the blessing of the board of directors and members of the conference, gifted leaders were hired and effective ministries were launched that have breathed new life into many churches and have seen the birth and development of new churches.

The work is ongoing and the end of the story is not yet written, but of this I am certain: Wherever He has called you to serve, and however He has called you to lead, with faith nothing is impossible. Without faith we cannot please God; we simply cannot! Matthew 13:58 says because of a lack of faith among the people, *he did not do many miracles.* If you see a giant but lack the faith to take it on, the place to begin is on your knees with other prayer warriors, asking Him to renew your faith. Then with His anointing step out and see what God will do!

Life Application Questions:

1. Why from God's point of view is faith so important for His chosen leaders?

2. What is your ministry facing that requires exercising faith (1 Timothy 2:1-2)?

3. What response is the Holy Spirit asking of you now?

93

God Knows His Plan for Us

"For I know the plans I have for you," declares the LORD, "plans to prosper you and not to harm you, plans to give you hope and a future" (Jeremiah 29:11)

A limitation of our humanity is we never know what tomorrow will bring. We may think we do, but we cannot know with certainty. This reality is a source of worry even for Christians, but God wants us to learn that though we do not know what the future holds, we have something far better – we have the One who knows His plan and who lovingly holds us in His hands.

In 2008 I traveled to South Africa to serve as Bible teacher at the annual meeting of the Evangelical Fellowship of Congregational Churches of South Africa. It was a sweet time of worship and fellowship. Pastors and delegates from churches across South Africa were in attendance. With only a few years gone by since the end of apartheid, I marveled at the unity and love among this ethnically diverse group of white, black, and Afrikaans Christians. As the only North American in attendance, I was the recipient of wonderful hospitality.

They had a number of customs that were strange to me, for which a sense of humor was helpful. One custom was their practice of having someone publicly address the speaker on behalf of the congregation at the conclusion of a sermon. I was not expecting this and the first night I was embarrassed by it. When I had concluded my message that night, one of the pastors came to the front and publicly expressed how God had used my message to challenge him personally, and how it had strengthened and encouraged all who were present.

Concluding his remarks he said, "In summary, Dr. Gammon, on behalf of us all I want to say, buy a donkey." At this the congregation wildly applauded, and as I recall some of them stood and cheered. I wasn't sure what to make of this, but when the applause had died down the pastor who was speaking said again, "Again I want to say, 'Buy a Donkey.'" Everyone was smiling, and I was sure he meant well, but I had no clue why he was telling me this. As it had been a long day, someone gave me a ride to where I would spend the night.

In the morning, the person who picked me up was the same pastor who spoke the previous night at the conclusion of my sermon, so I asked him my question. I said, "Twice last night you said something to which the congregation applauded, but it was confusing to me. Why did you tell me to 'Buy a Donkey'? What is the meaning of this phrase?"

He laughed. "You don't know?" he asked.

"I do not," I replied.

"'Buy a Donkey' is Afrikaans for 'thank you very much!'" he said.

Now I laughed! I had just learned my first Afrikaans words. You can guess how I concluded my teaching that morning. I thanked them for their attention and the warm hospitality they had shown me. Then I said, "In conclusion, I have one more thing I want to say from the depths of my heart. I want to say, 'Baie dankie' [Afrikaans spelling, though it sounds like 'Buy a Donkey']!" They all applauded.

It was after our final worship service that God especially reminded me that He knows His plans for us. The last service of the meetings took place on Sunday morning in the sanctuary of the closest member church. The building was memorable in that the neighborhood it was situated in was extremely poor. This was a black congregation who loved Jesus. They were rich in love and faith, but materially they had so little. Their sanctuary was a work in progress. It was built on a cement slab, with concrete block walls and a tin roof, but there were no doors or windows, as they could not afford them. I asked the pastor what they did when it rains, as the noise on the tin roof would be loud. He said they get closer together. As there was no heat in the building I asked him what they did when it is cold and his answer was the same, they get close. Their focus was not on their building; it was on worshiping and serving God.

The service that day was between three and four hours in length. All the clergy except me were dressed in their best clerical robes. The service was wonderful and the worship anointed. After the service, as was their custom, the clergy lined up in a receiving line leading toward the exit so the congregation could go through the line and receive a blessing from the clergy on their way out the door. I stood in the middle of this line as a crowd filed by one by one. That's when I met her.

A middle-aged, dark-complexioned woman greeted me and shook my hand while looking intently into my eyes. She then continued in the line toward the door. As I continued greeting worshipers, I noticed out of the corner of my eye that someone was reversing direction and pushing against the crowd to come back in. It was this middle-aged woman. It took her a few minutes, as she was swimming hard against a strong current, but in time she made her way back until she stood in front of me waiting for an opportunity to speak with me again.

Stepping back into line she took my hands, looked up into my eyes, and said slowly and very deliberately, "Dr. Gammon, the Lord has a message He wants me to give to you."

"Speak," I said. "I am listening."

"Jeremiah 29:11," she said. *"For I know the plans I have for you," declares the LORD, "plans to prosper you and not to harm you, plans to give you hope and a future."* She then said, "God wants you to know this promise is for you!" That was it! I thanked her for this good word and blessed her as she blessed me, and then she was on her way toward the exit.

In the years that have followed, as I have walked with God He has often brought me back to this promise. There have been times when I have had considerable uncertainty about what the future will hold. Perhaps you are in such a place now. Whenever we have such uncertainties, God invites us to hold on to the certainties of faith that are found in His Word. He invites us to trust His promise and know His Word is true. It is true for others, and it is true for me and you.

Life Application Questions:

1. What uncertainties are you currently facing, and how does this lesson apply?

2. The woman who spoke Jeremiah 29:11 had little materially, yet treasured this promise. How do the worries of this world affect your reaction to this promise?

3. What response is the Holy Spirit asking of you now?

Part XIII

WALKING WITH GOD INTO UNEXPECTED CHANGE

At one time or another we will all meet unexpected life change. What then? Even ministers of the Lord sometimes face something that seems to change everything, or almost everything. What then? How does faith and the experience of walking with the Lord in and through every life circumstance affect the way we approach unexpected change? What follows are key lessons the Lord has taught me as I walked with Him when unexpected change happened to me.

94

Fast, Pray, and Listen

But when you fast, put oil on your head and wash your face, so that it will not be obvious to others that you are fasting, but only to your Father, who is unseen; and your Father, who sees what is done in secret, will reward you (Matthew 6:17-18)

The nature of unexpected change is we do not see it coming. I have learned that I am far more ready for the unexpected changes God has in store if I am walking closely with and listening carefully to Him. Unfortunately, I can be so busy with tasks at hand that I fail to be still in His presence, to therefore hear what He is saying.

In His humanity Jesus often took time away from His many demands to enjoy His Father's presence and carefully listen (Luke 5:16). Before choosing his twelve apostles Jesus spent an entire night praying (Luke 6:12-16). It was as He prayed on a mountaintop with Peter, James, and John that Jesus was transfigured in heavenly glory (Luke 9:28-35). By example and words Jesus taught His disciples to fast, pray, and listen (Luke 4:1-10; 11:1-10; Matthew 6:16-18), lessons the early church actively applied (Acts 13:2-3; 14:23).

God intends for these disciplines to be practiced today by all His followers, especially those to whom He has entrusted leadership responsibilities. Though I know this, and though every time I have put these disciplines into practice God has blessed me, there have been times when I have neglected to do so. In such times I have been unable to hear what God wanted me to hear. This is particularly alarming when unexpected change is coming, as He desires to prepare us for it.

One Sunday in February 2011 the Lord got my attention and used children to do it. As I was not traveling that weekend I was attending with Helen our church home, Woodbury Community Church in

Woodbury, Minnesota. Helen was teaching her fifth and sixth grade Sunday school class and I was in an adult Bible class. At one point during the class Helen stepped into our classroom and asked if I could please bring my Bible and join her, as her children were asking questions she thought I was better equipped to answer. Grabbing my Bible I stepped into the hall. I inquired what questions they were asking and she said, "They will tell you."

She had a room filled with eleven- and twelve-year-old children who were eager to learn and were asking questions. They were studying the life of Jesus from the Gospels. The previous week they studied His baptism, and this week they were studying His forty days in the wilderness in which He fasted and prayed and Satan tempted Him. Their questions focused on Jesus' forty days of fasting and prayer. They asked, "Why did he do that?" "Are we supposed to fast and pray?" "Have you ever fasted and prayed?" When I told them that I had fasted and prayed from time to time they asked why I did it and what happened.

Jesus fasted and prayed to sharpen His focus and be prepared for what was coming.

Opening our Bibles I had them read various passages on fasting and prayer, and explained that in this way we choose in faith to push aside distractions of life, including our physical appetites, because we want to be more fully attuned spiritually. In so doing we declare to ourselves and God that our number-one desire is for Him and His glory and His will. I explained that when Jesus fasted and prayed for forty days He was facing a major change, as He was about to begin His public ministry.

Jesus fasted and prayed to sharpen His focus and be prepared for what was coming. I showed them how Jesus did not fast religiously, nor did He expect His disciples to (Matthew 9:14-15); yet he implied that this discipline would be part of their spiritual life (Matthew 6:16). He also promised that when we do this, *your Father, who sees what is done in secret, will reward you* (Matthew 6:18). I told them some of my own experiences through the years in fasting and prayer, and how God had rewarded me, often strengthening me and providing clear and new direction for me or the ministry for which I was responsible.

As I spoke with the children the Holy Spirit used the words I was

PART XIII ~ WALKING WITH GOD INTO UNEXPECTED CHANGE

speaking to convict me, as it had been some time since I had last cleared my calendar to devote a day for fasting and prayer. I was carrying various burdens pertaining to life and ministry, and I had not recently given Him full attention to listen for new direction. I therefore determined that the next day I would fast and pray. I am so grateful I did, as God had an unexpected change in store and that day He prepared me for it.

The next morning I was hungry for God and determined to spend the day with Him in my prayer chapel. As I fasted, I worshiped and prayed and read His Word, laying before Him personal and ministry concerns I was carrying. I expressed my hunger and thirst for Him and I asked Him to speak. Then I was still and listened.

I would have struggled with these unexpected orders if I had not taken the time that day to fast and pray and listen.

Through His Word and the still small voice of the Spirit I discerned He was asking if I would be ready for a move soon. This thought was unexpected as I liked where I was and the work was fulfilling and rewarding to me. I had been conference minister less than eight years, and my elected term would not expire until the following summer. My predecessor had served in that office for twenty-two years, and many told me they hoped I would remain a long time. The board of directors had encouraged me to think long term, even voting to offer me a three-month sabbatical, but that day God's whisper was louder than all other voices including my own. I heard the Lord say, "Are you ready for a move?"

I did not get huffy about it as I have in previous times when the Holy Spirit began telling me a move was coming. This time I did not argue, as God has taught me that I can trust Him. My only reply that day was, "Okay Lord, but it would help to know when and where you want me to go."

The next day I received His answer when I received a call from the chaplain of Commander Naval Reserve Forces Command informing me that I would be recalled to active duty. Within a few days I received orders to depart in April 2011 for Port Hueneme, California. Later in July 2012 those orders were modified to relocate to San Diego, California, and in November 2013 they were modified again to Guantanamo Bay, Cuba.

I would have struggled with these unexpected orders if I had not taken the time that day to fast and pray and listen. God blessed me with peace, and He blessed Helen too. I resigned as conference minister, trusting this was His plan for me and the CCCC, and grateful that He raised up Dr. Ron Hamilton to hit the ground running as our new conference minister.

Life Application Questions:

1. What has kept you from fasting, praying, and listening?

2. What is the connection between these disciplines and hunger for God?

3. What response is the Holy Spirit asking of you right now?

95

Proceed Boldly as the Spirit Leads

> *The Spirit told Philip, "Go to that chariot and stay near it." Then Philip ran up to the chariot.... When they came up out of the water, the Spirit of the Lord suddenly took Philip away, and the eunuch did not see him again, but went on his way rejoicing* (Acts 8:29, 39)

Along our journey there are times when God wants us to go somewhere or do something we cannot foresee. In such times He tells us to continue boldly as the Spirit leads. That is what Philip did. God told him to continue in a certain direction and he did. On the way *he met an Ethiopian eunuch, an important official in charge of all the treasury of the Kandake (which means "queen of the Ethiopians")* (Acts 8:27).

When the Holy Spirit told Philip to boldly approach this man he obeyed, and the man became a believer and follower of Christ. When that assignment was finished Philip and the eunuch never saw each other again, but went on their way rejoicing. This story is in the book of Acts for good reason. The Ethiopian eunuch undoubtedly brought the good news of Jesus back to his native land, and Philip offered an example of blessing that comes when we proceed boldly as the Holy Spirit directs.

During the years I again served on active duty, a number of occasions unfolded that required me to continue boldly as the Spirit directed. One such occasion required me to step out of my comfort zone and when I did, as in the story of Philip, God brought praise to His name and an African man went on his way rejoicing.

For more than a year I served in San Diego with part of my duties as chaplain for the Transient Personnel Unit (TPU), through which thousands of sailors came on their way to and from various seagoing commands. One morning as I entered the TPU buildings a leading petty officer approached me and reported that he had a transient sailor in very deep distress who needed to see me right away.

Some would say chaplains should not do what I did, but as a follower of Christ I am committed to obey Him without regard to consequences. Religious liberty is a treasured value that requires caring for all regardless of their faith perspective or lack thereof, and it means ensuring everyone has freedom to practice their faith. For military chaplains this requires living in the balance between providing religious ministries for people of our own faith which we can freely do, and proselytizing people of other faiths which we are not free to do. I am at peace with this tension because I know that I cannot convince any one of the gospel, and God alone opens spiritual eyes to see. Still, when the Holy Spirit says, "Do this," I do it.

> *I am committed to obey Him without regard to consequences.*

That is what happened when the young man entered my office. I welcomed him by name, closed the door, and we sat down. He leaned forward, holding his head in both hands. Looking at the floor and struggling for composure he spoke with a strong accent, unfolding his story. He had not slept in a day and a half because far away in his native African city his wife was dying. She was the love of his life and mother of their two small children. He told how he left them behind the previous year to join the United States Navy and prepare a way for them to join him. He described how hard it has been for him to be apart from her and their little ones, and that he had hoped for them to join him very soon. Now he was weeping.

A few days earlier his wife suffered a burst appendix. She went through surgery and now was very sick, her body filled with infection. Just two hours ago he spoke by phone with his sister who was now with his wife at the hospital. She reported that his wife is comatose and getting weaker and she has not responded in two days. He was losing his wife and the mother of his children. Far away from the ones he loved, he was terrified and grief-stricken.

Listening to his story I asked God to show me what to do. I knew I must confirm the faith of this young man and then pray in Jesus' name. I asked if he believed in the Lord Jesus. He said he did. I asked if he knew God was with us now and with his wife in her hospital room. He said he believed that. I asked, "Do you believe the Lord Jesus is able to heal your wife and raise her up from her bed?"

He said, "Yes."

I said, "Then we are going to pray." I boldly prayed in the name of Jesus that God would touch and heal her and get her up from her bed right now.

When I finished praying I shifted to what we did in such circumstances to initiate the process for emergency leave so he could travel home to his family. For that to happen we would need written confirmation of the medical emergency. Normally this comes through the Red Cross. I asked the young man if he had a phone number for the hospital. He said he could call his sister as she had a cellphone and was at the hospital with his wife. I asked him to call her in my presence.

When he did a transformation happened before my eyes. His countenance changed from great worry, grief, and fear to radiant joy. I could hear his sister shouting over the phone with joy. Just now his wife had awakened from her coma and at this moment she was getting out of her bed! All the glory is God's! How thankful I am that when the Spirit told me what to do I was obedient to do it. Until he moved on to his navy command, each time I saw that young man he was beaming from ear to ear, on one occasion running across a crowded room to embrace me and say, "Praise the Lord!"

Life Application Questions:

1. When has the Holy Spirit directed you to proceed boldly as He leads you?

2. How have you been compelled to obey Him without regard to consequences?

3. What response is the Holy Spirit asking of you now?

96

Say "Yes" Again

"So then, it was not you who sent me here, but God" (Genesis 45:8)

When Jesus asked Simon Peter if he loved him he said, "Yes," and he did! In the early days of the church Peter was eager to tell everyone about Jesus. He preached the good news on the day of Pentecost. He loved Jesus and was filled with the Spirit. He devoted himself to evangelism and making disciples. He followed the Lord all his days, but Jesus told him a time would come in his life when he would be led to places he did not want to go (John 21:18). Why do you suppose Jesus told Peter this? When that time came Jesus wanted Peter to recall this conversation and be at peace, knowing his Lord was still with him. Later in our life, even if the way ahead is not what we would choose, God wants us to say yes to Him.

There have been times when I have been led to places I would not have chosen to go, but when I knew God was in it I said yes. One such occasion brought me to Guantanamo Bay, Cuba. Entering 2013 I had every intention of retiring from the navy. Helen and I were praying about where God might lead us next. My navy responsibilities were to conclude by October, and I was awaiting His next orders. I expected it would be to a local church or to a civilian chaplaincy ministry. After twenty-four years in the navy I was ready to put away my uniforms.

Then an unexpected opportunity came. Someone was needed to serve as command chaplain for the joint task force at Guantanamo Bay, Cuba. My inclination was to dismiss it, but as I prayed I discerned the Holy Spirit was directing me to take another look. Speaking with some who had served there I learned about the unique challenges of this ministry, and that it would require youthful energy and at times be difficult. With the added prospect of being apart from Helen for so many months I was ready to say no, but as Helen and I prayed together I knew He was telling me to say yes. Though I did not really want to, after walking with God all these years I knew saying yes was required. When we say yes to God, even when the way ahead is difficult, we will surely see that God is faithful.

That is what happened to me. I was given orders to Guantanamo Bay, Cuba, and while there God provided countless divine appointments. This was a joint command with members of all military branches. Our troops served honorably and professionally, and I was privileged to serve with them. Leading and serving and mentoring other chaplains, and witnessing God's grace in many ways, this tour was among the highlights of my life and ministry. I am glad I said yes to God.

> *No matter how unexpected or daunting circumstances seem, if God is in them, say, "Yes."*

A time will surely come when you will face unexpected change and be asked to go somewhere or face a situation you do not want. In that day remember who you walk with and trust Him fully. Remember how the Lord was with Peter in his difficult time. Remember how God was with Joseph and blessed him when he was dragged away to Egypt. When at last he was reconciled with his brothers Joseph could say, *"So then, it was not you who sent me here, but God"* (Genesis 45:8). No matter how unexpected or daunting circumstances seem, if God is in them, say, "Yes."

Life Application Questions:

1. When has God called you to say yes to something you did not want to do?

2. What promises of God do you hold on to when facing such challenges?

3. What response is the Holy Spirit asking of you now?

Part XIV

WALKING WITH GOD TO FINAL BREATH AND BEYOND

We are all getting older, and the finite number of days remaining on our earthly journey are getting fewer. We might not like to think about this, but it is still a fact. I expect King David had this in mind when he wrote that *all the days ordained for me were written in your book before one of them came to be* (Psalm 139:16). Every year and day is to be treasured and lived to the fullest extent possible for God's glory. So how do we do that? What does He intend for us as we walk with Him to our final breath and beyond? What follows are key lessons God is teaching me as I walk with Him into the latter chapters of my life journey.

97

Keep Standing By for New Orders

So Abram went, as the LORD had told him; and Lot went with him. Abram was seventy-five years old when he set out from Harran (Genesis 12:4)

When God told seventy-five-year-old Abram to leave his country to go to a new place where God would direct him, he obeyed. Though he was no longer young, and though accustomed to life in a certain way, he did not resist God's new call. Abram went as directed, and through obedience he was blessed beyond his wildest imagination. A childless man when he left, he became Abraham, *a father of many nations.*

I want to be like Abraham. I want to go where He sends me and do whatever He calls me to do until my dying day. God reminds me that for the rest of my life this will require my willingness to accept new orders, perhaps even to go somewhere or do something I have not done before. If that is required, I will say yes.

Approaching my sixties and looking back now over a lifetime of walking with God, I can remember and celebrate so many times God gave me new orders. Sometimes His orders have surprised me, and sometimes they have overwhelmed me. Receiving new orders from God is always exciting because it reminds us that we are blessed to be in His service and to be used by Him. This is true for every disciple of Jesus Christ, no matter our age. In every new challenge in life we are reminded of our dependence upon Him to do what He is calling us to do.

It is common in military life for people to be awaiting new orders. Sometimes there is great consternation about it as we wonder what the next assignment will be. We may have our preference of where we want to go or what we want to do, but we do not have the final say, and when we receive orders, we carry them out.

This is Christian discipleship too, isn't it? Living under the authority of the Lord Jesus is our lifestyle for our entire lifetime. This privilege and commitment never stops. As we age we continue living daily in obedience to the Lord, and we say yes whenever He gives new orders, calling us to something new. He is Lord of all so He determines what our next orders will be. This is the way we want it.

I have prayed and counseled many people on this matter as they faced uncertainties and transitions. I have personally experienced God's faithfulness in times of transition, and I have seen Him reveal His will to those who walk with Him and who are ready to do His will. This principle never expires. It is true from childhood until final breath. As Abraham demonstrated, it remains true as we age.

As I write this I am again standing by for new orders from the Lord. I do not yet know where He will have me serve Him next, or even in what area of ministry I will serve. There are a few ministry possibilities before me, but I do not yet know where or when it will be. This I do know: God leads, He provides, He is faithful, and He is on time. I do not worry as I am standing by for His orders. By the time you read this I fully expect I will have received and responded to His next orders for me in His service. What a fantastic way to live, even as we age.

Are you getting older? Are you retired or nearing your retirement years? Is a change coming for you, but you're not yet sure what it will be? Lean on your Lord. Remember His faithfulness. Be ready and willing. Pray with availability. These are exciting days, for even now the Lord prepares your orders. Even now He prepares divine appointments and ministry opportunities where you will shine for Him. It might be to serve Him faithfully where you are. It might be to go somewhere you have not been before, or to branch out of your comfort zone into a new area of ministry. God has a plan for you from now until your last breath. Stand by for new orders, and when He gives them to you rejoice and do what He calls you to do.

Life Application Questions:

1. When has God given you new orders and how did you respond?

2. Are you ready to say yes if God calls you to something new?

3. What response is the Holy Spirit asking of you now?

98

Emulate Faithful Witnesses

*One generation commends your works to another;
they tell of your mighty acts* (Psalm 145:4)

Along the way of our earthly journey God gives us faithful witnesses to emulate, and He calls us to set an example for those who follow us. One faithful witness God gave me that I have sought to emulate is my grandfather Reverend Morley Durost. I wish you could have known him. Born in 1894 and called home to heaven in 1981, he was a man who loved his Lord and lived his faith. Like Noah he *was a righteous man, blameless among the people of his time, and he walked faithfully with God* (Genesis 6:9). For those who knew him he was a model of walking with God. Though only Christ is our perfect example, on this side of heaven we see in people of faith like Morley Durost how Jesus demonstrates Himself in someone fully yielded to Him. By their example we become motivated toward a closer walk with God. This is the effect my grandfather had on me.

> *He calls us to set an example for those who follow us.*

As a shepherd of God's flock I have come to appreciate the importance of having godly models to disciple us, demonstrating in life the faith they proclaim. We all need examples from whom we can learn and be inspired. My grandfather knew that. He wanted to pass on the faith he had lived and to tell how Christ blessed him. So in his later years when friends and family encouraged him to write about his experiences with God he did so. He wrote with evident faith of the times and ways God worked in his life, and of things God taught him along the way, praying someone might thereby be drawn to Jesus. That is what I have wanted to do.

Morley Durost faced significant challenges in life, including military service in France in the First World War when he was shot in both legs. Through it all God was with him and in each chapter of life he learned and enjoyed God's faithfulness. My grandfather was sixty years old when I was born, so when I knew him he enjoyed the perspective of having walked with God for many years, a perspective I now enjoy.

My last one-on-one conversation with him was immediately before my ordination service in February 1981. Before leaving for the church where he would pray over me my grandfather put his big hands on my thin shoulders, looked at me through coke bottle-thick eyeglasses with tears in his eyes and a smile on his face, and then said with obvious affection and passion, "Stephen, I wish I was sixty years younger and in your shoes and could do it all again." That passion for the Lord and His service motivated me then and motivates me still. This is what I want to do for others.

Life Application Questions:

1. What faithful witnesses has God given you to emulate?

2. In what ways is your life a faithful witness for others to follow?

3. What response is the Holy Spirit asking of you now?

99

Run the Race to the Finish Line

...my only aim is to finish the race and complete the task the Lord Jesus has given me—the task of testifying to the good news of God's grace (Acts 20:24)

I have looked, but nowhere in the Bible can I find anything to support the idea of retirement that is prevalent in our culture. Nowhere does God encourage His children to work hard as long as they must until they can afford to pursue whatever enjoyments they want. Jesus told a parable illustrating the foolishness of such an aim (Luke 12:16-21). The only place I have found in Scripture that even mentions retirement is Numbers 8:24-26, where Levites who served as worship attendants were to do so until age fifty, after which they were to shift their focus to assisting the next generation. This does not suggest a life of leisure, but a life of mentoring and passing on wisdom to those who will follow us.

When the apostle Paul was saying good-bye to the Ephesian church elders, he gave them an excellent example by suggesting as he approached the end of his earthly journey that he was not quitting but was determined to *finish the race and complete the task the Lord Jesus has given me* (Acts 20:24).

If we run with others we tend to do better, as we motivate each other along the way. For me, I always tend to pick up the pace when someone is running beside me. This illustrates the importance of Christian community. Running the race of life to the finish line while encouraging others along the way is important spiritually. When the race seems long and our souls are weary, God reminds us that He runs beside us. As we keep in step with Him we can know we will reach the finish line together.

When we live our lives like this, running to the finish line, you and I will be like athletes standing in the winners' circle holding high our greatest trophy, an eternal crown through Jesus Christ. Our training is not easy and at times it requires much discipline, but it is well worth it for the prize that awaits. Paul said, *Everyone who competes in the games goes into strict training. They do it to get a crown that will not last; but we do it to get a crown that will last forever* (1 Corinthians 9:25).

As we age we must learn to adjust our tempo.

As we age we must learn to adjust our tempo. I have become less focused on how much ground I can cover and more focused on doing every mile well. As we get older and some things become harder for us God reminds us that He is still with us. He teaches us to seize every opportunity to encourage others along the way.

Life Application Questions:

1. Have you asked God His plans for your "retirement"?

2. How is the race of life going for you, and who are you running with?

3. What response is the Holy Spirit asking of you now?

100

Tell His Story in You

Jesus ... said, "Go home to your own people and tell them how much the Lord has done for you, and how he has had mercy on you." So the man went away and began to tell in the Decapolis how much Jesus had done for him. And all the people were amazed (Mark 5:19)

When you have walked with God for any length of time you have a story to tell. God wants us to tell the story so in telling it we can point people to Him. That is what Jesus instructed the man to do who was delivered from a legion of demons, and it is what he did. He told his story and Jesus received the glory. That is what we are to do. Through my grandfather's life and ministry he told stories of God's grace, and in the process he pointed people to Jesus. In later years he wrote some of it. Though he never completed the project I am grateful for the stories he told.

There is one story he began to tell and perhaps even finished, but after his death only the first page was found. He described a time when one of his adult daughters contracted polio. It was the summer after she graduated from Maine State Teacher's College. She had already been hired and was looking forward to starting her first teaching job at the end of the summer, but she became ill. Her condition worsened as the summer progressed. She was hospitalized and then paralyzed. My grandfather informed the principal of the school where she was hired that his daughter would be unavailable for teaching that school year.

He described receiving a phone call from the hospital one evening telling him his daughter would likely not survive that night, so if they wished to see her before she died they must hurry. Rather than rush to the hospital, Morley Durost called the elders of the church to join him in prayer. They prayed for hours, claiming the promises of James 5:13-15, asking God for a miraculous touch. Their pleas before the throne of grace offered from a distant location is reminiscent of the centurion who from a distance sent a message to Jesus on behalf of his dying servant, asking the Lord in faith, *But say the word, and my servant will be healed* (Luke 7:7).

As with the centurion's plea, the prayers of my grandfather and those who prayed with him were answered. As I did not have the complete story in print I went to the one whose story was told. My mother is the woman in the hospital who was paralyzed and approaching death. When I asked her to share what she recalled about that night she described being in bed and unable to move, but she could hear. She heard a doctor say, "That young woman will never get out of that bed."

But the man who spoke those words did not know what God could do! He did not know that people of faith were storming the heavens for her. He did not know that Jesus Christ had already touched her. When she heard the doctor say, "She will never get out of that bed," she said these words: "Oh yes, I will!" Then she sat up and got out of her bed! The next week she was teaching school, and a couple of years later she married a ministerial student. In time they had six children, twenty-six grandchildren, and thus far eight great-grandchildren and counting.

Hearing this story I realized that if God was not a prayer-answering, miracle-working God, if Jesus was not lord of all and faithful to His promises, then I and many other people who are so dear to me would not have lived and I would not have had the privilege of telling you about His faithfulness. God is faithful! He is faithful in every generation and in every chapter of life and ministry! He is faithful in every moment, even in the troubling times, and He will be faithful forever! We have an abundance of stories to tell of His love and faithfulness. God wants us to tell them. There are more stories yet to be lived and told. As we walk with God through life and ministry, He continues telling the story of Jesus through us.

Life Application Questions:

1. What story has God given you to tell?

2. With whom can you share your story of what the Lord has done for you?

3. What response is the Holy Spirit asking of you now?

101

Walk with God into Glory

For I am already being poured out like a drink offering, and the time for my departure is near. I have fought the good fight, I have finished the race, I have kept the faith. Now there is in store for me the crown of righteousness, which the Lord, the righteous judge, will award to me on that day—and not only to me, but also to all who have longed for his appearing (2 Timothy 4:6-8)

For all of us the moment will come when our heart will beat for the last time. When that happens, what then? Jesus assured His disciples that He was going ahead of them, and would prepare a place for them, and then one day come again to take us to be with Him in the place that He has prepared (John 14:1-6). When the apostle Paul realized his days were numbered and that very soon he would breathe his last, he expressed peace and calm and resolve (2 Timothy 4:6-8). Paul wrote about this to Pastor Timothy to encourage him, and us, to be looking forward to that day when the Lord will welcome us into glory and bestow on us a victor's crown.

On the day that my grandfather died I was rushing from Rhode Island to Maine hoping to arrive at the hospital before he departed. I arrived too late, but was so blessed when someone who was with him at the end repeated his final words. They were, "I'm going home now." Then, he did just that. When your final moments come and you breathe your last, do you have such confidence? Because of Jesus I do. I will walk with Him into glory. What a wonderful day that will be!

Life Application Questions:

1. If today were your last day, what would your final words be?

2. How have God's promises affected your anxiety level about your own death?

3. What response is the Holy Spirit asking of you right now?

About the Author

Dr. Stephen Gammon is a third-generation minister and lifelong follower of Jesus Christ, and has walked with God since early childhood. A pastor since age 25, he has served more than 30 years wherever and whenever God has led him, including in two local church pastorates, as a denominational leader of ministers and churches (Conservative Congregational Christian Conference), and as an active duty and Navy Reserves chaplain. Steve and his wife, Helen, reside in Colorado Springs, Colorado. They have three adult children, a son-in-law, and a grandson.

Connect with the author
www.walkingwithgodforlife.com

Also by ANEKO Press

In the Jubilee Bible 2000 (JUB), the usage and context tends to define each key word so you don't need to depend on theological dictionaries or reference materials. Careful attention has been made to properly translate the first usage of each key word and through to the last occurrence. Then, as the word makes its way across the Old Testament and you make the correct match with the corresponding Greek word in the New Testament, an amazing pattern emerges. The Jubilee Bible is the only translation we know of that has each unique Hebrew word matched and mated with a unique English word so that the usage (number of occurrences and number of verses where the word occurs) sets forth a meaningful number pattern and a complete definition of what God means by each word.

www.ingramcontent.com/pod-product-compliance
Lightning Source LLC
Chambersburg PA
CBHW020354080526
44584CB00014B/1016